Praise for *The Gift*

W9-BMF-918

A *Working Mother* Book Pick
A *Fortune* Staff Pick
An *Education Week* Must Read for 2016

"'The ugly and wonderful truth about middle school,' [Lahey] says, is that 'failure is not an if-proposition, it's a matter of when.' Or it used to be. Now that parents shelter their children every step of the way, we have 'failure deprived' college students (as administrators at Stanford and Harvard call them) and entitled, anxious 20-somethings who can't function in a world that's sometimes cold or cruel or indifferent. So how can teachers snatch back their critical role and give children the necessary space to fail? They could start by making parents read Lahey."

—*New York Times Book Review*

"This wonderful book by Jessica Lahey is perfect for parents at all levels."

—Patrick Larkin, *Education Week*

"[Lahey gives] advice on how to let kids make their own mistakes, then turn their failures into future successes. It might make you feel better about your own bumps in the road, too." —*Working Mother*

"Lahey writes clearly and with much-needed humor, using anecdotes along with research to show us just how our tendency to try to 'save' our kids by making life easier for them does exactly the opposite. The lesson: If you want to raise resilient, confident adults, don't deliver forgotten homework for them. Don't stay up all night with the glue gun. Don't tell them they're loading the dishwasher wrong. Just let them do it—their way."

—Jennifer Reingold, *Fortune*

"A new book written by a schoolteacher has a simple yet compelling message for parents: Back off." —Associated Press

"Jessica Lahey, author of the new book *The Gift of Failure*, wants everyone to back off and let kids mess up. Because without experiencing failure, mistakes, and imperfection, she believes, they will grow up to become adults incapable of dealing with adversity. They may wind up being paralyzed by the fear of failure and will strive to experience less in their lives."

–Evan Grossman, *Men's Journal*

"[*The Gift of Failure*] gave me the permission to stand down and provided me with the push I needed to send my older son into the wilds of middle school without me hovering, smothering, or freaking out."

—Adrienne Wichard-Edds, *Washington Post*

"Lahey's book is surely a gift to parents, a wake-up call that reminds us that our job is not about making our children happy or successful today, but rather helping to nurture future adults who can do this for themselves."

—Lisa Heffernan, *The Mid*

"An important, thoughtfully balanced book aimed at shifting thinking and providing concrete steps toward encouraging positive—and realistic—self-image development."

—*Kirkus Reviews*

" 'Failure-avoidant' parenting would seem, on the surface, to be synonymous with good parenting. Children stay safe, get into good colleges, and seem happier, at least in the moment. Debut author Lahey proposes, however, that parents will ultimately serve their children better by allowing them to stand on their own abilities and experience the occasional failure. . . . Lahey has many wise and helpful words like these—ones that any parent can and should embrace."

—*Publishers Weekly*

"It's hard to overstate the importance of this book. *The Gift of Failure* is beautifully written; it's deeply researched; but most of all it's the one book we all need to read if we want to instill the next generation with confidence and joy."

—Susan Cain, author of *Quiet: The Power of Introverts in a World That Can't Stop Talking*

"This fascinating, thought-provoking book shows that to help children succeed, we must allow them to fail. Essential reading for parents, teachers, coaches, psychologists, and anyone else who wants to guide children toward lives of independence, creativity, and courage."

—Gretchen Rubin, author of *The Happiness Project*

"Finally, an antidote to the hysteria! Through an artful combination of anecdote and research, Jessica Lahey delivers a lesson that moms and dads badly need to learn and secretly wish to hear: That failure is vital to children's success. Any parent who pines for a saner, more informed approach to child-rearing—to say nothing of a sounder night's sleep—should read this book. A compassionate mother and dedicated educator, Jessica Lahey knows exactly, authentically, and authoritatively of what she speaks."

—Jennifer Senior, author of *All Joy and No Fun*

"Instead of lecturing us about what we're doing wrong, Jessica Lahey reveals what she did wrong with her own children and students—and how she systematically reformed her ways. A refreshing, practical book for parents who want to raise resilient kids but aren't sure how to start."

—Amanda Ripley, author of *The Smartest Kids in the World: And How They Got That Way*

"Lahey offers one of the most important parenting messages of our times: Unless we allow our children to learn how to take on challenges, they won't thrive in school and in life. Her extremely helpful book tells her story, compiles research, and provides hundreds of doable suggestions."

—Ellen Galinsky, author of *Mind in the Making: The Seven Essential Life Skills Every Child Needs*

"How can we help our children grow to be resourceful, happy adults? Lahey shows in practical terms how to know what your child is ready for and how to offer support even as you encourage autonomy. A wise, engaging book, steeped in scientific research and tempered with common sense."

—Daniel T. Willingham, author of *Why Don't Students Like School: A Cognitive Scientist Answers Questions About How the Mind Works and What It Means for the Classroom*

"Simply put, I think it's one the most important, thought-provoking, and helpful books about raising children that has been written in a long time. And because much of it has to do with a family's approach to how their child learns, I also consider it one of the most important books about education as well."

—Eric Messenger, *New York Family* magazine

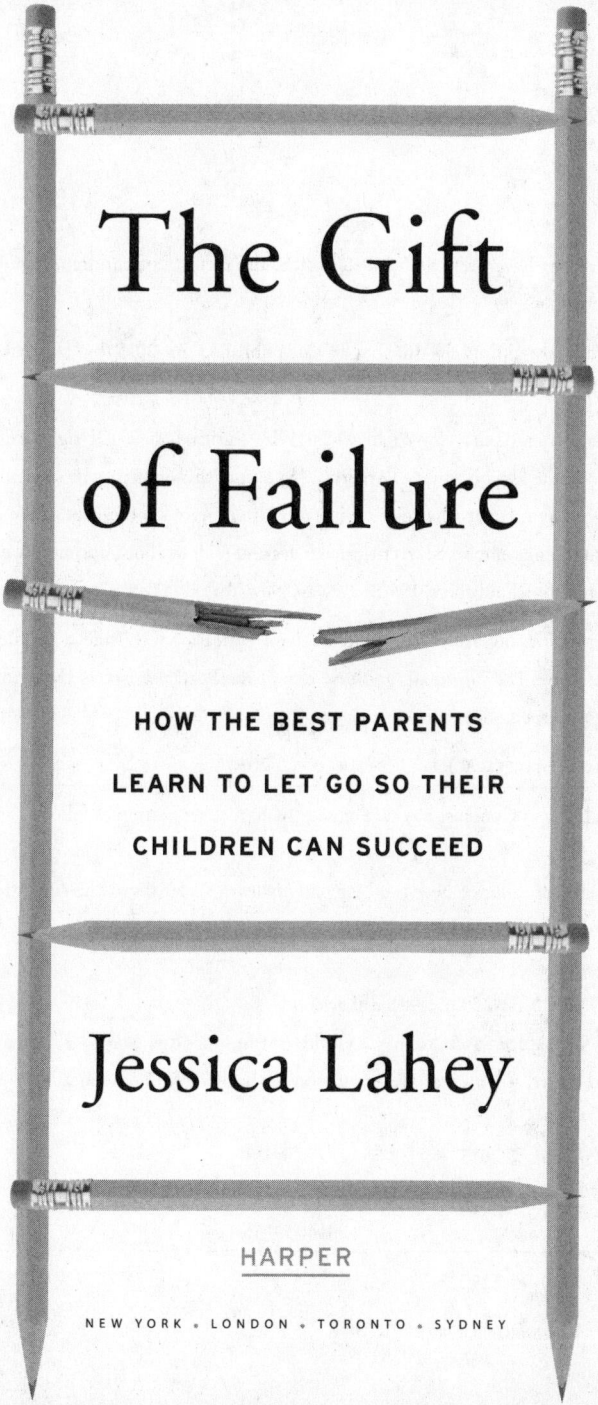

The Gift of Failure

HOW THE BEST PARENTS LEARN TO LET GO SO THEIR CHILDREN CAN SUCCEED

Jessica Lahey

HARPER

NEW YORK • LONDON • TORONTO • SYDNEY

HARPER

Some names have been changed to protect the identity of children described in this book.

A hardcover edition of this book was published in 2015 by HarperCollins Publishers.

THE GIFT OF FAILURE. Copyright © 2015 by Jessica Lahey. All rights reserved. Printed in the United States of America. No part of this book may be used or reproduced in any manner whatsoever without written permission except in the case of brief quotations embodied in critical articles and reviews. For information, address HarperCollins Publishers, 195 Broadway, New York, NY 10007.

HarperCollins books may be purchased for educational, business, or sales promotional use. For information, please e-mail the Special Markets Department at SPsales@harpercollins.com.

FIRST HARPER PAPERBACK EDITION PUBLISHED 2016

The Library of Congress has catalogued the hardcover edition as follows:

Lahey, Jessica.

The gift of failure : how the best parents learn to let go so their children can succeed / Jessica Lahey.

pages cm

ISBN 978-0-06-229923-9 (hardback)

1. Self-reliance in children. 2. Child rearing—United States. 3. Parenting—United States. 4. Parental overprotection. 5. Early childhood education—United States. I. Title.

BF723.S29L35 2015

649'.7—dc23

2014039146

ISBN 978-0-06-229925-3 (pbk.)

17 18 19 20 OV/RRD 10 9 8

FOR BENJAMIN AND FINNEGAN

I know you all, and will awhile uphold
The unyoked humour of your idleness.
Yet herein will I imitate the sun,
Who doth permit the base contagious clouds
To smother up his beauty from the world,
That, when he please again to be himself,
Being wanted, he may be more wonder'd at,
By breaking through the foul and ugly mists
Of vapours that did seem to strangle him.
If all the year were playing holidays,
To sport would be as tedious as to work;
But when they seldom come, they wish'd for come,
And nothing pleaseth but rare accidents.
So, when this loose behavior I throw off
And pay the debt I never promised,
By how much better than my word I am,
By so much shall I falsify men's hopes;
And like bright metal on a sullen ground,
My reformation, glittering o'er my fault,
Shall show more goodly and attract more eyes
Than that which hath no foil to set it off.
I'll so offend, to make offence a skill,
Redeeming time when men think least I will.

Prince Hal, Act I, Scene 2, Henry IV, Part I

CONTENTS

Introduction: How I Learned to Let Go *xi*

PART I FAILURE: A MOST VALUABLE PARENTING TOOL

1 How Failure Became a Dirty Word: A Brief History of American Parenting *3*

2 Why Parenting for Dependence Doesn't Work: The Power of Intrinsic Motivation *19*

3 Less Really Is More: Parenting for Autonomy and Competence *43*

4 Encouragement from the Sidelines: The Real Connection Between Praise and Self-Esteem *61*

PART II LEARNING FROM FAILURE: TEACHING KIDS TO TURN MISTAKES INTO SUCCESS

5 Household Duties: Laundry as an Opportunity for Competence *75*

6 Friends: Accomplices to Failure and the Formation of Identity *95*

7 Sports: Losing as an Essential Childhood Experience *119*

8 Middle School: Prime Time for Failure *135*

9 High School and Beyond: Toward Real Independence *157*

PART III SUCCEEDING AT SCHOOL: LEARNING FROM FAILURE IS A TEAM EFFORT

10 Parent-Teacher Partnerships: How Our Fear of Failure Undermines Education *181*

11 Homework: How to Help Without Taking Over *205*

12 Grades: The Real Value of a Low Score *223*

Conclusion: What I've Learned from Letting Go *241*

Acknowledgments *245*
Notes *249*
Bibliography *253*
Index *261*

INTRODUCTION: HOW I LEARNED TO LET GO

I BECAME A PARENT AND A middle school teacher in the same year, and these twin roles have shaped the way I've raised my children and educated my students. Over the course of my first decade raising two boys and teaching hundreds of children, I began to feel a creeping sense of unease, a suspicion that something was rotten in the state of my parenting. But it was only when my elder child entered middle school that my worlds collided and the source of the problem became clear to me: today's overprotective, failure-avoidant parenting style has undermined the competence, independence, and academic potential of an entire generation. From my vantage point at the front of a classroom, I'd long viewed myself as part of the solution, a champion of my students' intellectual and emotional bravery. However, as the same caution and fear I witnessed in my students began to show up in my own children's lives, I had to admit that I was part of the problem, too.

We have taught our kids to fear failure, and in doing so, we have blocked the surest and clearest path to their success. That's certainly not what we meant to do, and we did it for all the best and well-intentioned reasons, but it's what we have wrought nevertheless. Out of love and desire to protect our children's self-esteem, we have bulldozed every uncomfortable bump and obstacle out of their way, clearing the manicured path we hoped would lead to success and happiness. Unfortunately, in doing so we have deprived our children of the most important lessons of childhood. The setbacks, mistakes, miscalculations, and failures we have shoved out of our children's way are the very experiences that teach them how to be resourceful, persistent, innovative, and resilient citizens of this world.

As I stood there in my middle school classroom on the day of my personal epiphany, looking at the students before me and seeing my own parenting clearly for the first time, I resolved to do what I needed to do to guide both my children and my students back toward the path to competence and independence. The way isn't smooth, and the going certainly isn't easy, but that's kind of the point. We parents are going to have to step back, leave those scary obstacles lying in the road, and allow our children to face them head-on. Given our support, love, and a *lot* of restraint, our kids can learn how to engineer their own solutions and pave their way toward success that is truly of their own making.

THE DISCOMFORT I'D BEEN FEELING in my own parenting had been growing for a while, but I could not put my finger on where I'd gone wrong. I read all the parenting blogs, from the austere to the zealous, and read books by the experts on how to raise happy, healthy children. However, as I watched my boys approach their teenage years, something was amiss. They were good, well-adjusted kids, but I couldn't shake the sense that when it came time for them to head out on their own and make their way in the world, they were ill-prepared. As long as they stayed inside the safe haven I'd created for them, they were confident and successful, but when forced to venture outside, would they know how to function? I'd so successfully researched, planned, and constructed their comfortable childhoods that I'd failed to teach them how to adapt to the world on *its* terms.

I never meant to teach my children to be helpless or fear failure, and a life of anxiety is certainly not what I envisioned for them. On the contrary, I thought my kids would grow up brave, in the sort of wild, free idyll I experienced as a child. I wanted them to explore the woods with a pocketknife and a couple of cookies shoved in their pockets, build tree forts, shoot handmade arrows at imaginary enemies, and swim in the local watering hole. I wanted them to have the time and the courage to try new things, explore their boundaries, and climb one branch beyond the edge of their comfort zones.

But somehow, somewhere, that idyllic version of childhood morphed into something very different, a high-stakes, cutthroat race to the top. Today, careless afternoons in the woods seem like a quaint throwback because the pressure to succeed from an early age has ramped up for both parents and kids. It never lets up, and there is no longer room in our children's schedules for leisure time in the woods, let alone opportunities to problem-solve their way out of the muck and mire they encounter out there. In the new normal, every moment counts, and the more successful our kids are as students, athletes, and musicians, the more successful we judge ourselves as parents. The race to the top starts when children take their first steps and does not end until a six-figure income and socioeconomic upward mobility are secured. And, come on, what kind of negligent mother allows her kids to play alone in the woods during homework time, with pockets full of gluten and sugar, armed to the teeth with pocketknives and arrows?

Standing in my middle school classroom, frozen in that horrible realization of my own culpability in the epidemic of overparenting, I finally understood just how far off the path we parents have strayed.

We bring a beautiful, precious child into the world, and after those first moments of bliss wear off, we realize that our new purpose in life is to protect this fragile human being from harm. And if we are to believe the fear-mongering mass media, that harm is all around us. Baby snatchers disguised as maternity nurses, antibiotic-resistant germs, toxic chemicals, disease-carrying ticks, bullying kids, unfair teachers, murderous school shooters . . . no wonder we've gone nuts where our children are concerned.

However, this fear doesn't just cause us to overparent; it makes us feel overwhelmed, myopic, and much too credulous of those who seek to stoke our parental fears. It's easier to self-soothe by shielding our kids from all risk than to take a pause and figure out which risks are necessary to their development and emotional health. We protect our kids from all threats, whether real or imagined, and when we tuck our kids in bed at night, free of cuts, bruises, or emotional hurt, we have, for one more day, found tangible evidence of our parenting success.

We revel in their safety and reassure ourselves that there's plenty of time to teach them how to deal with risk and failure. Maybe tomorrow I'll let them walk to school, but today, they got to school safely. Maybe tomorrow they will do their own homework, but today, they are successful in math. Maybe tomorrow continues until it's time for them to leave home, and by then, they have learned that we will always be there to save them from themselves.

I am as guilty as the next parent; I have inadvertently extended my children's dependence in order to appropriate their successes as evidence and validation of my parenting. Every time I pack my child's lunch for him or drive his forgotten homework to school, I am rewarded with tangible proof of my conscientious mothering. I love, therefore I provide. I provide, therefore I love. While I know, somewhere in the back of my mind, that my children really should be doing these kinds of tasks for themselves, it makes me feel good to give them these small displays of my deep, unconditional love. I reassure myself with what feels like a vast expanse of childhood, stretching out for years, its eventual end invisible over the horizon. My kids will have their entire lives to pack their lunches and remember their backpacks, but I only have a very brief window of time to be able to do these things for them.

There's a term for this behavior in psychiatric circles. It's called enmeshment, and it's not healthy for kids or parents. It's a maladaptive state of symbiosis that makes for unhappy, resentful parents and "failure to launch" children who move back in to their bedrooms after college graduation. In 2012, 36 percent of adults age 18–31 still lived in their parents' home, and while some of that figure is due to declining employment and marriage statistics, these numbers are part of a trend that's been rising for decades. In order to raise healthy, happy kids who can begin to build their own adulthood separate from us, we are going to have to extricate our egos from our children's lives and allow them to feel the pride of their own accomplishments as well as the pain of their own failures.

WE ARE ALSO GOING TO have to knock it off with the competitive parenting, because we have managed to whip ourselves up into a frenzy of anxiety and paranoia. Our Facebook posts and soccer tournament sideline chat is jam-packed with passive-aggressive tales of academic honors and athletic glory. As our kids get older, we spin tales of coast-to-coast college tours, SAT prep and AP tutoring, because didn't you hear? According to the news, today's college degree counts as much as our high school diplomas . . . and in order to get that college degree, our kids will have to jump through all sorts of hoops we never had to deal with because colleges have become more expensive and selective . . . and there is no such thing as a safety school anymore . . . and as the economy is in the toilet, once our kids graduate from whatever college will deign to take them, they may have to work as minimum-wage baristas in order to be able to afford to share an apartment with sixteen of their friends.

We need to stop and take a very deep breath. Research shows that this behavior, this "Pressured Parents Phenomenon," is extremely contagious. Even when I've vaccinated myself against it ahead of time, I have fallen victim to it as well. Consequently, I am not the mother I hoped I would be. I hover over homework and obsess about grade point averages as the specter of college admission looms large on the horizon. It is as if the better angels of my nature have been cowed into silence, and I've bought into the hype: unless I push my kids to do more, *be* more, they will fail, and, by logical extension, I will have failed as a mother.

In my darker moments, I've cast around for others to blame for my plight, and I've found plenty of scapegoats. Reaction against the hands-off parenting of the fifties and sixties, extension of the attachment parenting we employed when our children were in infancy, and guilt over our failed attempts to strike an impossible balance between work and family. There does not seem to be a middle ground anymore, a safe harbor between having it all and having nothing.

The parenting pendulum swings back and forth over time, so the fact that it is currently hanging at its apex at the extreme end of the overparenting arc isn't really anyone's fault. It's part of the action and reaction that constitute the history of our species. Early in the twentieth century, parents were instructed not to touch their children at all lest we spoil them, but by the time the nineties swung into view, experts had latched on to attachment parenting, in which we were instructed to sleep, eat, bathe, urinate, and breathe without ever letting go of our kangaroo-style infants. Sure, the pendulum swung through a sane, middle ground between 1970 and 1980, and I am forever grateful I was allowed to play in its gentle shade as it passed overhead. However, that golden moment of equilibrium was over much too soon, and we began our upward swing toward the place we find ourselves in today.

If you grew up in the 1970s, some of you more than likely were latchkey kids, with both parents working outside the home. While some of us associate the term with a childhood lit with a rosy, romantic hue, others recall the lack of supervision as near-abandonment, and have begun making reparations to their children accordingly. In our efforts to make up for our own perceived lack of guidance, we are ever-present, ever-helpful, ever-reminding, ever-rescuing. As part of this reparation effort, some parents—mostly women—abandoned their executive offices for home, determined to mindfully parent their children as full-time caregivers. Often, mothers dove in to full-time parenting armed with the skills they had earned in higher education and in the business world, and they took no prisoners. How hard could parenting be? Guiding children into Ivy League colleges, like making partner in a Wall Street law firm, was simply a matter of organization, drive, and the meticulous management of academic and extracurricular resources.

Parents who remained in the workforce, meanwhile, were made to feel deficient for prioritizing work over their children, and felt obligated to show the world that they could do it all. Again, success was just a matter of scheduling and some sleight of hand. Cupcakes here, boardroom there. Parent-teacher conference here, Bluetooth Skype with clients on the way home in the car. Besides, the mortgage and child-care payments required two incomes to maintain, and as the economy tanked, the suggestion that one parent could simply kiss the stability of a paycheck and benefits goodbye in order to parent full-time seemed ludicrous.

We did the best we could with the skills we'd worked so hard to acquire. Schedules of meetings and project management schemes were repurposed into color-coded school activity and carpool calendars, scheduled down to the minute. Management skills formerly used to guide teams of employees toward quarterly sales goals were appropriated to plan semester-long campaigns to help children improve their grades. I know this, because I've used every trick in my college- and law-school-educated quiver. When I returned to work after my elder son, Ben, was born, I used spreadsheets and database software to chronicle his first words, the input and output of his digestive system, and his reading progress. These were the tools at my disposal, and since I'd worked long and hard to acquire them, it hardly seemed right to let them go to waste. I took comfort in these measures when faced with the silent, sucking void I found when I searched for clues that would validate my parenting. The only other ally I found in this endeavor was my son's pediatrician, who at *least* provided me with growth charts that plotted my infant's progress against all the other rival babies out there. If his weight and height were just above the 50th percentile on the growth chart, great. I'd done some good, solid mothering. If his BMI was a little lower than average, well done, me; I got some bonus points for staving off the epidemic of childhood obesity. At the end of the appointment, though, I needed the good doctor to bestow judgment and answer my unspoken plea: Do I qualify for honors or is this parenting business pass/fail? What about those other parents out there in the waiting room—did I beat them? Come on, help me out here, Doc: what's my grade?

Of course, the strategies that make us successful in the business world do not translate to the business of parenting. Reams of research papers on child development and behavioral psychology reveal that while these methods may work to motivate assembly-line workers, they are terrible tools for motivating children to engage in creative problem-solving, and they actually undermine long-term motivation and investment in learning. Even more damaging, the use of rewards and incentives prioritizes scores and grades over exploration and experimentation, which undermines a teacher's ability to foster self-directed and intrinsically motivated learning.

Despite the wealth of evidence regarding the folly of these methods, we continue to incorporate them into our parenting, and lacking regular performance reviews from some higher authority, many of us look to our children to provide the feedback we need in order to feel as if we are doing our jobs well. If our children are on the honor roll and make varsity soccer as a freshman, we must be great parents. Conversely, when a child fails a test or receives detention for neglecting to hand in his science paper, *we* must have done something wrong. Parents, after all, are judged by their children's accomplishments rather than their happiness, so when our children fail, we appropriate those failures as our own.

This is not only disastrous for parents' self-worth; it's shortsighted and unimaginative. Failure—from small mistakes to huge miscalculations—is a necessary and critical part of our children's development. Failure is too often characterized as a negative: an F in math or a suspension from school. However, all sorts of disappointments, rejections, corrections, and criticisms are small failures, all opportunities in disguise, valuable gifts misidentified as tragedy. Sadly, when we avoid or dismiss these opportunities, in order to preserve children's sense of ease and short-term happiness, we deprive them of the experiences they need to have in order to become capable, competent adults.

Failure is frightening enough when faced firsthand, but when our children wander too close to its jaws, we are overcome with a primal, overpowering need to protect. From an evolutionary perspective, this response makes perfect sense. We are programmed in our hearts and our DNA to shield our children from harm, so when tasked with shepherding our genetic offspring safely to adulthood, we are prepared to fight anything that threatens their success with all the ferocity our nails and teeth and smarts can muster. Unfortunately, when we are all hopped up on adrenaline and cortisol, our brains can't distinguish between genuine, mortal threats to life and limb, and the manageable threat of a soccer opponent flying downfield to steal the ball away from our child. Leaping in front of an attacking predator on the savannah and screaming at the referee for a bad call are just "two different manifestations of the same biological trigger." So when you want to push that little girl who tossed sand in your child's face or punch that teacher who threatened your child with a D on her science project, remember that while these actions are not sane, socially appropriate responses to minor stressors, their genesis comes from our shared biological nature. We all want our children to make it safely to adulthood, and it often feels as if it is all on us to make that happen.

Lacking saber-toothed tigers and precarious cliffs, failure feels like the greatest threat of all, the one danger our children can't afford to encounter in these times of academic pressure and exclusionary admissions. Yet history is filled with stories of extraordinary people, inventors and innovators, who learned how to appropriate the gifts of failure to their own advantage, who did not run from it, but stayed in its company long enough to become comfortable amid the jumbled wreckage of their dashed hopes and flawed plans. They learned how to salvage what was working while leaving these plans behind only to regroup and rebuild. As recent MacArthur Fellow and former middle school teacher Angela Duckworth has found, the ability to attend to a task and stick to long-term goals is the greatest predictor of success, greater than academic achievement, extracurricular involvement, test scores, and IQ. She calls this grit, and first discovered its power in the classroom, while teaching seventh-grade math. She left teaching to pursue research on her hunch, and her findings have changed the way educators perceive student potential. Gritty students succeed, and failure strengthens grit like no other crucible.

EVERY TIME WE RESCUE, HOVER, or otherwise save our children from a challenge, we send a very clear message: that we believe they are incompetent, incapable, and unworthy of our trust. Further, we teach them to be dependent on us and thereby deny them the very education in competence we are put here on this earth to hand down.

But here's the truth, what research has shown over and over again: children whose parents don't allow them to fail are *less* engaged, *less* enthusiastic about their education, *less* motivated, and ultimately *less* successful than children whose parents support their autonomy.

Decades of studies and hundreds of pages of scientific evidence point to one conclusion that sounds crazy, but it absolutely works: If parents back off the pressure and anxiety over grades and achievement and focus on the bigger picture—a love of learning and independent inquiry—grades will improve and test scores will go up. Children of controlling and directive parents are much less able to deal with intellectual and physical challenges than peers who benefit from parents who stand back and allow their children to try, and fail, and try again. Furthermore, the failure our children experience when we back off and allow them to make their own mistakes is not only a necessary part of learning; it's the very experience that teaches them how to be resilient, capable, creative problem-solvers.

The United States has been criticized for producing a generation of inflexible thinkers, students who can memorize and regurgitate, but who are incapable of manipulating information in order to answer questions in novel and innovative ways. This is due in part to the fact that our educational system relies on high-stakes standardized testing as a measure of its efficacy, and because today's parents simply are not allowing their child to muck about in the unpleasant, messy, experience of failure long enough to come to terms with the shortcomings of plan A and formulate plans B, C, D, and E. Lots of kids can ace a test using plan A, but it's going to be the kid who has tried and failed and regrouped in order to try again with twenty-five other plans who will create true innovation and change in our world. That kid is not only creative and innovative in his thinking; he is also unafraid to try out new strategies. He will have the courage and resolve to work through thousands of miscalculations as he pursues a working solution. He will be able to regroup in the face of repeated failures and like Thomas Edison, he will learn the lessons inherent in discovering the thousands of ways a lightbulb does *not* work before inventing the one lightbulb that does.

MY FLASH OF INSIGHT HAD been a long time coming. Yes, I'd been uncomfortable with my own overparenting for a while, but I have to credit my students (again) for teaching me what I was too blind to see. Each year, my eighth graders write essays about an experience that has shaped their education, and after much struggle, one of my most tightly wound and anxiety-ridden students handed in the following paragraph:

> Some people are afraid of heights, some are afraid of water; I am afraid of failure; which, for the record, is called *atychiphobia*. I am so afraid of failing that I lose focus on what actually matters; learning. In focusing on the outcome, I lose the value of the actual assignment and deprive myself of learning.

She went on to recount all the ways this fear has held her back in school and athletics, but those first few sentences stopped me cold. Her experience as a student, my professional experience with her parents, my own parenting, and my son's fears all came together in her admission. This student's parents are wonderful, kind, and caring, and they never intended to create this sort of fear in their child. And frankly, the fallout would be their own problem to deal with save for the fact that the private choices parents make that undermine their child's social, academic, and emotional development eventually come in conflict with a teacher's ability to educate their child.

Despite the unbridled optimism and energy of the thousands of new teachers who enter the educational workforce every year, the National Education Association reports that one-third of these teachers will quit after three years, and 46 percent will be gone within five years. According to Ron Clark, the winner of a Disney American Teacher Award, many of these fleeing educators cite "issues with parents" as one of their main reasons for abandoning the profession. In a 2011 interview with CNN, Clark related an exchange with a principal who had been named the administrator of the year in her state but had chosen to leave education. "I screamed, 'You can't leave us,' and she quite bluntly replied, 'Look, if I get an offer to lead a school system of orphans, I will be all over it, but I just can't deal with parents anymore; they are killing us.'" I love teaching dearly, but "issues with parents" have inspired elaborate fantasies in which I abandon the profession forever, move to Alaska, and raise sled dogs. "Issues with parents" are the stuff of my nightmares.

Now that I understand the root cause of parents' fears and worries, I do what I can to convince them that a small blip in their child's journey means so little in the big picture, and can actually serve as a great opportunity to teach their child about resilience. I back up, let those anxious parents slow their breathing, and help them see that they have a fantastic, kind, generous, and curious child. I reassure them that *he will be fine*; indeed, he will do wonderful and interesting things in his life and no one will remember whatever transgression or failure triggered our conference. Some parents believe me, but many more do not, and leave my office convinced that the B-minus their child received for the semester spells the end of their dreams for educational excellence, economic security, and a lifetime of happiness.

It's always been hard to be a teacher and equally difficult to be a parent, and there should be plenty of common ground for mutual sympathy. We are, after all, working toward a shared goal: the education of our children. Unfortunately, parents who put a priority on saving kids from frustration and teachers who put a priority on challenging their students often butt heads, and consequently, the parent-teacher partnership has reached a breaking point. Teaching has become a push and pull between opposing forces in which parents want teachers to educate their children with increasing rigor, but reject those rigorous lessons as "too hard" or "too frustrating" for their children to endure. Parents rightly feel protective of their children's self-esteem, but teachers too often bear the brunt of parental ire.

I've struggled to find the best way to support parents in their efforts to love and nurture their children while teaching them how to step back a bit and allow children the safe space they need in order to fail, particularly when those kids hit middle school. Middle school is prime time for failure, even among kids who have sailed through school up to that point. The combined stressors of puberty, heightened academic expectations, and increased workload are a setup for failure. How parents, teachers, and students work together to overcome those inevitable failures predicts so much about how children will fare in high school, college, and beyond.

And that way forward? In order to help children make the most of their education, parents must begin to relinquish control and focus on three goals: embracing opportunities to fail, finding ways to learn from that failure, and creating positive home-school relationships. In the chapters to follow, I'll explain each of these goals in depth and give you strategies that will help you achieve them.

THE DAY I FINALLY CAME to terms with my overparenting, I was determined to start making amends at home with my own children.

I needed to do something immediate, something symbolic, and I knew just where to start. My younger son, then a third grader, had never learned to tie his shoes. I blamed this oversight on the invention of Velcro and his preference for slip-on shoes, but if I'm completely honest, I knew I was falling down on the job. He freaked out when I mentioned the situation, even in my most enthusiastic "Won't this be a fun project we can do together?" voice. He got frustrated with my instruction, I got frustrated with his helplessness, and the entire endeavor dissolved into anger and tears. Tears. Over *shoelaces*. When I began to look closely at the source of his issue with the shoelaces, it all boiled down to his feelings of frustration and helplessness, which was my fault, not his. I taught him that.

For every time I tied his shoes, rather than teach him to do it himself, I reinforced his perception that I believed the task was too hard for him. Eventually he and I both began to wonder whether he'd ever prevail. One day before school, when he'd left his Velcro shoes at a friend's house and had to wear the backup pair with laces, he said he'd rather wear his rain boots than try to tie his shoes. He didn't even care that wearing boots meant he'd have to sit out PE all by himself.

This, right here, is what I had wrought: my son was so convinced of his inability that he was willing to forfeit an hour of playtime with his friends.

So that afternoon, I took out his backup sneakers, and prepared to remedy the situation. Over a snack, I told him I'd made a mistake, and that I thought I'd figured out how to be a better mom. I empathized with his worry and told him that while the task might be hard for him at first, with some effort and perseverance, I knew he could conquer it. I was so confident that we were going to stick with it until he mastered those darn shoelaces.

In less than an hour, the embarrassment he'd felt about being the only third grader who could not tie his shoes was gone. He had succeeded and I've hardly ever seen him so proud of himself. I felt like a supermom, and all it took was a little time, a little faith in each other, and the patience to work through the tangle of knots and loops.

No, it's not always going to be this simple. The stakes get higher and the consequences get bigger as our children get older. Lumpy knots and uneven shoelaces give way in the blink of an eye to flawed college essays and botched job interviews, and there's only so much time available to instill confidence and resilience in our children. The work begins the first moment our babies fail to grasp a toy or fall as they toddle across the room, and continues until they head out into their own lives. The sooner parents learn to appreciate the positive aspects of hardship and allow children to benefit from the upside of failure in childhood, the sooner all of us will have the opportunity to share in the moments of pride like the one I saw on my son's face as he secured those laces.

It's up to us. Parents have the power to grant this freedom to fail. Teachers have the ability to transform that failure into an education. And together? Together, we have the potential to nurture a generation of confident, competent adults.

Let's get started.

Part I

Failure: A Most Valuable Parenting Tool

1

HOW FAILURE BECAME A DIRTY WORD: A BRIEF HISTORY OF AMERICAN PARENTING

AS A CHILD, I WAS obsessed with the *Little House on the Prairie* books. I wanted to live in a sod dugout on the banks of Plum Creek or a tiny cabin in the Big Woods under the strict but loving guidance of Ma and Pa Ingalls. I wanted to be Laura, who bravely roamed the dangerous and exciting world around her, and made plenty of mistakes as she made her way across the prairie. When she returned home to face the music, her parents responded not with anxiety and fear, but with interest in her adventures and an eye toward her education in the great big beyond.

I strove to be tolerant of my sister, just as Laura was of Carrie. When the extravagant gift I coveted did not appear under our Christmas tree, I reminded myself of the year Laura received only a small tin cup, a piece of candy, a small cake, and a penny, and tried to be grateful. Remnants of my "What would Laura do?" mentality survived into adulthood, and I could not wait to read the *Little House* books to my own children, to teach them about Laura's world of clear-cut morality and balloons made of pig bladders. We read and relived their favorite moments—dribbling syrup on snow to make candy, coloring butter with the juice of grated carrots, and tracing patterns in the window frost with a thimble. I encouraged them to wander our not-so-Big Woods, even as I worried about bears and hunters and deep cellar holes. I did my best to be that reassuring, firm, and loving Ma for my sons.

Ma and Pa set clear limits and goals for their children. Right was right, wrong was wrong, learning arose from failure, and when parents had to discipline, consequences were swift and just. And so, when I became a parent, "What would Laura do?" became "What would Ma do?" and I strove to raise my children according to that ideal. I try to remember that their mistakes and failures are a necessary and inevitable part of their growing up.

The fact that I turn to the late nineteenth century for advice says a lot about how complex and confusing parenting has become. Ma and Pa understood that the job of a parent is to raise self-sufficient, capable, and ethical adults. I envy their clarity, because sometimes, I'm not sure what my job is. One day it is to be my son's friend so he will feel comfortable enough to confide in me, the next it is to stand firm as an authority figure and teach him to write thank-you notes whether he wants to or not.

If I'm confused by my role, he must be, too. No wonder I yearn for the simplicity of parenting in the Big Woods. I fear, however, that even capable Ma and Pa Ingalls would be overwhelmed and confused by the shifting expectations and lack of solid footing in today's parenting landscape. In order to get our bearings in this confusing territory, to understand how we arrived in this state of confusion, we need to find the signal in the noise of our collective parenting history.

PARENTING IN A SIMPLER TIME

Parenting in Colonial New England was simpler in terms of its hierarchy of needs, defined as it was by risk and loss. Parents could expect to lose one in every ten children, even in the healthiest and wealthiest communities. In cities such as Boston, where urban poverty and close living quarters facilitated the spread of disease, childhood deaths were two to three times higher. When disaster struck, as it did during the 1677 smallpox epidemic, a fifth of the population died, most of them children. Parents to whom the sight of a dead child was "a sight no more surprising than a broken pitcher" were preoccupied with basic needs—the daily struggle for shelter, food, and safe drinking water—rather than the education, social life, and emotional health of their children. Reason, rather than emotion, dominated early American childrearing. The voice of parenting philosophy in Colonial America, as far as such a thing existed, was that of John Locke. Where today we explain why it's not nice to bite the neighbor lady via a long-winded treatise accompanied by a supplicatory lollipop, Locke favored a simpler solution, one that stressed clearheaded reason over emotion, for "[l]ong discourses and philosophical reasonings at best amaze and confound, but do not instruct children." Children were meant to be seen and not heard, and to always behave in the best interest of the family. They certainly were not allowed to make a scene. Toddler temper tantrums in the 1690 equivalent of the grocery store? Please. Locke advises "crying is very often a striving for mastery and an open declaration of their insolence or obstinacy: when they have not the power to obtain their desire, they will by their *clamor* and *sobbing* maintain their title and right to it" (emphasis Locke's, and I can almost hear the derision dripping from those *horrid*, *emotional* words). When children faced hardship and the consequences of their mistakes, Locke advised parents, "by no means bemoan them. This softens their minds and makes them yield to the little harms that happen to them, whereby they sink deeper into that part which alone feels, and makes larger wounds there than otherwise they would." In other words, correct and comfort, but do not pity or make a big deal out of children's hardship and failures because "the many inconveniences this life is exposed to require [that] we should not be too sensible of every little hurt." Locke was very much in favor of encouraging children to get back up and try again when they failed. "In the little harms they suffer from knocks and falls, they should not be pitied for falling, but bid do so again; which, besides that it stops their *crying* is a better way to cure their heedlessness and prevent their tumbling another time than either chiding or bemoaning them. But let the hurts they receive be what they will, [it will] stop their *crying* and that will give them more quiet and ease at present and harden them for the future" (again, the emphasis and disdain are Locke's). Colonial parents loved their children, and I'm sure they comforted them when they "suffered knocks and falls," but these obstacles were considered a part of daily life as one contributed, quietly and obediently, to the survival of the family in a harsh and dangerous land. Children grew up surrounded by the ups and downs of life and parents had more to focus on than the happiness of their offspring around the clock.

Parents pushed their children out of the nest much earlier in life than we do today. In the words of writer and American revolutionary Thomas Paine, "Nothing hurts the affections, both of parents and children, so much, as living too closely connected, and keeping up the distinction too long." Children married young, had their own children soon after, and had to be ready to maintain their own trade, farms, and households before they left what we consider middle adolescence, so parents were under pressure to pass down an education in survival and independence from a very early age.

The American Revolution saw the birth of a new nation and a new philosophy regarding the nature of children and their place in family and society. Just as our nation rebelled against the rule of an English king who required blind allegiance and submission, writers and thinkers promulgated an analogous vision for American children. As Steven Mintz points out in his book *Huck's Raft: A History of American Childhood*, this move toward individuality can be illustrated by the concurrent shift in baby-naming conventions. Until the American Revolution, children were typically named for parents or a close relative in order to reinforce the significance of lineage and honor for the family over the individual. By the mid-eighteenth century, however, parents began to bestow unique names on their children, sometimes paired with a middle name in an added display of individuality. Other customs that paid service to political, social, and familial hierarchies, such as children bowing to their parents, fell out of favor and the spirit of revolution began to seep into the minds and habits of a citizenry who refused to view themselves as subjects of any master, political or otherwise. Americans began to look toward the future of their new country, a nation of educated citizens that depended on children who would not bend to tyranny but value individual rights in service to freedom.

Despite the promise and heady idealism of this hard-won American independence, children still lived lives of quiet desperation. Up to half of all children lost a parent before they reached marriageable age, so many carried the weight of their own childhood work, as well as the work of a parent, on their narrow shoulders. Farm children as young as five were put to work and expected to do their share in order to secure their family's future. In cities, children had household chores, learned trades, and helped with the piecemeal work families brought into the home in order to earn extra money, such as laundry and sewing.

By the end of the nineteenth century, as the American population and its economy moved away from the farm and toward the city, one out of every six children between ten and fifteen was employed. Mills and factories employed children because of their handy, compact size. They could squeeze their small bodies under industrial machinery in order to free snags and malfunctions, and they were a cheap and expendable form of labor.

The early part of the twentieth century marked a new awareness of the danger and horrors children endured in the workforce. Unsafe child labor practices led to the creation of child labor laws that prevented children below a certain age from working outside the home. Just as child labor was outlawed, mandatory school attendance became the law of the land. Children who used to work for the financial security of the family were now occupied with the work of education. These reforms were wonderfully beneficial, but from the perspective of the family and a society that measured a child's worth by his utility, children had become superfluous, and over the course of a generation, were transformed from "useful to useless," profitable to priceless. As more children were born and raised into a life of leisure, parents were left to cobble together new parenting goals in order to raise these very expensive, nonproductive children.

THE RISE OF THE PARENTING EXPERT

By the time *Parents* magazine appeared on newsstands in 1926, the debate over parenting philosophy had taken hold in American culture and parents were eager for advice and information on how to raise their children in an increasingly confusing century. Thus began the era of the Parenting Expert, and a temporary lapse in society's faith in the competence of American parents. Where childrearing had once been absorbed into the fabric of everyday life, it now became a full-time job, requiring expert advice and training. Society no longer viewed children as miniature-sized adults, capable of work and resourceful problem-solving, but vulnerable dependents requiring a great deal of well-researched and precise care. As the number of children per family shrank over the years, parents focused more on the individual child's emotional and psychological needs. All those idle children had time to express their psychological issues, and new theories of developmental psychology emerged to address those issues. Behaviors that would have been described in judgmental terms by John Locke were deemed emotional conditions to be treated rather than irksome behaviors to be corrected. Gone were the days of the sturdy, resilient child; the era of emotionally dependent children and anxious parents was officially under way.

Parents heard the message of late-nineteenth and early-twentieth-century experts loud and clear: mothers had no business raising a child without the advice of doctors. Women used to counsel other women on childrearing, gathering advice in the form of wisdom handed down over generations, but as pediatric medicine emerged as a specialty, the wisdom of generations past was treated with distrust, if not overt disdain. These experts advised women to turn a "deaf ear" to "the grandmother . . . [whose] influence is particularly pernicious, as she is supposed by her previous experience to know everything about babies." Before the twentieth century, parents (mostly mothers) took care of children's health-care needs at home. Mothers kept a medical text, such as William Buchan's *Domestic Medicine*, in the home, and functioned as doctor, therapist, dentist, and teacher for their own children. At the turn of the century, however, the number of books on childrearing and child care exploded, and more significantly, their tone changed. Parenting had become a field of study and the experts writing the curriculum for this postgraduate specialty had little faith that mothers could ace it on their own.

The 1920s also marked the emergence of professional child care. Nursery schools were increasingly used as a way to educate all those ignorant mothers on the latest scientific advances in parenthood. Dependence on childrearing books, manuals, pamphlets, and professionals was strongly encouraged, and an avalanche of these publications emerged on the scene. They were full of the advice parents were told they needed about how to keep their children safe from the threat of germs (another popular topic thanks to the discovery of the germ theory in the late nineteenth century) and attend to their children's ever-changing and newly pressing emotional needs, concerns that would have been laughable to parents just fifty years before. The mental and emotional state of children was a novel concept, and the "psychologizing of childrearing" implied that parenting was not instinctual but a skill to be studied and learned. The consequences of improperly parenting a child included grave psychological damage and emotional distress, leading to psychological syndromes such as sibling rivalry, phobias, sleeping disorders, and teenage rebellion. Freud popularized the theory of psychosexual development and warned parents about the dangers of neuroses due to improper toilet training, heaping the burden of adult psychological illness on improper mothering. Psychologist John Bowlby alerted parents about the grave harm that can result from incomplete attachment to our children; if we did not hold them enough, they would become maladapted juvenile delinquents. Children increasingly became the focus of their parents' lives, and by the time the fifties rolled around, the United States had become fixated on the care, feeding, and entertainment of its young.

Full faith and credit in experts persisted until a certain warm and fuzzy physician gave parents permission to trust themselves again.

YOU KNOW MORE THAN YOU THINK YOU DO

Dr. Benjamin Spock's *Common Sense Book of Baby and Child Care*, published in 1946, sold three-quarters of a million copies in its first year, and marked a shift in the tone parenting experts adopted when handing out advice. Dr. Spock's book began with the shocking yet somehow comforting assurance, "Trust Yourself," and "You know more than you think you do." With those introductory sentiments, Dr. Spock handed power back to parents. He hoped to halt our nation's overdependence on experts, and it seemed he might just be the savior of common sense. Women still turned to doctors and psychologists for consultation, but Dr. Spock, through his gentle tone and comprehensive manual, encouraged parents to exercise common sense and ownership of their parenting. While many found Spock's vote of confidence in parents a step back toward sanity, some people—experts who were losing their authority and parents who were frightened by the sudden lack of direction—found this freedom anxiety-provoking. Vestiges of antiquated theories about the fragility of infants and the lifelong impact of bad parenting decisions remained, so when paired with a new freedom from the inflexible instructions of experts, many parents were paralyzed with the weight of their own power to tragically and irreversibly screw up their kids. As the fifties came to a close, a generation of children bent on rebellion and anti-establishment sentiment gave those experts plenty of ammunition in the case against Dr. Spock's brand of feel-good parenting.

The 1960s exploded in bursts of social and political activism, and its children began to believe in the power of a younger generation to change the world. John F. Kennedy, the youngest president ever elected, succeeded the oldest, and the civil rights movement gained energy and momentum thanks to a generation of young activists. They were loud, they were gaining power, and there were simply more of them than ever before; the baby boom following World War II reduced the median age of the American population to less than twenty years old. Adulthood, and the responsibility that came with it, lost its allure, and "power" lost its positive connotation as this younger generation was urged to actively question, rather than blindly follow, authority. Adolescence became a time of rebellion, experimentation, and the search for identity, and as it expanded further and further into what had traditionally been seen as adulthood due to prolonged schooling, delayed marriage, and jobs made scarce in a weak economy, Americans sought to stretch out the endless summer of childhood. Consequently, adults who had been raised in a more authoritarian era, operating under the long-standing assumption that adulthood began at eighteen, felt increasingly powerless in the face of this rebellion. Many parents put their hands up in defeat, and the media jumped on these parents for their overly permissive childrearing. Remember, child psychologists still espoused the theory that parents were likely responsible for the misdeeds of their children, particularly if they mucked up their child's infancy, so it made perfect sense that the media blamed parents for the historically unprecedented rebellion of America's children. Permissive parents were labeled neglectful parents, as illustrated in Jules Henry's 1963 study, *Culture Against Man*, in which Henry pinned the blame for the insolence and insensitivity of America's adolescents on "the overly intense child-centered postwar family [that] produced children who found it difficult to break the umbilical cord during adolescence."

In the meantime, the family was falling apart, at least relative to the quickly dwindling nostalgic glow of the 1950s. At the beginning of the 1960s, half of all women married before they were out of their teens, had a couple of kids in the first years of marriage, and remained at home with their children. However, as the decade progressed, young women went to college, got jobs, and put marriage off as they established their place in the world. Divorce rates doubled between 1960 and 1970, and the number of couples living together outside marriage increased sixfold.

Older, more independent and confident parents finally settled down to have children, and when they did, they parented according to the attachment method, the natural extension of Spock's "Trust Yourself" sentiment. Attachment parenting sought to strengthen the parent-child bond through constant, close contact and nurturance. The idea was that strong bonds established in infancy persist over a lifetime. John Bowlby, Harry Harlow, and T. Berry Brazelton strengthened public sentiment around the importance of attachment parenting, and by the time the American public bore witness to a prime-time broadcast about the tragically neglected children discovered in Romanian orphanages, the theory of attachment parenting had become a dire warning: wear your children in a sling 24/7 or risk attachment disorder like those Romanian babies. However, this message was incompatible with the reality most parents faced in the 1970s and 1980s. Women flooded the workforce in the wake of the feminist movement and were finally beginning to fulfill—and be recognized for—their potential as thinkers, innovators, and leaders. More significant, women *had* to work as inflation soared and recession settled in after the economic expansion of the 1960s. Women were torn between the needs of home and work, children and financial security, attachment parenting and the psychological need to detach from the restrictive labels of motherhood and expand their rights as individuals.

Hence, mothers were fertile ground for seeding the self-esteem movement of the 1970s. Nathaniel Branden's 1969 book, *The Psychology of Self-Esteem*, kicked the movement off with a bang. His message, that self-love is vital to emotional health, and that a person's self-evaluation "is the single most significant key to his behavior," appealed to parents who sought to assuage their guilt and fill the gaping hole left by their own esteem-fueled search for self and career-fueled detachment. The individual, and her sense of self-worth, eclipsed the value of community or family, and the American self-esteem movement took off. Unfortunately, it did not accomplish what Nathaniel Branden hoped. Branden envisioned a world in which children so valued themselves that the opinions of others would bounce off like some self-esteem force field, and we'd all live in a state of blissful self-exploration, self-satisfaction, and self-love.

A GENERATION OF NARCISSISTS

That's not quite how it worked out. Jean Twenge and W. Keith Campbell place the blame for *The Narcissism Epidemic* squarely on the back of the self-esteem movement. According to Twenge and Campbell, the self-esteem movement may have bolstered

Americans' self-esteem, but the result is not a happier, healthier citizenry; it is a generation of self-admiring narcissists focused on superficial appearances and personal gain. Worse, the self-esteem movement with its emphasis on individual happiness was the final nail in society's distrust of collective action and government.

The self-esteem movement promised that we could feel good about ourselves in everything we do, that kids would always like their parents, and that we would feel great about our parenting all the time. But this is not how life—let alone effective parenting—works. Children who like their parents all the time are not apt to be children who are corrected when they misbehave, called on for their mistakes, or asked to consider the needs of other people. It does not *feel* good to punish or correct our children; no one wants to be the cause of tears and hurt feelings. It *feels* great to hand our kids cookies just before dinner with a conspiratorial finger over the lips, bonding us to our kids in a shared, secret treat. It *feels* wonderful to swoop in and rescue when we take that forgotten homework to school, saving our kids from the disappointment of recess detention and the stern glare of a teacher. The catch is that what *feels* good to us isn't always what *is* good for our children. We are not used to putting off what feels right and good for us in the short term in order to do what is right and good for our children in the long term.

The lure of short-term happiness and permissive, feel-good parenting became even more tempting as we heaped on guilt over increasing divorce rates, more hours spent at work, and less time spent in leisure with our children. Treats traded hands in exchange for the quality time we could not spend with our families. When we did have time for them, we wanted to spend it in relative peace, not in squabbling over rules and consequences. It takes more time to teach a child how to clean a toilet than to clean the toilet ourselves, as is the case with about every worthwhile lesson, and we just did not have that kind of time anymore. I'm not casting stones here, and the windows in my glass house are well overdue for a cleaning. My children are quite limited in their ability to cook, simply because I want and need that time in my kitchen to myself. It is my refuge from a day spent in the classroom or in doing things for my own children. I'll teach them how to cook someday, just not today.

As we move through this new millennium, parents are caught in a bit of a catch-22. We are expected to feel good about ourselves and our parenting as we raise our children naturally and intuitively, while poring over more parenting books and magazines than ever about how to raise smart and creative and empathetic children who practice piano on their own, sleep nine hours a night, and play varsity soccer as freshmen. We are expected to take up the mantle of those authoritarian experts we abandoned in the fifties and function as professionals both at home and at work. As we sift through the reams of parenting advice, we are left to strike our own balance between work and home, trust in our instincts, and trust in the experts. Today, parenting is less oxytocin-soaked rosy glow, more adrenaline-fueled oncoming-headlight glare.

According to a post on *Parenting* magazine's website about today's most pressing parenting questions, we parents are concerned with the minutiae of parenting, such as "Will I spoil my baby if I pick her up every time she cries?" and "My baby does not reach his motor milestones as quickly as other infants do. Should I be worried?" While our focus has shifted from matters of life and death to the small details of children's mental, physical, and emotional development, the concluding item on the list exposes the concern at the root of all these parenting details. When we beg for answers to all those other nitpicky, insignificant questions, what we really want to know is "How will I know if I am a good parent?"

The answer, for most of us, is found in the moments when parenting feels good. I feel good when my children are safe, warm, and fed, of course, but what really feels good, what makes me feel like an A-plus parent, is when I show my kids I love them by rescuing them from disappointment. Those times when I remember to pick up a book from the library I know my son will like, or when I show up at the last second before a soccer game with a forgotten mouth guard so he can play, reassure me that, "Yes, you *are* a good parent today."

Most of my adult life has been dedicated to the work of raising my children, and until recently, that meant I spent my life protecting them from failure, all wrapped up in the safety of my loving embrace. But that's not working for us anymore, and it's certainly not working for my students and their families. I was afraid to abandon what felt good, afraid to put my needs aside and expose my children to the parts of life that hurt a little. Afraid I wouldn't hear my inner "Yes, you *are* a good parent today" anymore.

GIVEN THAT THE SELF-ESTEEM MOVEMENT is a failure, and doing what *feels* good has fostered a generation of narcissistic, self-indulgent children unwilling to take risks or cope with consequences, what will work? What parenting practice can help our children acquire the skills, values, and virtues on which a positive sense of self is built?

Parenting for autonomy. Parenting for independence and a sense of self, born out of real competence, not misguided confidence. Parenting for resilience in the face of mistakes and failures. Parenting for what is right and good in the final tally, not for what feels right and good in the moment. Parenting for tomorrow, not just for today.

2

WHY PARENTING FOR DEPENDENCE DOESN'T WORK: THE POWER OF INTRINSIC MOTIVATION

I'VE KNOWN THE MOTHER SITTING in front of me for years, and we have been through a lot together. I have taught three of her children, and I like to think we've even become friends during our time together. She's a conscientious mother who obviously loves her children with all of her heart. I've always been honest with her about their strengths and weaknesses, and I think she trusts me to tell her the truth. But when she hits me with the question that's been bothering her for a while, all I can do is nod, and stall for time.

"Marianna's grades are fine; I'm not worried about that, but she just doesn't seem to love learning anymore."

She's absolutely right. I'd noticed the same thing about her daughter over the previous two or three years, and I have an answer, right there on the tip of my tongue, for what has gone wrong. Yet I'm torn between my responsibility to help Marianna and the knowledge that what I have to say is a truth I'm not sure this mother is ready to hear.

The truth—for this parent and so many others—is this: Marianna has sacrificed her natural curiosity and love of learning at the altar of achievement, and it's our fault. Her parents, her teachers, society at large—we are all implicated in this crime against learning. From her first day of school, we pointed her toward that altar and trained her to measure her progress toward that goal by means of points, scores, and awards. We taught her that her potential is tied to her intellect, and her intellect is more important than her character. We taught her to come home proudly bearing A's, championship trophies, and college acceptances, and we inadvertently taught her that we don't really care how she obtains them. We taught her to protect her academic and extracurricular perfection at all costs and that it's better to quit when things get challenging rather than risk marring that perfect record. Above all else, we taught her to fear failure, and that fear has destroyed her love of learning.

I look at this mother with concern on her face, her eager pencil poised to write down my words of wisdom, and struggle to find a gentle way to explain that the daily nagging about points and grades both perpetuates Marianna's dependence on her mother's interventions and teaches her that external rewards are far more important than the effort Marianna invests in her education. Marianna is so concerned with pleasing her parents that the love she used to feel for learning has been crowded out by her craving for their validation.

This mother's hovering comes from a place of love, that's clear. She wants the world for her children, and yet the very things she's doing to encourage the sort of achievement she feels will help them secure happiness and honors may be undermining their future success.

Marianna is very smart, and her mother reminds her of that on a daily basis. However, Marianna does not get praised for the diligence and effort she puts in to sticking with a hard math problem or a convoluted scientific inquiry. If that answer at the end of the page is wrong, or if she arrives at a dead end in her research, she has failed, no matter what she has learned from her struggle. And contrary to what she may believe, in these more difficult situations she *is* learning. She learns to be creative in her problem-solving. She learns diligence. She learns self-control and perseverance. But because she is scared to death of failing, she has started to take fewer intellectual risks. She knows that if she tries something challenging or new, and fails, that failure will be hard evidence that she's not as smart as everyone keeps telling her she is. Better to be safe. Is that what we want? Kids who get straight A's but hate learning? Kids who achieve academically but are too afraid to take leaps into the unknown?

Marianna's mother has been extremely successful in school and business, and she knows the value of that hard work in her own life. Her own mother allowed her to fail and play and learn for the sake of learning, but now that she's parenting her own child, she's lost sight of the value of struggle. She is too worried about Marianna's future achievements to allow her to work through the obstacles in her path. She wants to give Marianna everything and yet she forgets that the very best experiences of her own childhood likely arose from the thrill of facing challenge, from the moments she lost herself in the trying, and when she failed, trying again to accomplish something all on her own, simply for the adventure and pleasure inherent in learning something new.

I know this mom because she's just like me, and telling her the truth is hard both because I'm afraid she'll get defensive and angry, and because it means I have to cop to all the same mistakes she's made in my own parenting. Maybe it's time to share some truths with her as I figure out where I went astray, and together we can help our kids rediscover their intellectual bravery, enthusiasm for learning, and the resilience they need in order to grow into independent, competent adults. With a little luck, they will look back on their childhood and thank us; not just for our unwavering love, but for our willingness to put their long-term developmental and emotional needs before their short-term happiness. To let their lives be just a little bit harder today so they will know how to face hardship tomorrow.

I take a deep breath, cross my fingers, and tell her the truth.

INTRINSIC MOTIVATION: THE HOLY GRAIL OF PARENTING

Here's what I told her: The less we push our kids toward educational success, the more they will learn. The less we use external, or extrinsic, rewards on our children, the more they will engage in their education for the sake and love of learning.

All kids begin life motivated by their own desire to explore, create, and build. When babies take their first step, it is because they are driven to discover and master their environment. If there's any trick to parenting, it is to keep our children from losing that internal drive. Unfortunately, parents and teachers rely on the same sort of reward system used to train monkeys and seals. It works great at the circus, but bananas and herring—or iPads and pizza—do not work for humans. Rewards may get results in the short term, but when it comes to encouraging long-term drive and enthusiasm for learning, rewards are terrible motivators.

When I read about the research on rewards, first in Daniel Pink's *Drive*, and later in the original research of psychologists Harry Harlow and Edward Deci, I was thrown. Nearly everything I do in my classroom and in my home revolves around external rewards, but Harlow's research into what motivates monkeys had me doubting my practices.

In 1949, Harlow became curious about what motivates primates (and, by extension, humans), so he gave eight monkeys, each in its own cage, a latch attached to a piece of wood, and waited to see what they would do with it. He didn't have to wait long; the monkeys loved playing with the latches, and fiddled with them over and over again until they opened up. The monkeys were opening the locks just for the fun of the activity, or, in Harlow's words, "the performance of the task provided intrinsic reward." That's all the monkeys needed to spur them on.

Once Harlow realized the power of intrinsic motivation, he was curious about whether an "extrinsic reward" such as a raisin would improve their performance.

In the second phase of his experiment, Harlow gave half of the monkeys a raisin as a reward for opening the locks. The monkeys were quite good at opening the locks, so surely, given a reward, they would open them even faster, right? Nope. The monkeys who received raisins actually opened the locks more slowly, and with less frequency, than they did when no reward was offered. Something about the extrinsic reward interfered with their intrinsic motivation and threw them off their game (or latch, in this case).

The human analogy is simple: when a kid is fascinated by a task, he will be much more likely to persevere, even when he falters, even when the task gets more challenging, and yes, even when he fails to master the task the first time around. Think back to the explorations of your newly mobile baby, crawling around the living room floor, pulling the cat's tail, and clearing the books off the bottom shelf of the bookcase. My sons drove me crazy, dropping spoons down into the heating vent in the living room and repeatedly attempting to climb the stairs on their own. That same drive that allows kids to learn the name of every god in the Greco-Roman pantheon or the scientific name and genus of every dinosaur that lived during the Cretaceous period fuels their learning early on in school. As kids get older, our goal should be to preserve this natural curiosity and thirst for discovery at all costs. Unfortunately, the methods we use to motivate our children, such as rewards, are in direct conflict with what keeps kids engaged and interested. Put simply, if you'd like your child to stop doing his schoolwork, pay him for good grades.

Once, many years ago, I had a student who was, according to her father, "a bad speller." No matter what the student did, she failed her weekly list of ten spelling words. Her grades hovered around a B, but that pesky spelling grade kept pulling her down into B-minus territory. Her year-end grade was, in fact, a B-minus, and her parents were livid. Not with her, but with me. They demanded an immediate parent-teacher meeting and asked some key school administrators to attend as well. They made it very clear in the meeting that their daughter wasn't "a B-minus student." The mother explained that despite all the support their daughter was being given she was intrinsically a bad speller and shouldn't be penalized for that. The meeting took about an hour and a half, and for much of that time, I was berated by the parents for being an ineffectual teacher and warned that my actions had lowered their daughter's self-esteem to the point that she cried every Thursday night before her Friday spelling quiz.

I used all of my best parent-teacher skills: I listened, kept my body language relaxed, and empathized with their frustration. I also made them a promise. I promised them that if they would allow the B-minus to stand, and encourage their daughter's effort rather than her grades, they might find that this

B-minus "crisis" would be one of the best things that ever happened to her. They were not exactly mollified. They left that meeting extremely angry that I would not change her grade, and I left feeling frustrated and wary of the fact that I would be teaching their daughter again the following year. I hoped that some of what I offered up as advice might sink in, and that one day, we could all laugh over this B-minus.

That next fall, their daughter returned to school with renewed vigor and a commitment to her education. Whatever had gone down at their house over the summer, *something* was working. She studied hard for her spelling quizzes and hit the ground running with a 10/10 on her first quiz. The perfect quiz grades continued, and about a month into the year, I graded her quiz and congratulated her on a perfect score while I was proctoring a study hall. I motioned to the recycling bin and raised my eyebrows in a silent "Would you like the quiz back, or should I recycle it?" She walked up to my desk to retrieve the quiz and told me, "I have to have the quiz or I won't get my ten dollars."

Ah. She'd been getting paid a cool ten bucks for each perfect score. I was mildly irked, but then again, what's the harm? Her parents had the money to spend on the weekly, ten-point quizzes, she had some spending money in her pocket, and her past as "a bad speller" seemed to have faded into an unpleasant memory. Besides, she was happy. The arrangement seemed to benefit everyone, and it even worked. For a while. Sometime after the holidays, her spelling grades fell again. I asked, and yes, her parents were still offering ten dollars for every perfect score. It was a busy year for her, she said, but she would bring her scores back up to where they were before, she promised. Except those scores never did come back up, and she ended the year, spelling-wise, about where she'd been, the year before.

So what went wrong? If the ten dollars were incentive enough for that first month or two, why did the reward stop working? There are a couple of issues at play here. First, rewards don't work, because humans perceive them as attempts to control behavior, which undermines intrinsic motivation. Second, human beings are more likely to stick with tasks that arise out of their own free will and personal choice. Given the choice between sticking with a "I have to" task or doing something else, most people would choose anything that is the product of their autonomy and self-determination.

Psychologist Edward Deci, author of *Why We Do What We Do: Understanding Self-Motivation*, provided the human extension to Harry Harlow's work on intrinsic motivation in monkeys. Deci sought to find out why younger children are so clearly fueled by curiosity and a desire to understand their world, and why that internal drive is often lost in older children. "I had the fleeting—and surely blasphemous—thought that maybe all the rewards, rules, and regimentation that were so widely used to motivate schoolchildren were themselves the villains, promoting not an excited state of learning but a sad state of apathy."

To expose these villains and prove his theory, Deci needed an inherently interesting task and some subjects. He discovered the Parker Brothers game Soma, "The World's Finest Cube Puzzle Game," and was immediately hooked on the challenge and feeling of accomplishment he discovered when he solved the puzzles. According to Deci, the Soma challenges were quite addictive, and he found himself solving puzzles in his head, even after he'd put them down. He then invited student test subjects into his lab to solve the puzzles. Some of the students received a dollar for every puzzle solved, and some received nothing and had to rely on their own feelings of satisfaction. After the subjects had solved a few puzzles, Deci would leave the room for eight minutes to complete an administrative task, and the subjects were left alone in the lab with the puzzles and an array of magazines. During those eight minutes, the subjects were secretly watched by the experimenter to see how they spent their free time. The students who were being paid to complete the puzzles were much less likely to play with them, while the subjects who were not being paid continued to play, just for their personal enjoyment of the activity. In Deci's view, money does not motivate, so much as it controls, and that control disrupts our sense of intrinsic motivation.

After a few more studies in this vein, he concluded that just about anything humans perceive as controlling is detrimental to long-term motivation, and therefore, learning. Want to hover over your kids to make sure they dot their *i*'s and cross the *t*'s on their homework? Detrimental. Feel the need to impose some of your goals on their learning? Detrimental. Itching to impose a deadline for your son's rough draft on that science project? Detrimental.

Don't believe me? Try this simple exercise. Go into a young child's room and ask to play Legos with her. If you play according to her script, everything will go fine. However, if you start to impose your goals on the project or attempt to force new directions based on your wants or needs, the fun will end, and quickly. Your child will either lose interest or get angry, but either way, your child is done with that project. The quickest way to kill off your child's interest in a game, topic, or experiment is to impose your will on her learning.

So what is a parent to do to if we can't bribe, supervise, or impose goals or deadlines? Believe it or not, the answer, no matter how counterintuitive it might feel, is to back off. Allow kids to have the control and autonomy they crave even if it means struggling with the task or situation at hand. In an experiment that built on his initial results in the Soma puzzle research trial, Deci offered half of his test subjects a choice of puzzles, and predictably, the half who were given a choice spent more time playing with the puzzles and reported having more fun than the subjects not given any choice. As soon as your child is capable of working on his own, and maybe even a little bit before he is completely independent, give him choices. This is a well-known and wonderful strategy for toddlers, who are stuck in a developmental stage in which they have very little control over their world, and yet their need for autonomy is high. Offering limited choices to toddlers—*do you want to wear the blue or the red sneakers*—gives the impression of control without allowing so much control that anarchy and chaos result.

Give school-aged children control and autonomy over where, when, and how they complete their schoolwork and let them make choices about the other important aspects of their lives such as friends, chores, and sports, subjects we'll address in later chapters. Establish nonnegotiable expectations, such as "Homework will be completed thoroughly and on time," or "Curfew is at ten and I expect you to be here or call if something comes up." After those expectations are made clear, older children should be allowed the autonomy to figure out the precise manner and strategy they will use in order to fulfill these expectations. As long as your expectation is that homework will be completed thoroughly, and on time, where, when, and how they complete their homework should be up to them.

DON'T WORRY; THIS DOES NOT mean teachers and parents have no say in our children's learning. It just means that we have to abandon our current strategy and get creative. Putting this knowledge into practice in my classroom was a challenge; I'm not going to lie. I *love* standing at the front of a classroom, dictating the whens, wheres, and hows to my students, assigning my carefully thought-out lessons, grading that work when students hand it in on the due date. I had been teaching this way for ten years, but given Deci's research, I was moved to shake my teaching up a little bit and see what happened. Luckily, teachers all over the country are moving toward project-based learning, in which students create real-world problems or questions and then figure out how to find answers themselves. Students define the scope, goals, and steps in the project, and therefore feel a real sense of ownership over the learning. My first attempts at handing the educational reins over to my students were encouraging, and I used Deci's work as a blueprint for my lessons. The more I pulled back and allowed my students to come up with the details of their own projects, assessments, and learning, the more invested they became in those projects. I had to upend my thinking in the classroom, but as I saw my students engage more enthusiastically in their learning at school, I realized I had to try these new strategies out at home with my own kids.

I took the guidelines I'd gleaned from Deci, set aside time alone to talk with my husband, and laid it all out for him: if intrinsic motivation happens when kids feel autonomous, competent, and connected to the people and world around them, those three needs must inform our parenting.

AUTONOMY: IN WHICH KIDS FIND OUT THAT SELF-RELIANCE FEELS GREAT

Autonomy and independence are similar beasts, but their roots reveal a key difference. Independence is the linguistic opposite of dependence, but autonomy is something more. It comes from the Greek *auto*, which means "self," and *nomos*, which means "custom" or "law," so to be autonomous, a child has to have internalized a system of rules for living independently. In order to help foster the formation of this self-rule, parents have to help kids come up with a system of guiding principles so they will be able to problem-solve and think creatively while remaining rooted in tried-and-true principles of behavior. When parents are overcontrolling, kids tend not to think about why and how they act in the world. Their choice is to respond to our rules or not. When they are given more control over their worlds out of our sphere of influence, they are more likely to make solid, rule-based decisions. It's a win-win situation for parents, really, because autonomy begets autonomy. As kids realize they have control over their worlds, they want more control over their lives and become more responsible.

While the research on intrinsic motivation shows that attempting to exert control over kids undermines their sense of autonomy, this does *not* mean that we should not make demands of our children. Just the opposite. Children of all ages need limits and guidance from parents and teachers. Without limits, chaos ensues, and a chaotic classroom or household does not foster learning. I've spent a lot of time in other teachers' classrooms, and when those teachers have poor classroom management skills and fail to set expectations for behavior, standards, and character, their students tend to be anxious, confused, and inattentive. In classrooms where teachers establish respect for the educational process and make their expectations clear, students are able to relax and focus on learning.

One way parents and teachers try to impose control over children is to offer rewards: bribes, gifts, money, and yes, even praise in exchange for performance. As we saw in that example of the student who was being paid for perfect spelling scores, rewards for academic performance work only for the short term. Is your goal an A on next Friday's algebra test, or your child's interest in learning math over the long term?

I know. This is hard information to swallow. Reward for performance is the American way, capitalism at work, pay for play, right? As we learned back in high school science, when B. F. Skinner gave his lab rats rewards for pressing a lever, it worked. Those rats pressed that lever over and over again, and he proved that animals continue to perform a particular behavior as long as the reward is forthcoming. And there's the key problem with using rewards to fuel behaviors. Animals continue to perform a particular behavior *as long as the reward is forthcoming.* But, as Deci notes, when was the last time you saw a seal balance a ball on his nose without a trainer standing there with a fish in the offing? No fish, no trick. Rewards work for repetitive, uncomplicated, or boring tasks, but when it comes to creativity and nuanced learning, they are lousy motivators. One of my favorite research studies on the subject sums up the effect of money on learning in its title: "Money enhances memory consolidation—but only for boring material."

Applying pressure in the form of control is the single most damaging thing parents and teachers can do to their children's learning. Whether in the form of threats, bribes, deals, surveillance, imposed goals, evaluations, or even rewards and praise, control is the enemy of autonomy. We parents are all guilty. Full disclosure: There's a chore chart on my refrigerator, and on top of that same refrigerator is my son's favorite toy, a stuffed creature named Stinky, currently being held hostage until his room is clean, and Finn is nearly apoplectic. I had a moment of weakness fueled by frustration and accidentally reached into my old bag of parenting tricks when I made the decision to take Stinky away, and once I did it, I had to follow through. Parenting is hard, and even those of us who know what works in the abstract fall victim to old habits. That said, the research of Deci and others is clear: any strategy that undermines autonomy is probably not going to work if long-term learning is the goal.

Another drawback to offering rewards as incentive is that this strategy inhibits creativity and risk-taking. When rewards are at stake, emphasis is on the end result, so what's the point of creativity? If my students know they will receive an iPod for an A, they will take the safest route to that A because they don't want to risk the iPod reward. The student who is motivated by the process of problem-solving and intellectual exploration learns for the sake of learning, and if the A comes, or the iPod falls into her lap, great. This is why intermittent rewards can work even if routine, expected rewards do not. The thrill and surprise of a reward when you least expect it can jump-start motivation, but again, only when it's not part of a routine practice.

Weaning children off a reward-for-performance system doesn't happen in a day, particularly if pay-for-play has become your default parenting strategy. Keep those trained seals in mind and expect that the behaviors you have been eliciting with rewards may well stop as soon as the rewards disappear. This will likely be frustrating to both you and your child in the short term, so it might be worth talking to your older children about why you are ending the system they have come to expect. You are the model for your child's behavior and attitude toward failure. Children need to see examples of adults admitting to their mistakes, learning how to be better parents and people, and adopting new strategies when a previous one has failed. Make sure they know that you truly believe learning springs from failure, and encourage them to view failure in the same light. Anne Sobel, a lecturer in cinematography and directing at Northwestern University in Qatar, has fought back against her students' inclination to play it safe, by incorporating risk-taking and failure into her grading. "I tell students that if they attempt a challenging project, I will take that into consideration when I grade, even if the film falls short of their vision."

In my own teaching, I make it a practice to model a constructive and adaptive reaction to failure. I admit to my mistakes, and am honest about the moments my teaching strategies have failed my students, and those admissions have led to some of the most productive and cooperative moments in my classroom. Children need to understand that mistakes are simply a part of my efforts to become a better teacher, and that education never really ends. Modeling is a powerful educational strategy—far more powerful than the offer of an iPod or ten bucks.

For some reason, it was easier for me to admit to my mistakes in the classroom than in my own home. In the middle of an argument with my teenager, or when I'd grabbed the reins on some household task that had spiraled out of control, I could feel my heels digging in, even when I knew I'd screwed up. I had to push my pride aside and admit to my mistakes, and show my kids that I have the courage to fail, face it, take the lessons to heart, and move on.

When my husband and I stopped dangling rewards in front of our kids, we decided to try using something I had been using for ages with my advisees at school: goals. My former middle school uses an advisory system, and teachers meet weekly with students to help them set goals regarding everything from school to social issues to handwriting. I think goals work well for students because they are rewards that remain squarely under the kid's control.

Sometimes, when I feel my advisees could use a sense of renewal or a clean slate, we talk about starting from scratch with new goals for a semester. For example, one of my advisees set goals to get over her shyness, and we devised plans for talking to teachers and asking other adults for help. She made huge strides that semester, because it was *her* goal, to be completed according to *her* parameters, and if she failed, so what? She was accountable to no one but herself for those failures. Self-imposed goals are about the safest place there is for a kid to fail. If kids make up their own goals, on their own timeline, according to their criteria, then failure is not a crushing defeat. Goals can be amended, changed according to circumstances, and even postponed to maybe next week. For kids who are particularly afraid and anxious about failing, goals offer a private proving ground, a safe way to take risks, fail, and try again.

If we really want our kids to invest in long-term goals, those goals have to be their goals, not ours. A friend of mine figured this out recently when her son pleaded to stop taking piano lessons. She was finally swayed when he told her, "Mom, I think playing piano is *your* goal, not mine." This can be hard to keep in mind, particularly when a student is having problems, but for a goal to work, the child has to own it.

Teenagers may resist the practice of goal-setting, particularly if you have been a controlling parent until now (I believe my older son mocked the entire idea the first couple of times I brought it up). However, once they realize that you have turned over a new leaf and want to help them achieve *their* goals, their trust in your motives will return. And remember, this goal-setting does not have to be conducted like a business meeting. The best discussions are relaxed, calm, and casual. My favorite conversations take place in the car, on walks, and in all those moments that pop up when you least expect them. Teenagers are not always ready to listen or talk, and sometimes you simply have to be ready to meet them where they are and when their minds and spirits are willing.

Be supportive of their goals. Some goals are going to seem trivial, but if they are important enough for your child to verbalize, they are important enough for your respect and support. Deci calls this strategy "autonomy-supportive," but I call it smart parenting.

COMPETENCE: CONFIDENCE BORN OUT OF EXPERIENCE

You can prop your child's confidence up with lavish praise, but you cannot create competence through praise alone. Competence requires both ability *and* experience, and confidence alone can lead to disaster. Recent studies have shown that while kids need to engage in free play that includes risk-taking, risky play is much more dangerous for kids who have never been allowed to engage in it than for kids who grow up knowing how to manage risk. Knowing how to manage risk through experience is real, hard-earned competence, and it makes them feel great about themselves.

When my neighbor's son was five, he was absolutely positive he could operate his father's power tools. As his father had not yet taught him to use any of those tools, this belief was built on confidence rather than competence. On one visit to his house, he led me over to his father's new wood splitter, an insanely dangerous and decidedly not kid-approved piece of machinery. He looked up at me with great hope (and a hand on the power key) and asked if I'd like to see him operate it. I declined his offer (and alerted his mother), as I knew his confidence was dangerous, grounded in nothing more than his deep love of power tools. Now that he is nearly twelve, and his father has spent hours teaching him how to operate the machinery safely and effectively, he has become a competent carpenter, woodsman, and handyman. That competence stems not just from a belief that he could work these tools, but also from a place of real ability and hours of experience under his father's guidance.

Children who possess competence through experience will be safer in the world because they will not launch themselves headlong into risks they are unprepared to handle. A child who believes he's ready for the deep end of the pool because you praised his incredible talent as a swimmer when he flopped through his first two freestyle strokes is in much more danger of drowning than a child who has a realistic sense of his abilities. Be honest with your children. Praise them for their resilience and the efforts they make to recover from their mistakes. Above all, keep your eye on the prize: intrinsic motivation. Protecting kids from the frustration, anxiety, and sadness they experience from failure in the short term keeps our children from becoming resilient and from experiencing the growth mindset they deserve.

Encourage competence in your child whenever possible. Watch a child master fixing her own lunch, or listen to a teenager recount the moment he made a goal in soccer practice. Competence and mastery are incredible motivators. Once children get a taste of success, particularly success born of their own efforts and persistence, it becomes addictive. This is the lovely thing about competence: it's a self-fulfilling prophecy.

I have seen what can happen when a child who has previously been bribed and cajoled suddenly discovers the wonder of mastery. It's as if the sun has broken through the clouds and is shining directly on that child's face. He lights up, he wiggles with excitement, he beams. The best part of this moment is that once a kid masters a skill through his own self-directed efforts, he enters a positive feedback loop that keeps on giving. The buzz can last for years if it's nurtured. I've even seen this sense of competence overshadow and replace years of frustration and negative self-image.

The key is that competence must come out of a child's own efforts. Keep this in perspective as you begin to withdraw rewards (false praise, gifts, unnecessary adulation) and shift to a more autonomy-supportive system. The day your child comes home from school having finally understood a complex and challenging concept, all radiant with pride and mastery, the magic of competency will become clear.

CONNECTION: RELATIONSHIPS ARE WHAT MAKE AUTONOMY AND COMPETENCE MEANINGFUL

This last element of intrinsic motivation comes down to your child's relationships with you, with teachers, and with the world at large. Humans are social animals, and we need to know that our efforts mean something to other people and the world. The good news is that autonomy-supportive parenting tends to strengthen bonds between child and parent, while controlling practices weaken them. Again, this does not mean that parents who set strict limits are bad parents. One of the most effective mothers I've ever known is incredibly strict, but her children understand why she sets the limits she does. She reminds me a bit of Ma Ingalls, because above all else, she's reasonable and supportive of her children's autonomy and sense of competence. Consequently, her children—even her teenagers—admire and adore her, and feel connected to her to a degree that is rare these days. Foster autonomy and competence, and connectedness will follow.

In order to foster autonomy while strengthening that connection to your kids, they need to know that you believe they can grow into your new, greater expectations. Here's where the idea of "mindset" comes into the picture. Stanford University psychology professor and *Mindset* author Carol Dweck divides people into one of two mindsets: fixed or growth. A person with a fixed mindset believes that intelligence, talent, or ability are innate, and remain the same throughout life, no matter what he does. A person with a growth mindset, however, believes that these qualities are simply a starting point, that more is always possible through effort and personal development. Those with growth mindsets are motivated to learn for learning's own sake because they believe that by pushing and stretching themselves they can do more and become more accomplished. They thrive on challenge and understand that failing and trying again is part of becoming smarter, better, or faster. If they discover limitations in themselves, they search for ways to overcome these challenges. "The hallmark of successful individuals is that they love learning, they seek challenges, they value effort, and they persist in the face of obstacles," writes Dweck. To put this research in practical terms, kids with fixed mindsets will be far less likely to persevere when school gets challenging because they don't believe they can stretch beyond their perceived limitations. Kids with growth mindsets will push on even when they fail to understand something the first time around because they know it's a matter of exerting more effort until they succeed.

Sadly, overparenting undermines so much of what contributes to a growth mindset and therefore inhibits intrinsic motivation. Overparenting teaches kids that without our help, they will never be able to surmount challenges. When we save them from risk and failure, we communicate to our kids that we don't have faith in their ability to grow, improve, and surmount challenges, and we encourage a fixed mindset. The sort of dependence created by rescuing and overparenting may feel like connectedness, but because it communicates our lack of faith in them, it undermines healthy connectedness by emphasizing control rather than love and support.

Just as connectedness with parents shores up kids' confidence at home, kids are much more likely to take academic and emotional risks at school if they feel connected to their teachers. As I see it, this idea of connectedness goes beyond the classroom to the larger world outside. An understanding of geometry is abstract and meaningless until it is connected to the beautiful and powerful angles of bridges, architecture, and astronomy. Without building a connection between Roman culture and the roots of modern languages, Latin truly is a dead language, and unlikely to inspire passion or drive in my students.

So one of the most important things parents can do for their children is to show them that they are not alone in the world, that they matter in the big picture, and that their parents are there to support them as they find their place within it.

DESIRABLE DIFFICULTIES LEAD TO MASTERY

While autonomy, competence, and communication sound like great concepts in the abstract, allowing kids to make the mistakes and face the failures that flow from increased autonomy goes against our parenting instincts. It's hard to watch, and it's even harder to not jump in when we see our kids frustrated or upset. I get frequent emails from parents whose kids were frustrated by an assignment, or a quiz question wasn't phrased precisely the same way I'd phrased the material in class. We want life to be smooth sailing for our kids, but interesting research shows that smooth sailing isn't where real, deep learning happens. Small failures, when the stakes are relatively low and the potential for emotional and cognitive growth is high, are what psychologists Elizabeth and Robert Bjork call "desirable difficulties." Learning that comes with challenge is stored more effectively and more durably in the brain than learning that comes easily.

Learning occurs when we observe something—we hear, see, or otherwise experience information in some way—and our brains transform that perception into a representation our brains understand. This is called *encoding*. We perceive hundreds of experiences all day long, and yet we don't necessarily hold on to all of those perceptions in our long-term memory. In order to turn those ephemeral perceptions into long-term memory, we must *consolidate* them. Consolidation is the process of organizing, sorting, and ordering perceptions and experiences into something the brain can store away and pull up later. Finally, in order to really nail that memory down, we must tag it for retrieval later on. This final part of the process, *retrieval*, is vital to learning because it solidifies knowledge through the process of pulling the information back out of the brain in order to apply it to novel situations and contexts. This is why rote memorization and regurgitation are ineffective teaching tools; they do not go far enough toward creating durable learning.

A popular buzzword in education today is *mastery*, and mastery demands retrieval. Students need to be able to recall information and apply it, connect it to other disciplines, demonstrate it for someone else, or otherwise render that information useful in their world. Teachers understand that you don't really know something until you can teach it to someone else, and this is because being able to teach information requires all three parts of the learning equation: encoding, consolidation, and retrieval.

But here's the catch. It turns out that the easier it is to retrieve information, the less durable the information is in your brain. So the harder you have to work to retrieve and apply knowledge in a novel way, the more durably that knowledge will be encoded.

That is why aversion to failure is a handicap. As the authors of *Make It Stick: The Science of Successful Learning* explain, errors are an integral part of learning. If kids are terrified of making mistakes, they will shy away from taking chances to the detriment of their learning and personal growth.

IN MY WORK AS A teacher, I talk to parents all the time who claim that their child simply can't abide failure, that it makes kids anxious, upset, and frustrated, which in turn makes parents anxious, upset, and frustrated. They worry that even if they adopt a rosy view of failure, their child is too afraid to fail. I tell them to watch their child undertake a task they love, under their own motivation and control, and see just how afraid of failure that kid really is. A child who flips out over a challenging fractions equation during homework time is often the same child who will sit down to play Minecraft for three hours, gleefully overcoming repeated obstacles in order to construct the perfect lofty tower to house his stash of treasures and show off his architectural prowess. Our kids have not entirely lost their ability to face failure; they have simply misplaced it among their trophies and ribbons and award certificates.

Children can be taught how to rediscover their willingness to fail and tap into their intrinsic motivation, even when they have become reward junkies, slaves to praise, and dependent on our interventions at every turn. It's not going to be easy, especially in the transitional stage, but I promise, the ends will more than justify the challenge of the means.

3
LESS REALLY IS MORE: PARENTING FOR AUTONOMY AND COMPETENCE

WHEN MY HUSBAND AND I started to transform our own parenting, we knew it would be a shock to the flawed system we'd been cultivating in our family for fifteen years. Rather than leave our kids to wonder whether their parents had suddenly been taken over by aliens, we sat down one night with them and laid it all out—our parenting transgressions and our plans to reform. Yes, the teen rolled his eyes. Finn asked to be excused from the table about two minutes into the discussion. But when we admitted that we had been doing things all wrong, and that we believed that changing the way we parent would make them better, more independent, confident, and *competent* people, I think I caught them listening. We told them that the more competent they became, the more we would let them do for themselves. The more we saw that they could handle difficult decisions, the more we would trust them to make them.

There were some initial hiccups and setbacks, maybe even some pushback and tantrums, but once the kids figured out we had no plans to go back to our old ways of dependent parenting, they stepped up. My older son, who has always been fairly independent, started to take responsibility for everything in his life I did not need to be a part of anymore. He started using the alarms on his calendar as a backup for his spotty memory. He made checklists to help him remember the things he needs to do before the start of the school day. He organized his forms for high school and gave me what he needed me to read and sign. He took control of ordering his back-to-school supplies, packed for two weeks of camp, and left notes for me on the counter when people called. My younger son, who is usually willing and eager to let me do everything for him (recall our adventures in shoelace-tying), suddenly took charge of his morning tasks without being asked and even made a checklist after forgetting his towel one day at our local pond. He cleaned his room, organized his desk, and figured out where and when he planned to complete his homework every night. Best of all, he saw that my older son could do the laundry and asked to be taught how to use the washer and dryer, too.

TWO WEEKS INTO OUR BLISSFUL honeymoon period, my younger son, Finnegan, suffered a bit of a setback in his journey toward autonomy and competence. As the door slammed closed on the last kid heading for the school bus, I noticed his math and spelling homework lying on the living room coffee table. I looked out the window at the bus stop, and there he was, oblivious to his oversight, twirling his hands in the air while explaining some detail of an imaginary world to his friend Pierce. I looked back down at the homework. And back out the window. And back to the homework.

And then I did my best to get on with my day, knowing that I was scheduled to stop by the school later, and it would be so easy to deliver Finn's homework to his classroom, maybe even surreptitiously slide it into his locker or backpack. He'd done such a good job on it, too, so conscientiously completing it in his neatest handwriting, effort now wasted. I picked it up off the table, looked at the neat letters and numbers, and put it down again.

Flummoxed, I turned to Facebook and posted,

> For those of you who think this whole letting my kids mess up thing is easy, know this. One of my sons left his homework assignment on the living room table, completed in a timely and neat fashion. I have to go to his school anyway to drop something off. Leaving that homework on the table, knowing it will cost him his recess today, is KILLING ME. I've looked at it twenty times, even picked it up once. But there it is. And there it will stay, waiting for him to see when he gets home and realizes what he could have done to make sure that homework made it into his backpack and his teacher's hands.

Facebook friends began responding immediately, many with their pledges of support and enthusiastic approval and lots of "Likes," but one friend posted her strong disapproval.

> Jessica I admire you greatly, as I hope you know, but I could not do this. I forget things every day. I have driven things to my husband's office that he has left on the kitchen counter. I think a certain level of distraction is inevitable in our lives, no matter how hard we try, and high school kids are the most overwhelmed by it. I would be so happy that the homework was done, on time,

> neat and ready that unless I was unable to do so, I would take it to school. I would save my consequences for homework that was not done or was not done well.

I thought about her words for the rest of the morning. I had to admit that yes, I *would* go out of my way to deliver a friend's forgotten wallet, or my husband's forgotten power cord, so why would I treat my children any differently?

Because I'm not raising those other people. I treat my children differently because I have a greater responsibility to them than to make them happy and grateful for my love and support. In order to raise competent, capable adults, I have to love them enough to put their learning before my happiness.

THIS SHIFT IN THE WAY I understood my role as a parent was the hardest part of our switch to a more autonomy-supportive parenting style; harder than watching my kids mess up, harder than knowing they were going to mess up before they did and not preventing those train wrecks. I had to stop equating the act of doing things for my children—saving them from themselves, scoring a smile and a hug when I showed up at school with a dropped mitten or toy—with good parenting. It still feels good to do things for them, and I still do—all the time. But the things I do for them are different now, and my motivations are based on an evaluation of *their* needs, not mine. Before, I was doing the things they could do for themselves to feel good about my parenting. Now, when I choose to do things for my children, I know my actions come from a place of genuine love, and I think my kids sense that, too.

WHEN I PUSH PARENTS TO give their kids autonomy, I don't mean to imply that parents should drop all parental oversight and walk away, hoping the kids will respond by stepping up to the plate with newfound autonomy and intrinsic motivation. Autonomy-supportive parenting is not negligent parenting, and it is not permissive parenting. Autonomy-supportive parents establish specific and clear expectations, make themselves physically and emotionally present, and offer guidance when kids get frustrated or need redirection. The best part about being an autonomy-supportive parent is that all the negative stuff we do to get our children to do the things we want them to do—nagging, nitpicking, hovering, directing—stops. These parenting techniques are destructive to our relationships with our kids, anyway, so parenting in their absence is a more peaceful and enjoyable affair all around.

Autonomy-supportive parenting gives kids what they need. Children are starved for responsibility and a role within the family, and all the jockeying for power, and the mischief that arises when their hands are idle, stems from our failure to give our kids a clear way to contribute to the family's well-being. Kids thrive on our expectations and they flourish when given responsibilities of their own and the education they need to carry them out successfully. That said, a certain degree of parental involvement is crucial for children's learning and emotional well-being. For example, study after study shows that a strong family-school bond leads to better educational and emotional outcomes, and when teachers are polled, they point to "involved parents" as one of the most important elements of school success. This is still true despite headlines over flawed, myopic research studies that have claimed parental involvement is overrated. Teachers love parents who show up for parent-teacher conferences, who help out with class trips, and offer their support when it is needed. There is a difference, however, between being involved in your child's learning and taking over. The line between overparenting and autonomy-supportive parenting can be hazy, but there is a clear difference between the kind of parenting that results in dependent, unmotivated, and unsuccessful children, and the kind that produces resilient, driven, intrinsically motivated kids.

In order to draw a line, and clarify why it's so important to support autonomy rather than dependence, I have to return to the research for a minute. Psychologist Wendy Grolnick has done some fascinating work on the impact that autonomy-supportive versus controlling parenting has on children's motivation. In her lab, she videotaped mother-child pairs for three minutes and rated mothers' interactions with their child as controlling or autonomy-supportive. When Grolnick invited these mother-child pairs back to the lab for a second visit, the children were put in a room by themselves to work at a task independently and the results were "striking." Children who had previously been directed in their play by controlling mothers gave up when faced with frustration in their solitary play.

Stop for a moment and realize what this means. The kids who were being raised by controlling or directive parents could not complete tasks on their own, but the kids who were being raised by autonomy-supportive parents stuck with tasks, even when they got frustrated. Kids who can redirect and stay engaged in tasks, even when they find those tasks difficult, become less and less dependent on guidance in order to focus, study, organize, and otherwise run their own lives. These competent, more autonomous kids enjoy their work more. Children who rely on their parents to direct them through tasks, however, continue to require guidance and direction, and as the complexity of the task escalates with age and maturity, the complexity and nature of the parental intervention usually escalates as well. These are the kids who need their parents to help them with homework into middle school and beyond. These are the kids who can't manage their schedules and priorities as they approach adulthood.

Sure, the leap from a controlling parenting style to autonomy-supportive parenting is challenging, but changing any habit is a challenge at first. Keep your eye on that brass ring of the positive feedback loop: the more independent you allow your children to be, the more independent they will become.

Making the switch from controlling to autonomy-supportive will require some investment of time and patience. If your child never learned to pack his own lunch, do the laundry, clean out the car after school, load or unload the dishwasher, or do any of the many tasks any kid should be able to do by the time she hits middle school, there's going to be a steep learning curve. The tasks may not get done to your exact specifications the first time around and there may be pushback as your child balks at his new responsibilities, but the rewards come, and sooner than you may expect.

While our children tend to love us no matter what we do or how we parent, I would rather my children think of me as the sort of parent who guides rather than directs, supports rather than controls, the sort of parent who is more concerned with my child's competence and the strength of our connection than the alignment of the dishes in the dishwasher or a stray white sock tossed in with the colored load of laundry.

Autonomy-supportive parenting is not the same thing as permissive parenting, because discipline, respect, and rules all have an important place in this approach. Children need rules and behavioral guidelines. Most of all, children need structure.

Young children test the boundaries of their capabilities but find it reassuring and safe when adults provide limits on their explorations. Toddlers test limits in order to be reassured that nothing has changed and that their world—including their parents and the rules they impose—can be relied upon. They test, we reassure, they relax, and the cycle repeats ad nauseam until that toddler finally gets shipped off to Siberia or enters kindergarten.

I try not to mention this in front of my middle school students, but tweens and teens present a variant on the toddler's cycle of testing. They test their curfew, we reassure them that it's still ten o'clock, and they relax. They test our resolve regarding boy-girl sleepovers, we reassure them that no, we still don't allow it, and they relax. They test our standards for their behavior, we reassure them that we still expect them to be kind and respectful toward us, and they relax. And the cycle repeats ad nauseam until the teenager gets kicked out of the house or starts college.

Testing limits is a way of testing independence, and that's a good thing, even if it makes us want to stick a fork in our heads. It's exhausting, yes, but it's a necessary part of creating independent kids. One way to make this testing easier is to establish clear expectations for their behavior, and more important, stick to those expectations and employ consequences when those expectations are not met. This limit-setting is a key element of autonomy-supportive parenting. Limits are structure. Limits give kids reassuring information about what to expect and how to act according to those expectations. Limits make kids feel safe and cared for.

Parents who establish high standards and subsequently enforce those high standards are not *necessarily* controlling. In fact, there is plenty of evidence to show that children react favorably to parents who hold children accountable for lapses in behavior or failure to uphold expectations. However, when parents resort to controlling behavior in their attempts to hold children to standards—when they offer bribes, rewards, excessive monitoring, or pressure—this corrodes a child's sense of autonomy and therefore his intrinsic motivation (and, as we have established, his success in school and life).

CREATING NEW HABITS

Once I'd weaned myself off my need to save my kids, I had to help them learn how to be in charge of their own lives. We taught them how to use the appliances and complete all sorts of household tasks but we also had to teach them how to form new habits; how to remember all those responsibilities and make them a part of their daily life. In *The Power of Habit*, Charles Duhigg explains that habits come out of a basic feedback loop: a cue, the routine, and the reward. As an example, he writes about his habit of eating a cookie every afternoon around three. The cue (hunger or boredom) triggers a habit (going to the cafeteria), and the reward for the routine is both the satisfied hunger and the relief from boredom. In order to create new habits, you have to create a new cue, establish a routine tied to that cue, and find an appropriate reward for the routine to close the feedback loop.

As we've seen, rewards may be antithetical to creating long-term success, but they can be powerful motivators when it comes to mundane, repetitive tasks. We held a family meeting to decide on our cues. I asked my sons to think about what they do when they get home from school. My younger son said that he likes to do homework immediately after school so he does not have to think about it and can play with his Legos or draw in peace. We agreed that his cue would be his after-school snack. He'd come home, *prepare his own snack* (emphasis his!), and start his homework. He agreed to check in with me when it was done, and his reward would be the feeling of satisfaction he gets from finishing his homework thoroughly and with his best effort. Find what works best for your child, and make that the routine.

The most important habits we all vowed to adopt have to do with technology. We all agreed that part of our routine for homework includes shutting down phones, iPods, and other devices that distract us from our work. We all agreed that the cue none of us can resist is the sound of an email or text arriving in our inbox. If we omit these cues, we won't even be tempted to engage in the routine of checking email and can enjoy the reward of homework completed without distractions. In our home, checklists have become a favorite cue, and I was surprised to find that praise for mastery and effort can be a powerful motivator. I assumed we'd have to come up with elaborate reward ideas, but in the end, increased independence is the reward my children have been craving all along.

Change is never easy, particularly in the first days. It definitely does not feel good, and there were moments along the way when I was feeling like a really mean and terrible mother. Given some time, and persistence, however, change happens, and it doesn't just feel good, it feels great. Your kids will still make a stink here and there when they don't want to do something that needs to be done, but that's realistic. They are children. Even Laura Ingalls protested having to do her chores once in a while. But once your kids have detoxed off rewards, and the overparenting withdrawal symptoms have subsided, your kids might just do for themselves because they can, and because they want to. Because it feels good to be of use, first in our family, and later, in the big, wide world.

BECAUSE I SPENT MONTHS FUMBLING about in the hazy, gray area between controlling and autonomy-supportive parenting, I came up with some guidelines to clarify the difference:

CONTROLLING PARENTS GIVE LOTS OF UNSOLICITED ADVICE AND DIRECTION.

That's not the right way to load the dishwasher. Always wash the plates before putting them in and stack all the large plates on the left side. Don't leave the dishes in the sink and come back later. Do it this way. Do it now. Do it later.

We all have our own way of doing household chores so there's every possibility that your child may not load the dishwasher precisely as you'd like it done. Unsolicited advice and direction, commonly known as "helping" from the parent's perspective or "nagging" from the child's, interferes with her sense of autonomy, conveys a lack of faith in her competence, and, because it's irritating and upsetting to both of you, undermines your connection.

When the child who loaded those food-laden plates into the dishwasher unloads the dishwasher, she will discover that crusty food on the plate, and you will have the opportunity then to explain how to prevent that mistake in the future. Offer guidance when the child is stuck, and seize the big learning moments, but otherwise hold your tongue. The mistakes she makes and corrects on her own are learning moments. The mistakes you anticipate don't benefit anyone, save for you in that brief moment when it makes you feel better that the plates are stacked north-south instead of east-west.

CONTROLLING PARENTS TAKE OVER.

I'll just do it, you go play. We have to get to school, I'll just do it myself when I get home. No, not that way, just let me do it.

Sometimes it's just easier to take over, particularly if you are under a time crunch or exhausted. Remember, the goal is for children to learn how to do for themselves, not for the task to get done. Sometimes it's going to be more important to be a minute late, particularly when a child masters something he's been struggling with. Step back, breathe, and remember what's really important in the big picture.

CONTROLLING PARENTS OFFER EXTRINSIC MOTIVATORS IN EXCHANGE FOR BEHAVIORS.

You get one jelly bean for every toy you clean up. If you walk the dog every morning, I'll buy you new sneakers. If you load and unload the dishwasher for an entire week without being asked, I will get you that video game you've been asking for.

As long as you keep rewards to a minimum and space them out, it's fine to celebrate or acknowledge in some way a child's accomplishment on the way to a more autonomous self. But many basic household responsibilities, such as walking the dog or taking out the garbage, should be viewed as part of family maintenance, not as endeavors deserving of hoopla or a grand reward. Everyone should contribute to what needs to be done around the house, and rewarding these kinds of basic activities suggests that doing them is heroic as opposed to expected.

CONTROLLING PARENTS PROVIDE SOLUTIONS OR THE CORRECT ANSWER BEFORE THE CHILD HAS HAD A CHANCE TO REALLY STRUGGLE WITH A PROBLEM.

But honey, you know five times four is twenty, you just did that down here. I'll just look that word up for you while you do the spelling list. Just give me that pencil and I'll show you. Not like that, like this.

Not all answers come immediately. Give children time and silence to think. Not only will it teach them to value quiet; it also shows them that you value the process of coming up with the answer as much as the answer itself.

CONTROLLING PARENTS DON'T LET CHILDREN MAKE THEIR OWN DECISIONS.

Do your math first, and then your spelling. Do your homework here at the table where I can see you. You should play tennis rather than baseball this season.

Sometimes it's better to allow your child to experience the ownership and rush of independence that comes from choosing one sport over another or one game over another, and that ownership is often more important than the activity. Decision-making is a complex process that takes a lot of practice, so give your child that opportunity to try on her autonomy for size.

AUTONOMY-SUPPORTIVE PARENTS GUIDE CHILDREN TOWARD SOLUTIONS.

I know you know what five times three is, so what happens when you add another five? Why do you think the cold glass broke when you poured hot water into it? Try holding the protractor so you can read the numbers right-side up.

Parenting is teaching, and teachers look for the teachable moments in just about everything we do. Find those moments and lead your child toward answers. Discoveries children make under their own steam will always be remembered longer and understood more deeply than the answers you hand them out of impatience.

AUTONOMY-SUPPORTIVE PARENTS ALLOW FOR MISTAKES AND HELP CHILDREN UNDERSTAND THE CONSEQUENCES OF THOSE MISTAKES.

It's no big deal that you dropped that glass, I'll show you how to clean it all up, and you can remember to carry fewer next time. Pick out the lumps in the oatmeal, and I'll show you how to avoid that mistake for next time. The mop bucket spilled because it's too short to hold the weight of the mop handle; just clean up the mess and use the other bucket next time.

It can be so hard to keep our sense of humor and patience when there's shattered glass or dirty water all over the kitchen floor, but if we show our kids that mistakes are part of the process of learning, they will be more positive about their abilities and better able to bounce back from mistakes in future attempts. If we teach them that messing up means the world will crumble around them, we only succeed in reinforcing fear of failure.

AUTONOMY-SUPPORTIVE PARENTS VALUE THE MISTAKES AS MUCH AS THE SUCCESSES.

I'm so proud of you for sticking with that worksheet even though it was hard for you. What could you have said to your brother that might have helped him understand you rather than throw his toy at you?

One way to teach our children that we value mistakes as an educational tool is to support and love them as much during the mistakes as we do during the successes. Find the lessons in the failures. Help them discover new ways to cope and rebound from their mistakes in order to do better next time. Empathize and love them when they have messed up, because that's when they need our support the most.

AUTONOMY-SUPPORTIVE PARENTS ACKNOWLEDGE CHILDREN'S FEELINGS OF FRUSTRATION AND DISAPPOINTMENT.

I get mad, too, when I can't do something right the first time, but I keep trying until I figure it out. Remember yesterday, when I did not get that job I wanted? That was really disappointing, but I know I'll figure something else out if I work at it. I can imagine how frustrating this math must be for you, but won't it feel great when you know how to do it?

Let your child know that you understand that algebra is hard sometimes, and it must have felt terrible when Kayla refused to sit with her at lunch, and that yes, it can be really frustrating when the teacher marked up that paper she worked so hard on. We all need to feel heard and understood, and this is when connection happens. Show your child that you empathize with her feelings, and subsequent problem-solving will be much easier to hear.

AUTONOMY-SUPPORTIVE PARENTS GIVE FEEDBACK.

Look down at your buttons; something looks off—can you figure out what's wrong? If you forgot to carry the two in that other problem, maybe you made the same mistake on this problem?

Effective feedback supports effort and guides the child toward seeing her mistakes. Kids value supportive observations that encourage them to solve their own problems more than specific directions because the solutions are their own, not yours.

AS YOU MAKE YOUR WAY through the gray areas and begin to discern black from white, try to remember that the line between controlling and autonomy-supportive parenting is not always going to be easy to see. Sometimes it's going to be downright blurry, and some controlling behaviors, such as rewards and praise, can easily be mistaken for positive parenting.

You will make mistakes. We all do. But as long as we love our children, and make it clear to them that our love is not contingent on their performance, they will be fine. Research has shown that the worst kind of controlling parenting is the type that either withholds affection or makes it contingent on performance. This type of parenting hits kids where they are most vulnerable: their basic sense of safety and fear of abandonment. Even subtle withdrawal has a deleterious effect on children's sense of security, so be careful about how you interact with your children when you know you are disappointed in their performance. As long as we steer clear of this type of parenting, we can make a lot of other mistakes along the way.

Abandoning rewards and other forms of controlling parenting may seem counterintuitive at first. But as parents get tired of parenting dependent children, and the positive effects of autonomy-supportive parenting catch on at home and in the classroom, all of this will begin to feel a lot less revolutionary and a lot more like common sense.

AS FOR MY OWN DILEMMA over that forgotten homework, I fretted and puzzled over my decision. Why not just be a nice mom, and give him a break, this one time? When it came time to head over to the school, and that homework whispered to me one last time, I realized why I could not, why bailing my children out and saving them from the consequences of their failures is different from doing my friends or husband a favor here and there. I went back inside the house to post my eureka moment to the Facebook thread:

> As my discussions with Finn over the last couple of weeks have been about packing away homework the night before so it does not get lost in the rush of morning, this is a perfect way to drive that point home. And Finn *does* know I have his back. I make sure he knows that every day, in every way, and yes, I forget and lose things, too (my keys, like 10 times a day) but those mistakes cause me to come

up with strategies to help remember the next time. This homework is a specific response to a specific deficit in his planning, and will pay huge dividends in the end in terms of a teaching moment.

When Finn came through the door at the end of the day, he was greeted by the smell of cookies baking. If I could not feed my need to feel like a good mom by delivering his homework and saving the day, I figured a batch of warm cookies might serve as a suitable alternative. All the love, none of the rescuing.

As he dumped his backpack on the floor and began to unpack his lunchbox, I asked him how his day went. I raised one eyebrow and pointed to the homework, still sitting on the coffee table. What did his teacher say, I asked, when he found out the homework was missing?

"It was okay. My teacher and I talked about how to remember my homework, and he said I could bring it tomorrow."

"That's it?" I asked. "No staying in from recess or giving up your free time?"

"Oh—yeah. I had to do some extra math practice during reading time, but I can just read some extra time tonight. And he made me promise to write a note in my homework book to help me remember to take my homework in tomorrow."

And he did just that. He wrote himself a note, and he remembered his homework the next day, and (almost) every day since. Facing the consequences of his failure taught him so many things that day. He learned to own up to his mistake, and talk to his teacher about solutions. He was encouraged to think about how to keep from making the same mistake again, and devised a system that worked for him. And, as we discovered when we sat down together after that night's homework was done, our cookies were warm, delicious, and guilt-free.

4

ENCOURAGEMENT FROM THE SIDELINES: THE REAL CONNECTION BETWEEN PRAISE AND SELF-ESTEEM

ONE DAY, WHILE PICKING RASPBERRIES with my friend Elena, we started talking about her daughter, Olivia. A year before, Olivia had suffered a severe head injury and lost her memory. At first, everyone thought it would return, but her life before the accident—her family, pets, friends, school—never came back. After about a month of waiting for her to remember the previous sixteen years of her life, Elena and her husband realized it was time to move on and make do with what Olivia had left. She was—and is—an otherwise capable and intelligent individual, albeit one without a past. I asked Elena how her parenting had changed over the past year, and reaching past me for a berry, she remarked,

> I've totally changed the way I praise my kids. I used to just tell them how smart they were, how talented and amazing, but once Olivia lost her memory, praising her just for being smart and

> talented didn't feel right. She was working so hard to improve and to figure out who she was and who she was going to be that it made more sense to praise her for her effort, for sticking with this crappy, horrible deal she'd gotten. The kind of praise I was giving Olivia became the kind of praise I gave all of my kids, and it changed them, especially the younger ones. I can see a real difference in the way they think about themselves and their potential.

Americans are huge fans of praising kids at every turn. But as I dug into the research on praise and motivation, I found that praise is a slippery and tricky parenting tool, one that can lift a kid up or tear him down, depending on how it's used. It can be the best parenting and teaching tool in your toolkit, the kind of encouragement and support that makes kids want to risk failure and reach for greater challenges. Or it can destroy self-esteem. Most recent studies have shown that the worst of the destruction happens in the hearts of kids who already suffer from low self-regard, the very kids we most want to help.

All praise is not equal. "You are a smart kid" is very different from "You worked so hard on that French homework; it must have felt really good to have done well on that assignment." The first statement makes a judgment, and even if it seems like a positive and loving judgment, it has a negative effect on performance. "You are smart" judges and labels the person, not the product. If I tell my son that he's smart, I'm telling him that I value him for being smart, and he's going to be a lot less likely to try things that might damage his "smart" label, lest he fail, which, in his kid brain, could cause me to withdraw my love and approval. However, if I tell him that I am proud of him for the effort he put into editing the short story he wrote last week, I am reinforcing behavior, not judging him.

Kids who are praised for effort are more likely to have a growth mindset, the understanding that intelligence and capability can be improved with effort. In her book *Parenting Without Borders: Surprising Lessons Parents Around the World Can Teach Us*, Christine Gross-Loh writes that Americans are more prone to a fixed mindset and are drawn to terms such as *talented*, *gifted*, and *prodigy*, and therefore more apt to praise for these inherent qualities. Americans are much more interested in the story of a child who can pick out a Bach concerto on a keyboard at the age of five than a violinist who has put in ten thousand hours of practice in order to rise to first seat in the orchestra. While our view of intelligence tends to be one of a fixed potential, other cultures, such as Korea and Japan, view potential as a package deal, made up of innate traits and deliberate effort. Gross-Loh reports:

> In Japan, there is less labeling. In school, students aren't separated according to ability. There is no "gifted" education, and most learning-disabled children are integrated into the regular classroom. Instead of dividing kids up, there is a pervasive belief—reinforced in school—that it's less about what you're born with than what you do. Up to a certain point *everyone* is capable of cultivating skills, even in art or music. So, while in America art and music are looked at as things for all kids to dabble in, but serious training or cultivation is reserved for kids who show talent, in East Asia there is a common belief that anyone can and should be able to achieve a certain degree of mastery in a variety of areas, whether it be mathematics, art, music, or physical education. It just takes effort.

The research on the harm we can do when we create fixed mindsets is best summed up in one of Carol Dweck's experiments.

Dweck and her associates gave several hundred adolescent students ten test questions. After the test, half the students were praised with "Wow, you got [say] eight right. That's a really good score. *You must be smart at this.*" The other half heard, "Wow, you got [say] eight right. That's a really good score. *You must have worked really hard.*" The two groups did about the same on the test before they were praised, but after the praise was lavished, they began to look like two very different groups of kids. The half who received praise for their smarts adopted a fixed mindset. When given a choice between tasks, they rejected the more challenging option in favor of one they could more easily master, thereby keeping their "smart" or "talented" label intact.

Children look to their teachers and parents to help them understand their place in the world, and if we lavish praise for inherent qualities in an attempt to bolster their self-esteem, we do them a huge disservice. Not only are we instilling a fixed mindset; we are planting the seeds of distrust. When a teacher moves around the room, praising each kid, "Great job! You are so smart!" the students figure out pretty quickly that someone is being lied to. They know they can't *all* be geniuses, and they begin to doubt our honesty—or at the very least, our judgment.

Stanford University education professor William Damon describes the damage praise can wreak on children and their trust in our opinion of them: "Even when spawned by the best of intentions, less-than-honest communications to children inevitably create unfortunate complications. One such complication is that, sooner or later, children see through all inaccurate statements about themselves."

This sentiment was echoed by Lisa Endlich Heffernan, writer of the parenting blog Grown and Flown, and mother of two.

> The single most important thing we have with our kids, beyond our enduring love, is our credibility. By telling kids that they are good at something when they are patently not, we ruin that credibility and do little for their self-esteem as the truth at some point will be revealed. When my kids do not have an aptitude for something, I don't shy away from telling them, but this means that any praise I do give them has that much more value. Our trustworthiness as parents should not be sacrificed on the flimsy altar of acclaim.

Kids who have been taught to pray to that altar and have been overpraised for their smarts and talent are easy to spot in the classroom. They do the bare minimum required to get by; they never take up the gauntlet of challenging extra work and are reluctant to risk saying anything that might be wrong. These students are frustrating to teach because they won't stretch themselves or take any intellectual leaps of faith for fear of not living up to their parents' expectations and whatever label has been bestowed on them. The truth I try to impart to every single one of my students is this: it all gets hard eventually, even the stuff you have a talent for.

Imagine when a kid who has been told that he has a talent for math first sees a complex algebra formula in class and can't understand it. He thinks: "My parents tell me I am smart, but I can't be, not if I can't understand this right away, and I can't let them find out the truth." This is a terrible bind to put kids in and it drives them underground. They feel terrible about themselves as they suffer through a crisis of confidence and identity, and reject help at the cost of the image they are desperate to keep intact for the sake of their parents' affection and approval.

THE MOST STRIKING PART OF Dweck's work on praise and mindsets lies in what comes after these growth or fixed mindsets take hold and begin to shape children's identities. After Dweck praised students either for effort or smarts on a fairly easy test, they were then given a much harder test designed specifically to elicit some failure and frustration. The kids who had been praised for their smarts tended to give up, whereas the kids who had been praised for effort tried harder. The students did not give up because they did not take the failure personally; they did not think that their inability to correctly answer the problems right away meant that they were not smart. And here's my favorite part, the detail that warms the cockles of my teaching heart: the kids who accepted the challenge problems said *the hard problems were more fun*.

While the kids with the growth mindsets were having fun, the fixed-mindset kids tanked. Even when Dweck backed off on the level of difficulty and gave the subjects more of the easy problems, the fixed-mindset kids did poorly. They could not bounce back from defeat, and did even worse on the easy problems than they had in the first round. In a final, sinister, yet illuminating twist, Dweck asked the subjects to write down their thoughts about the problems for future students and, while they were at it, write down their scores. Forty percent of the kids who were praised for smarts lied about their scores. As Dweck wrote in her book *Mindset*, "we took ordinary children and made them into liars, simply by telling them they were smart."

In order to understand how praising kids the wrong way can turn them into liars, I turned to Professor James M. Lang, author of *Cheating Lessons: Learning from Academic Dishonesty*. He writes that we "good-job" kids into a state of overconfidence and an overinflated sense of their skill level, which can lead to all sorts of negative consequences, such as a tendency to understudy. The ability to judge one's own level of knowledge, skill, or thought process is called metacognition, and it's what allows kids to gauge whether or not they are prepared or knowledgeable on a topic.

Students with good metacognitive skills are more likely to achieve what Lang calls "self-efficacy," or a belief in their ability to succeed. Not confidence in their ability to succeed, not magical thinking based on parents' effusive praise, but a belief based on experience and repeated effort in a skill or task. Yet we continue to believe that if we tell our children how wonderful and talented they are by throwing empty platitudes, trophies, and blue ribbons at them, we will bolster performance along with self-esteem. We plaster our car bumpers with stickers, advertising "My Kid's an Honor Student at Springfield Middle School." Every time your kid glances at that bumper, he is reminded that the thing you value in him is not how hard he works, or how long he sticks with a challenge, but his grades and standardized test results. Recent studies have shown that the very kids we hope to help the most with all this praise, kids with low self-esteem, are actually the worst off for our efforts, and suffer even lower self-esteem than if we'd just left them alone. Imagine what those kids with low-self-esteem could do if their parents and teachers started praising them for their hard work and diligence, hard work that pays off in increased autonomy, competence, and connection. That's the kind of esteem I'd like my students to have, the sort of self-image that's been earned, hard-won, and deserved.

IT'S A REAL CHALLENGE TO switch from a fixed to a growth mindset, and even harder to change the language that flies out of our mouths when our kids do something well, or come up short. Don't worry if it takes a while to get the language right; we have become accustomed to the praise and encouragement we heap on kids for innate and effortless accomplishment. Even Carol Dweck admits to slipping up once in a while, praising her family for brilliance rather than efforts, but the point is to create new habits that have the potential to communicate a sense of self-efficacy and an accurate representation of our children's abilities. Here are some ideas that can help reorient the way you praise your child, and may just help him adopt a growth mindset and strong sense of self-efficacy:

PRAISE FOR EFFORT, NOT INHERENT QUALITIES.

Instead of "Great job on that test! You are so smart!" try "Great job on that test! What did you do this time in your preparation that worked so well?" Instead of "I love that drawing! You have real talent in art!" try "I'm proud of you for working so hard on the shading and perspective." Kids who believe that intelligence grows with effort and diligence will be less distraught about failures, more likely to stick with tasks through those failures, and may even have more fun as they do so.

ADOPT A GROWTH MINDSET IN YOUR OWN LIFE, EVEN WHEN IT MAKES YOU UNCOMFORTABLE.

When your kids see you stretch yourself, even if you fail in the process, they will be more likely to stretch themselves. Better yet, let them see you continue to stretch yourself after you fail so they will understand that failing at a task does not mean that the person is a failure. You are your child's first and greatest role model, so show him that you are dedicated to the idea that success is tied to effort, not innate talent. Find the thing you believe you cannot do, and give it a shot. Failure and rejection are a part of the learning process, particularly when we butt up against our comfort zones, but it's amazing what can happen once we break through that zone and glimpse the possibilities beyond.

DON'T REINFORCE MALADAPTIVE REACTIONS TO FAILURE.

We all react differently to failure, but some of those reactions are healthier than others and have the potential to teach us more. Denial, for example, tends to exacerbate and prolong failure. Be honest with your children. If your child has failed at something because she did not work hard enough, say so. Teach your child to see the realities of her shortcomings and failures and react accordingly. When we tell children how talented and gifted they are at a particular skill when all evidence points to the contrary, they know, and their faith in us is subsequently weakened.

MAKE SURE YOUR CHILD KNOWS HIS FAILURES DO NOT LESSEN YOUR LOVE OR OPINION OF HIM.

Your love and emotional connection buffer and soften the pain and embarrassment children may feel from failure. Further, knowing that you will be there to support, rather than judge or offer false praise, offers kids a secure and safe haven from the anxiety they experience in their lives.

LET YOUR CHILDREN FEEL DISAPPOINTED BY FAILURE.

Sit with the emotions and don't try to jump in and resolve the situation. After all, these are his failures, not yours, and it is unfair and counterproductive to try to make it all better for him. What you are teaching him through your patient silence and inaction on his behalf is that he has the inner strength to move on from failure.

DO NOT OFFER TO RESCUE YOUR CHILD FROM THE CONSEQUENCES OF HIS MISTAKES.

Your offer to rescue implies that you don't believe he has the ability to find a solution himself. Help him problem-solve and find lessons in the failure rather than viewing it as a devastating blow to his self-image and confidence. Your goal should be to help him regain a sense of control over the experience of failing. The real learning happens when kids begin to understand how to pick through the wreckage, find the pieces that still work for them, and devise a strategy for future success.

OLIVIA EVENTUALLY HEALED FROM HER injuries, and despite having lost most of her knowledge base, she was able to return to high school, graduate with her classmates, and go to college. I can't be certain that the changes Elena made in her parenting had anything to do with Olivia's success, and a sample size of one is hardly statistically significant. I do know that when Elena began supporting Olivia's efforts rather than her intelligence, she increased the likelihood that Olivia would survive the many failures she encountered as she worked to regain a sense of normalcy. Better still, she gave Olivia a great lesson in how to be the sort of parent who will one day inspire a growth mindset in her own children.

Part II

Learning from Failure: Teaching Kids to Turn Mistakes into Success

5
HOUSEHOLD DUTIES: LAUNDRY AS AN OPPORTUNITY FOR COMPETENCE

ONE AFTERNOON, I WALKED INTO my English classroom and overheard an eighth grader complaining to her friends about how hungry she was. I asked her if she'd forgotten her lunch and she replied, "No, but I hate what my mom packs for me." Rather than point out the obvious solution—that she should plan and pack her own food—I asked if she could think of any way to solve her unsatisfactory lunch situation.

"I could buy lunch . . . ?" she offered, ending her sentence in an implied question mark, and looked for my reaction.

"Or . . ." I prompted.

" . . . or . . . I could . . . tell my mom what I like, so she can pack stuff I want to eat," she said more confidently, pleased that she had come up with such a brilliant plan.

"Or . . ." I repeated.

She was puzzled. What other option could there be? I turned to her classmate, who packed her own lunches.

"Elsie, what else could Kate do to make sure she gets exactly the kind of lunch she wants, one she can't possibly complain about?"

Elsie turned pink.

"You could pack your own lunch. That's what I do. Sometimes I even pack lunch right after we eat dinner, because all of the food is already out, and then I don't have to do it in the morning when I'm in a rush."

It was Kate's turn to blush.

"Oh . . . yeah. I could do that."

And do that she did. In the first week or two, she even made a point to mention how much she was enjoying her lunch whenever I was in earshot. About a month later, on her birthday, she turned up in the door of my office bearing a large tray of cupcakes.

"It's my birthday. Would you like a cupcake? I made them myself." She was beaming, absolutely thrilled with this opportunity to make sure I knew how far she'd come in her culinary skills. I took one and watched her hand out the rest to her classmates, mentioning every thirty seconds or so that she'd made them herself. "Even the frosting!" she proclaimed.

Children want to feel capable, and we used to let them, before we took the onus of household duties away from them. Instead of teaching our children how to be responsible, reliable members of a family in which children contribute, we do everything for them. Worse, we don't expect competence from them, and when they do give household duties a shot, we swoop in, and we fix.

We swoop in after our kids make their beds and smooth out the lumps and bumps. We swoop in after they fold the laundry and straighten the misfolded towels. I've actually taken the sponge out of my son's hands because he was making more of a mess of the milk he was supposed to be cleaning up. I have sent him out of the room and told him to "just go play" when he was not doing something as quickly, or as precisely, as I would have. I understand the impulse to want things done better, or faster, or straighter. But to what end? So much more than speed and perfection are sacrificed when we swoop in and fix.

What's more important—that the dishes are immaculate, or that your child develops a sense of purpose and pride because he's finally contributing in a real and valuable way to the family? That the bed is made without wrinkles, or that your child learns to make household tasks a part of his daily routine? All this swooping and fixing make for emotionally, intellectually, and socially handicapped children, unsure of their direction or purpose without an adult on hand to guide them.

It's important that my student plans and prepares her own lunch, not because she's spoiled or I want her to "toughen up," but because the failures she will experience when she screws up making that lunch are important. She needs to be disappointed in her own choices once in a while. She needs to find out that when she packs yogurt under the ice pack rather than on top, it gets squished, and the entire lunch bag becomes a sticky, vanilla mess. She needs to know what it feels like to clean that sticky lunch bag and avoid the same mistake next time. She needs to discover all the small details, workarounds, and solutions we devise in order to avoid the million small disasters that plague ordinary, everyday obligations.

A friend told me recently after she'd had a car accident that left her unscathed but chastened that in the midst of the crash, she'd realized she needed to make lists of all the small details her family would need to know if she was not there to take care of them. Her son needed to know that his soccer clothes had to go into the laundry on Sunday so he'd have what he needed for Monday's practice. Her daughter needed to know which fabrics can go in the dryer and which cannot, and what happens when wool sweaters sneak into the dryer by mistake. The kids should know how to fix the toilet when it clogs, and reset the water pressure tank after a power outage, and change a fuse, and winterize the lawn mower, and the million other things she'd taken care of herself rather than burden her kids with.

I pointed out that if she were to die in a car accident, the location of the reset lever on the water tank would be the least of her family's worries, but I understood her point. When we don't allow our children to participate in the business of running a household, they are quite helpless without us, and she'd gotten a glimpse of just how paralyzed and incompetent they'd be in her absence. This was a wake-up call for her in large and small ways.

Protecting our kids from failure, from experiencing small disasters and learning how to cope with them, isn't doing them any favors, and not just in my friend's near-death glimpse. Whether we overparent and protect out of a need for perfectionism, a desire to show affection, or a need to prove our own parenting excellence, we deny our children the opportunity to be full members of the family with their own duties and responsibilities. We withhold the gift of failure, forgetting that some of our best parenting moments happen in the midst of disaster.

My friend and *New York Times* editor K. J. Dell'Antonia loves to tell the story of the day a friend's car veered off her icy driveway into a snowdrift. The adults were stressed-out and angered by the accident, but the six or seven kids on hand were thrilled and excited by the opportunity to pitch in and help get the car back on the road. They rallied together, fetching cat litter for traction and shovels, and devised all sorts of ramps and levers and pulley configurations in order to maneuver the car back onto the driveway. K.J. still marvels at the optimism and enthusiasm that the kids brought to an otherwise frustrating situation. It was as if they were waiting for a crisis, an opportunity to prove just how ingenious and helpful they could be. They tried—and failed—at their many schemes to free the car, but they reveled in each new inspiration. K.J. speaks of that afternoon as one of her favorite memories of the winter, and when I asked her son about the afternoon, he immediately broke into a smile as he launched into a retelling of the day's adventures.

When we exclude our kids from household disasters, we lose an easy opportunity to recover from these failures; household tasks can be daunting at first. We encourage them to be freeloaders and stick with the things they are good at: watching, being waited on, and making that face of perplexed impatience, hoping an adult will pass by and rescue them from their inability to solve problems. We teach our kids that they only need to worry about themselves, and risk pushing them over the line between ineffectual and incompetent right into lazy and narcissistic. Ineffectual and incompetent can be remedied with some patience but the reeducation of a narcissist is a much bigger challenge.

In talking with teachers about what children are capable of doing around the house, it has become clear to me that teachers have much more faith in children's abilities than parents do. When I asked teachers for lists of skills that kids can do on their own, skills their parents don't believe they can handle, I received pages and pages of suggestions. One teacher, when faced with the question of what her kindergarten students could do if given enough time and patience, smiled, and said, "everything." I have written my fair share of secondary school and college recommendation letters, and I can't begin to recount the number of times I've reviewed carefully cultivated and well-planned transcripts, complete with extensive accounts of the students' commitment to service—time spent serving up dinners in homeless shelters, sorting donated clothing, building latrines in Costa Rica—yet I know for a fact that the child in question has never done her own laundry. We currently spend huge amounts of energy and money on service trips and charity work and obsess about how these efforts will look on a college application, but a child's education in service to others should begin at home, for her own family, and sooner rather than later.

Just because your child has never done the laundry, or loaded the dishwasher, does not mean she is not capable of doing just that. Kids are creative and resourceful, and even tasks that seem unmanageable due to limits of heights or dexterity can be accomplished with the aid of a step stool and simple directions. Those dishes that belong in the high cabinets above the counter? It took a half hour, but when my younger son was first assigned dishwasher duty at six or seven, he dragged a chair from the living room to reach the shelves. One by one, he put those plates away where they belonged. When I had asked him to "unload the dishwasher," I'd forgotten about the high shelves, but he'd figured a way around that obstacle himself. The look of pride he gave me when I said, "Wait—you did *all* of it? Even those plates?" was utterly gratifying. Failure has been a part of that process, of course. Since that first day, he has broken dishes in the process of learning how best to carry, stack, and load them, but who cares? I'd trade ten broken plates for his smiles of competence and pride.

Children have been deprived of a sense of contribution and purpose for a couple of generations now, and it's time to give it back. Household participation is a first, and I'd argue essential, step toward building a purpose-driven and fulfilling life. When physicians examine causes of depression and suicidal ideation in adolescents, "lack of purpose" is mentioned over and over in the academic literature as a main factor. Purpose is what saves us all from despair when the details of life become overwhelming or boring, and it is what fuels the determination, resourcefulness, and resolve that will see our children through to their goals.

There are a lot of reasons parents give for not granting their children the space and opportunity to find purpose, among them:

- It's faster if I do it myself.
- They will just do it wrong anyway.
- Kids should be kids while they can; they will work when they grow up.
- My house will look disgusting and people will judge me.
- My kids will look disgusting and people will judge me.

Enough. It's time to grant our kids the opportunity to contribute. Allow them the chance to step up, try, fail, and try again until they get it right.

First, we must expunge the word *chores* from our household vocabulary. Amy McCready, parenting coach and founder of Positive Parenting Solutions, told me, "I've always encouraged parents to ditch the word *chores* and replace it with 'family contributions.' Calling them 'family contributions' doesn't make kids enjoy them any more, but it sends an important message about significance, that when you help out, you make a big difference for this family. We all have a hardwired need for significance and this is a great way to foster that in all kids, from toddlers to teens."

As your child discovers her significance and purpose, it's important to keep in mind that she's going to fail. She's going to make a mess of things from time to time as she learns. Her contribution to the household is not simply an item on a checklist you post on the refrigerator, but a process, an education. You know how to fold laundry just the way you like it folded; your daughter does not. Let her muck it up the first couple of times; give her the opportunity to notice that her folded shirts look different than the other ones in her drawer. Let her brother get frustrated with her because his pants are inside out and damp because the dryer twisted the leg in a knot. Let her discover for herself that when she leaves the clothes in the dryer overnight, her favorite shirt becomes hopelessly wrinkled, and maybe next time, she won't let that happen. Your house might be a little less perfect than usual as she learns how to become useful, and your kids may have to go out in public wearing those damp pants and wrinkled shirts, but if you care about the judgment of teachers, friends, and neighbors more than you do about your child's sense of competence, that's something you should think about. Eventually she'll become competent in the details of doing the laundry, not just to completion, but well. Given enough time, and lots of opportunities, she may even figure out how to fold a fitted sheet.

As our children's first teachers, parents are in the best possible position to teach kids how to focus on goals and face everyday responsibilities and challenges with courage and a good attitude. If we are easily defeated, they will learn to become easily defeated. Children who view obstacles as overwhelming and insurmountable give up on their goals. Kids who have witnessed their parents' resolve and resourcefulness, and been allowed to develop great problem-solving skills, don't give up. They get down to the business of using pulleys, levers, and all the other tools at their disposal to move obstacles out of their way and finish the job. Here's how the magic happens.

GREAT EXPECTATIONS AND GENUINE ACCOUNTABILITY

Set clear expectations and hold your kids accountable when they don't meet those expectations. No bribes or rewards of cash payment—remember, those kinds of short-term incentives can be used to kick-start motivation, but don't work as a long-term strategy. Besides, the message should not be that one contributes to a family in exchange for money, but that one contributes because one is an integral part of a cooperative unit, a group of people who depend on each other for both labor and love.

Explain to your children from an early age that you expect them to contribute to the running of the household. If they are older and have never been asked to contribute before, be honest. Cop to the fact that you failed yourself, and have been underestimating their abilities all along. Brainstorm as a family about jobs the kids are capable of learning, and come up with a list of expectations. You can post or not post this list—that's up to you—but the expectations have to be clear and age-appropriate. One mom I know draws pictures of dishes, or a washing machine, or a lunchbox for her little kids who can't yet read, while the lists are written out for her older children.

STEP AWAY AND HOLD YOUR TONGUE

Once you've outlined your expectations for your children, explain that you will not be nagging them until they complete their responsibilities. If your daughter's job is to clean up her place after meals and rinse the dishes before putting them in the dishwasher, and she forgets, leave the dishes out. This is where the teachable moments happen. Explain to her that the once easily rinsable food dries over time, and it will be much harder to clean it off when she finally gets around to it, but the dishes will remain on the table, waiting for her to clean them up.

This is going to require a lot of restraint on your part. Nagging and pestering is the fastest way to destroy motivation as well as destroy your connection and relationship with your child. Even if that dish sits on the table for two days, don't nag or hover, and absolutely no swooping or fixing, but be present and help problem-solve. Parenting coach and author Vicki Hoefle calls this method "duct-tape parenting" because yes, sometimes keeping our mouths shut and holding ourselves back from interfering in these learning moments requires something as strong as duct tape. Keep the concept of autonomy-supportive parenting in mind and offer support, not control. Be there to help if he is not sure about a cycle setting on the washer, or if something goes horribly awry with the fabric softener, but find something absorbing to do while he goes about the work. No butting in, no prompting, and no correcting unless asked. Oh, and one last thing. If you go behind your child's back and redo the chore he has just finished to his satisfaction, even if it's after he's left the room, he'll notice. You will be telling him through your actions not only that he is incompetent, but that you will finish the job if he's careless. That is one lesson you don't want to him to learn, both for his sake and for yours.

Praise your children for the effort they put into the chores, particularly if they really had to problem-solve or had to stick with a task that was not going well. When I praised my son for putting those plates away in the high cupboards, I was not praising him for taking on the task, because he knew I expected that of him. Rather, I was praising him for the extra effort, determination, and perseverance he showed when he hit a roadblock.

DITCH THE LOLLIPOPS

If your child has become addicted to the rewards you have been offering for helping out, you have a little extra work ahead of you to reorient her thinking. Questions of "What do I get if I do that?" and "How much will you pay me?" must give way to a new motivation, and the transition can take time and patience. First, stop using rewards as your default strategy. If you must reward for household duties, try to put off the reward for as long as possible in order to disengage the reward from the actual task, or make the reward nonmaterial. Keep in mind that little kids can only wait for a short period of time, but older kids can wait for much longer. The goal is to remove the task from the reward and shift their focus back toward internal motivators. As you move away from material rewards, talk about how rewarding it is to do a job well. Explain why you are not offering material rewards and why household participation is so important. Reward with praise the effort and patience your child had to exhibit in order to complete the task, even if it took many tries. *Especially* if it took many tries.

ONCE YOU HAVE REORIENTED YOUR own thinking about your children's role in the household duties, and have shelved the rewards, here are some suggestions for what, and how, you can put your grand plans into action.

HOUSEHOLD DUTIES FOR THE PRESCHOOL SET

The key to successfully instilling a sense of responsibility and pride, and helping children understand that they have a role to play in the family dynamic, is to start young. Even toddlers, with their diminutive hands and limited attention spans, can begin to explore their ability and competence in shared household responsibilities. When dealing with younger children be sure to make your expectations clear and age-appropriate. Katie Hurley, child and adolescent psychotherapist and mother of two, gave me her perspective on how she empowers her young children with their household contributions:

> My kids are still little, and certainly responsibilities change and attitudes toward those responsibilities change over time. I think what I've done well with mine is instead of creating some nagging revolving wheel of chores, I established age-appropriate expectations and I adjust those as they grow. Telling Riley she can use the special wood cleaner and clean all of the wood furniture in the house empowered her to feel more responsible. Giving Liam the power of the Swiffer dry mop gave him a bump in his confidence. We have family cleaning days where we all pitch in and then do something fun after, but I try to keep it mellow and don't place undue stress on it. Our mentality here is that we all live here and we all help each other out. They might not make their beds the way I would, but the beds are made and they have pride of ownership—win/win. I see a lot of very controlling parents in my practice. Everything has to be perfect or punishments are the result. That's a mistake, and only ends up creating resentment and anxiety.

Communicate family participation as a privilege, or even a game, and toddlers can accomplish more than you might expect. Here are some examples of the kinds of tasks toddlers are capable of learning:

- Put their dirty clothes in a basket or hamper.
- Dress themselves with clothing that's not too complicated.

- Fold simple items of clothing or linens such as pillowcases or washcloths.
- Put their clothes away in drawers.
- Follow two- or three-step directions in order to complete tasks (get your toothbrush, put toothpaste on it, brush your teeth).
- Throw trash and recycling away in the proper place.
- Put toys away in tubs and baskets when they are done playing with them.
- Get out and put away their dishes as long as you arrange their cups and bowls on a low shelf.
- Feed the dog or cat.

As children graduate from toddlerhood and move toward preschool, start teaching them how to manage more complicated duties. Kids between three and five are big fans of counting and sorting, so give them jobs around the house that encourage them to practice these skills while instilling responsibility. Ask them to put five books on that shelf, or ask them to count out five oranges and place them in a bag at the store. Kids this age are perfectly able to:

- Make their bed.
- Straighten their room.
- Sort and categorize items, such as utensils in a drawer, or socks in the laundry.
- Water plants.
- Clear their place at the table.
- Learn to not freak out and cry about spills, but get a towel or sponge and clean them up by themselves.
- Prepare their own snacks.

Children as young as five can understand and accept the consequences of their actions (and inaction), but only if they experience those consequences. Left her bagel on the coffee table and the dog ate it? Don't make her a new one and she will remember not to leave it within reach of the dog's mouth next time. Forgot to put her favorite DVD away in its case after she watched it? The next time she wants to watch that movie, don't help her look for it in the pile of loose DVDs, and remind her why she can't find it. Refuses to put her clothes in the hamper? She won't have her favorite pink sweatshirt to wear to preschool. Left her favorite stuffed animal at school? She won't have that particular nighttime friend to cuddle with when the lights go out.

These responsibilities and the lessons they carry are not really about DVDs or stuffed animals. They are about learning how to be responsible, to show initiative, and to follow through. They are about learning how to be the sort of person who will be able to manage the demands life will place on them. If you constantly bail your child out, she learns a lot from that, too. She learns that self-sufficiency is not really necessary because you'll always pick up the pieces and that there's no real need to come up with any sort of system or plan for remembering her responsibilities in the future.

THE HABITS OF HIGHLY EFFECTIVE SCHOOL-AGE KIDS

Once kids have entered kindergarten, they are able to conquer tasks of much greater complexity and begin to develop solid habits for completing household duties. It can be a real challenge to establish habits during the unpredictable toddler and preschool years, but once kids are in kindergarten, it's time to nail down some routines. Make your child's jobs a daily event rather than an intermittent expectation. Habits are powerful motivators, and tasks can't become habitual unless they are regular and expected, and, well, habitual. As habits require three elements—a cue, a routine, and a reward—in order to turn the occasional moment of "helping out" into a habit, it must be regular enough to become ingrained as a pattern.

Let's take loading the dishwasher as an example. Your child's cue to clean up after herself is the dirty dish in front of her at the end of a meal. The routine is the cleaning of that dish, and the reward is the sense of accomplishment and competence that comes from having completed her task. Again, this does not mean a material reward such as money or the promise of a toy or treat. The enduring reward is the sense of a job well done. Here's the best thing about habits: once they are formed, and your child completes her work as a matter of course rather than as a result of nagging, your household becomes a much more peaceful and harmonious place.

As I mentioned earlier, there are some exceptions to the no-rewards rule. Rewards can be a fun and effective way to jump-start motivation when it begins to flag. My favorite example comes from the book *All-of-a-Kind Family*, by Sydney Taylor. The book tells the story of an Orthodox Jewish family living on the Lower East Side of Manhattan in the early 1900s. The girls are responsible for household duties on a rotating basis, and when the five daughters tire of the hated task of dusting the living room, their mother hides pennies in hard-to-find locations, locations that would only be revealed through a thorough job of dusting. Once enthusiasm has been restored for the task, and grumbling has been replaced with requests to be assigned to the task, she uses the game intermittently, just often enough to spark renewed motivation, but not frequently enough for it to become an expected reward. Once, in my own little twist on this lesson, I tucked a beloved missing toy into a pile of stuff I wanted my son to put away, and suggested that if he cleaned his room up, he might just find what he'd been looking for. My first impulse had been to shout to the heavens that Super Mommy had found the toy, and bask in the glow of my triumph, but that strategy would not have resulted in a cleaner room or the happiness and discovery he experienced when he came across the toy himself.

BETWEEN THE AGES OF SIX and eleven, children should grow more and more capable. They understand the concept of cause and effect, and can predict that if the clothes don't go into the laundry basket, they won't get clean. If the dog does not get fed, she will be hungry. Capitalize on this understanding and help children see how being proactive around the house can lead to positive effects. At this point, kids are able to be responsible for all sorts of household tasks, such as:

- Peeling and chopping vegetables (teach knife safety early, and always use a sharp knife, which is safer than a dull one).
- Laundry—all of it, from sorting to putting it away. Post a list on the washing machine and dryer after you've conducted the requisite one-on-one lessons in order to provide reminders for all the steps. One mom pointed out that dry-erase markers write and erase well on the side of washers and dryers, so she simply writes instructions on the appliance itself.
- Replacing the toilet paper when it's gone. Leave the direction the roll spins to your child's discretion!

- Setting and clearing the table.
- Outdoor work such as raking leaves, weeding, and hauling wood.
- Vacuuming and mopping floors.
- Helping to plan and prepare grocery lists and meals.

WITH ADOLESCENCE COMES GREATER RESPONSIBILITY

From twelve on up, I can't think of many household duties beyond their abilities. The more competent teens I talked to for this book are responsible for:

- Household repairs, such as painting, replacing lightbulbs, and simple car maintenance.
- Grocery shopping (given some teens' quirky dietary habits, some parents provide pretty specific lists).
- Planning and preparing more complicated meals.
- Caring for and teaching younger siblings about their role in the household responsibilities.
- Taking the dog to the vet for his shots.
- Cleaning out the refrigerator.
- Chopping kindling and firewood.
- Clearing leaves out of the gutters.

When I asked adolescent psychologist Jennifer Hartstein about the role household duties play in a teen's life, she noted that when responsibilities are understood to be a basic and foundational part of family life, they provide positive and effective opportunities for teens to gain the competence they are going to need as they move into adulthood.

> Encouraging your teen to be a competent and involved member of the household sets the stage for them to be successful in life. If an adolescent knows that he/she doesn't have to "work" for things, this often translates into an inability to "work" in the real world. Having to be responsible for things at home (i.e., chores, laundry, walking the dog, etc.) helps to teach teens what it means to take care of the important things in their lives. Ultimately, this will cause teens to have better self-esteem, feel more effective, be more productive, and be more motivated to continue this into their adult lives.

It's never too early—or too late—to teach children how to contribute and problem-solve under their own power. Despite all the protests to the contrary, kids want to play a useful role in their family's success. As parents have slowly, but systematically, deprived them of that role, we owe them the patience and time it takes to give that purpose and responsibility back. Sure, this restoration of order will be a challenge, but it will also be worth it, both in the short and long term. The contribution of your children to the daily work of keeping a house and running a family will not only be a boon to the family now, but your kids' increased competence and sense of responsibility will set them apart from their more coddled peers when they head off to college or land their first job. While their peers stand around helplessly, waiting to be told what to do and how to do it, your kids will know how to take charge and forge ahead, armed with the competence, experience, and the skills they learned by your side, in your home. They have had opportunities to fail, to mess up and fix their errors, and won't be fazed by a misstep here and there as young adults. As an added bonus, the stories about the time the washing machine foamed over because your son used dish soap in the place of laundry detergent, and the afternoon you all worked together to solve some "funny-in-retrospect" family emergency, will be the tales you weave in and out of your holiday celebrations over a lifetime. Better to understand now that perfection is not what holds a family together; the bond forged through shared struggle is what endures over the long haul.

6
FRIENDS: ACCOMPLICES TO FAILURE AND THE FORMATION OF IDENTITY

THE DAD RUNNING BACK AND forth between the play structure and the sandbox meant well, we could tell, but watching him work himself up into a sweaty lather was exhausting, even from a distance. My friend and I watched from our bench in the shade, quietly nibbling our children's cheddar crackers, diverted by his feats of extravagant overparenting.

One of his children, a girl of about six, was playing in the sandbox with my friend's daughter and two other girls. They were playing well together, but there was the usual jockeying for power going on between them, and they occasionally erupted in shouting as they fought over the coveted roles in their communal game. His other child, a toddler, was gleefully testing the limits of his strength and agility, repeatedly attempting to pursue a much older child up a slippery slide.

Both of his children were having a grand time in the moments they were allowed to play on their own. The father, however, was nearly apoplectic with worry. He could not simultaneously supervise the details of both children's play, so he ran back and forth between the two, sometimes towing the toddler under his arm as the boy screamed in protest. Every time the girl's voice rose to a shout, or one of the other girls shouted at her, the father rushed in to sort out their issues, soothe, or bribe the girl with the promise of a snack if she would "just play nice." When one of the other girls spoke harshly to his daughter, his eyes swept the crowd, searching for backup in the form of the other girls' parents. My friend wisely kept her mouth shut and averted her eyes when he looked in her direction. Meanwhile, his toddler seized on the opportunity of his father's momentary inattention to run back to the slide, which made the father so nervous that he abandoned the management of his daughter and ran back across the playground for round two.

I can only imagine how tiring and stressful the "play" session was for that dad. As for the kids, I can't imagine they enjoyed all his meddling. They seemed to have fun in fits and starts, but as soon as they gathered momentum and the play took on a life of its own, it was shut down due to noise or conflict. What that overwrought father did not understand as he struggled to manage his kids' every move was that he was defeating the very purpose of their playtime.

Our children's social lives begin in infancy when they gaze up at our faces and mirror our smiles, or convey the soggy discomfort of a wet diaper with a wailing cry. Once those babies move beyond the close company of their parents and venture into relationships with other children, however, they begin a lifelong education in rules of social conduct and the vocabulary of the subtle cues human beings use to communicate with each other. Fluency in the language of human social interaction will determine the success of all their future relationships, and failure to develop fluency is a significant handicap in life.

Much of the foundation for this fluency is taught through free play with other children. In her book *The Nurture Assumption: Why Children Turn Out the Way They Do*, psychologist Judith Harris argues that parents matter much less in the development of our children's nature than we'd like to believe, and that peers, not parents, shape much of our children's behavior and experience of the world. Peers teach our children how to interact and negotiate with other people, and this education starts in the sandbox, where children learn to play cooperatively, respond to the needs of others, and construct their own imaginary worlds. Play is a vital part of human development for many reasons: board games teach logic and planning; making forts spatial and construction skills; basketball pickup games teamwork. But the most important lessons of play and friend time are interpersonal, and these lessons are best learned when uninterrupted and free of adult manipulations and machinations. Adults should give kids the space and freedom to learn this language and work out the tough social moments for themselves, because those fights, tussles, silent treatments, and breakups are, despite the tears and heartbreak they cause, invaluable opportunities for growth. The social conflicts of childhood are all part of our education in human relationships, and failure to negotiate also provides its own lessons. Squabbles are opportunities to be valued, not emergencies to be managed. That father on the playground leapt in to intervene at the first sign of discord, and in doing so, short-circuited each one of those potential lessons. Children used to play on their own, away from the eyes of parents, and were allowed to work out these social dynamics free of parental interference. No longer.

When the troublesome, sand-throwing girl from the playground is removed from the squabble, she never learns to deal with her own anger, let alone the anger of her intended target. Worse, she never witnesses the rage and upset she caused. She needs to appreciate fully that she has failed at a social interaction and sit with those confusing, bad feelings. The target of the sand attack, who does not appreciate having sand thrown in her face, will send a message about acceptable sandbox behavior. In the end, the conflict will pass, and those two girls will likely heal their rift, closer and wiser for the conflict. Sure, throwing sand is a failure to communicate effectively, but when adults intervene, the lessons laid out by peers don't get the chance to settle in and do their work on the child who has failed. Children develop empathy by seeing and hearing other people's reactions and emotions, and when we don't allow our children to experience the full brunt of those uncomfortable moments, we deny them a glimpse into the consequences and impact of their actions on others. One missed lesson in the sandbox is no big deal, of course, but when that child grows up under the wing of parents who continue to rescue—from playground dust-ups, to tween misunderstandings, and the inevitable volatility of adolescent friendships—that child becomes an adult with no clue about how to negotiate, placate, reason with, and stand up to other adults.

Andrea Nair, a psychotherapist and parenting coach, explains further in an email:

> The cost of over-protecting is that the child does not develop the skills to fight back, speak up or get the hell out of the way. If a child is taught by their parent that an adult will swoop in and fight for them or save them from any form of challenging situation, that child will keep expecting that to happen and not look

for solutions to help herself. That child will also not learn valuable communication skills that are necessary during the heat of emotional flooding during an argument.

If the emotional and social benefits of not swooping in to rescue kids from conflict are not sufficient to convince you, how about this: the ability to enjoy uninterrupted and unrestricted free play is also predictive of academic success.

In her book *A Nation of Wimps*, Hara Estroff Marano points out that social interactions cultivated during free play are "so important that social behavior at recess in kindergarten predicts achievement at the end of first grade, as measured by class work and standardized tests of general knowledge, early reading, and math concepts. By a whopping 40 percent, peer play is significantly more predictive of academic success than standardized achievement tests. Free play, and the social interactions that it fosters, are undervalued in our children's social and emotional growth. It is a gross mistake to think that play is time unproductively spent." Sadly, many schools are so closely monitoring recess and managing children's social dynamics that kids don't have the opportunity or freedom to let recess and lunchtime dramas play out to their logical (and sometimes illogical) conclusions. This shortsighted and misguided move away from unsupervised free play means children have fewer opportunities to process the lessons they learn in school and are left with no outlet for the physical and emotional energy that builds up during the day. Later, when those recess-deprived children arrive home from school, they are no longer being kicked out of the house to fend for themselves until dinner; they are shuttled from organized activity to structured lessons and asked to silence their urge for unstructured play and skirmishes with their siblings.

A group of New Zealand schools heard researchers and sounded the call. As part of a study based at the Auckland University of Technology, eight elementary schools agreed to eliminate recess rules, relax supervision, and stop intervening in students' playtime. Consequently, those schools saw a reduction in bullying, fewer rule infractions, reduced need for adult supervision, and an improvement in attention and behavior during class time. Grant Schofield, one of the investigators in the study, explains that backing off on adult supervision and interventions during free play allows kids "to think for themselves and sort [social interactions] out." When we interfere with our kids' social lives, they are deprived of yet another opportunity to learn how to sort out feelings, convictions, and personal limits. The goals and lessons of children's social lives shift over time, but as they move from toddlerhood to adolescence, it's important to view friendships for what they are: opportunities for them to develop their own personalities, identities, and choices and for us to gain perspective and feedback on who our children are becoming.

THE PUSH AND PULL OF PLAYDATES

In toddlerhood, friends are usually plucked from whichever kids are closest in age or proximity. Unfortunately, parents are increasingly opting for digital companions over living, breathing ones, but I beg you, put the tablets, game consoles, and televisions away, and arrange playdates with a variety of real, live children. Playdates don't just give you five minutes to breathe and enjoy your own social time with another parent; they give your child an opportunity to figure out what she likes and does not like in a companion. Give her that opportunity to learn about friendships by giving her space. Don't take charge of the playdate. Provide a safe environment and observe from afar. Unless injury is imminent, kids don't want or need you interfering in their play. Even preverbal children convey their wishes to playmates, and as they mature into their words, they will begin to voice their opinions, likes, and dislikes. Feel free to instruct those squabbling toddlers to "use their words" but understand that they may not have the words to use. They are still developing the vocabulary they need in order to express their frustrations, and until they become more verbal, they may use their hands, teeth, and feet to express displeasure.

SIBLING RIVALRY AND RESOLUTION

These rules of disengagement apply to sibling social dynamics as well, but it can be hard to remember when the screaming and squabbling become overwhelming. I've been known to intervene just to get the noise to stop, and don't really care what the argument is about by the time I've reached my breaking point. Siblings are our children's first friends, enemies, and teachers, and it's really important to let them work out their issues with each other on their own time and terms. I asked Julie Cole, writer, cofounder of Mabel's Labels, and mother of six, how she handles the chaos and conflict.

> With six kids close in age, there's a lot of fun, a lot of love, and a lot of laughs. There's also a lot of bickering and getting into each other's business. In fact, I've been known to call them "The Bickersons" on occasion. I learned early on that I have better ways to spend my time than inserting myself into every disagreement. Short of putting them in a soundproof room, instead I laid out

the ground rules for how to "fight fair" early on, and as such, they seem to be able to resolve most things on their own. To me, "fighting fair" means only bickering about the issue at hand, never bringing up something from the past to use against a sibling, and no name calling. This means after an argument, they are back playing together five minutes later without ever remembering they had a disagreement. "Fighting fair" means I can step away and let them solve their own problems, which prevents me from pulling my hair out and being a full-time mediator.

PLAYMATE PROXIMITY TO PLAYGROUND POLITICS

Elementary-school-age children tend to pick friends based on shared interests rather than proximity, and their play gets much more complex. As independence grows and dexterity improves, they invent games and construct elaborate adventures with complex rules for the imagined worlds they conquer. This type of play is an important learning process because it's the beginning of their move toward independence and autonomy. No wonder superheroes are their idols; kids mimic the power, strength, and sense of justice those heroes represent in order to feel powerful in their own lives. They are used to obeying our rules, but as they step away from the parental sphere of influence, they discover the power of autonomy and self-regulation. They explore their own power to create and destroy entire realms, and negotiate those power struggles with the other children involved in the game. As the influence of their friends begins to gain in power, it's a good time to begin to talk to your child about peer pressure and what she might do if she is placed in a situation that makes her uncomfortable. Think ahead to middle and high school and get her thinking about the moments she will have to rely on her internal moral compass and judgment in order to deal with peer-pressure risky play.

IN TALKING WITH SOME MOMS about how they deal with their children's friendships, one mother confided that she's newly uncomfortable with her third-grade daughter's ability to pick and choose friends that may or may not be a good influence, though she is also realizing how much her daughter is learning from these relationships.

> My daughter has a burgeoning friendship with a girl in her class who isn't a "bad" kid, per se, but I'm troubled by what I hear about her. She lies, she is rather boy crazy, and she is rude. But she also seems to have a pretty horrific home life—which makes me feel really awful for her. I don't want to completely discourage the friendship because I do feel like some kids can "turn it around." Also, the friendship seems to be teaching my daughter compassion. She knows the child is quite poor, and she has been begging me to buy the little girl things since they became friends—things that my daughter used to take for granted, but now realizes her friend does not have.

Kids are not born knowing how to negotiate for themselves and their friendships; they learn this skill through years of trying, and failing, to manage their lives and their relationships. When a child learns how to say no to an older kid who asks to play doctor behind the toolshed, he also creates the emotional groundwork for someday being confident enough to stand up to a bully or demand fair treatment from an adult.

Parents need to step back and allow minor playground squabbles to play out because these conflicts give kids a chance to learn how to handle themselves in an increasingly powerful bully culture. We need to remember that if Johnny pushes another kid down on the pavement, but is not allowed to receive feedback from his peers because teachers or overprotective parents whisk him or his victim away before resolution can occur, Johnny does not receive the benefit of peer feedback. In the absence of peer feedback, empathy can't develop, and he will become the sort of kid who can't understand how his actions impact his classmates and friends. All those adults who intervened in the necessary lessons of his playground days are to blame. Unfortunately, a few years later, when he looks around the middle school classroom and realizes no one wants to play with him and his teacher must inform his parents that he has "issues with his social skills," Johnny's social and emotional problems will be much harder to remedy.

The good news is that given time, and some space from adult intervention, kids learn these social skills on their own. If we allow them to mess up, anger other kids, fight, and make up, they will learn how to be a good friend, how to stand up for themselves, and how to say no to behaviors that make them uncomfortable.

Research shows that children are less upset by their parents' arguments when they witness the emotional healing that results from making up, so it makes sense that kids benefit from seeing fights with friends through to resolution. Given that conflict is less upsetting to children than lack of closure, when you jump in to resolve a sandbox argument or forcefully arrange détente with the mean girl who has been ignoring your daughter, resolution is not being allowed to happen naturally in its own time and place. Unresolved conflict triggers anxiety for children and gets in the way of the healthy process of making up and healing rifts with friends, moments that cement long-term relationships that will endure through the next disagreement.

FRIENDSHIPS IN THE MIDDLE YEARS

As kids move to middle school, the focus shifts from shared interests to social acceptance. Cliques and other exclusionary social situations can be extremely stressful for middle school children, so it will be important to make sure that your child continues to participate in sports, music, and other extracurricular activities that bridge the divide between social groups. One mother from New Jersey admits that her own experiences with parents who allowed her autonomy in her social life inform her own autonomy-supportive parenting today.

> My parents left me to decide on my own friendships, and this was a great thing. I sometimes got my feelings hurt because I wouldn't do what [my friends] were doing, so they ousted me from their clique. It made me tougher and gave me pause when choosing friends.

Rather than dictate whom your child can associate with, make your home a comfortable gathering place for your kid and his friends, and set the expectation that when your child is not in your house, he will let you know where he is. Understand that kids' social lives are constantly evolving, and do not attempt to intervene when you feel your child has been excluded. You can be sympathetic to your child's sadness but don't try to fix a situation that is, and should be, out of your control. It can be painful to see your own child fail to make friends, or smooth over disagreements, but these are important trials and lessons your child must experience and learn from.

As a teacher, I have seen far too many kids arrive in middle school still unsure of how to handle social situations, but nothing upsets a child's social maturation more than parents who fight their children's battles for them and overreact to the normal social jostling that takes place in middle and high school. When parents overreact to everyday social interactions and label it bullying, children never learn how to figuratively push back and demand respect. Bullying is a real and terrifying fact of life in schools today, but in our attempts to halt bullying before it ramps up into dangerous territory, teachers and parents tend to overreact to the normal social and emotional ups and downs of the adolescent social scene and inadvertently saddle their kids with a victim mentality.

In talking to educators and administrators, it is clear that they are aware and alarmed by the impact bullying can have on kids, but they are also frustrated by the way some parents feed the bullying dynamic while simultaneously trying to short-circuit it. At a recent speaking engagement, a high school teacher told me:

> I recently taught a student who had been the target of a few of her classmates' ire because of a disagreement, and when the disagreements and behaviors rose to the level of bullying, the school bent over backwards to make sure this girl was protected and safe. However, the parents—and consequently the child—became so hyper-alert and oversensitive to what they saw as bullying that the teachers were forced to become secret agents. The entire class orbited around that one child's needs, from classroom seating charts, to teacher supervision during the walk between classes. The mother sent daily emails to the teachers and administrators,

> quoting her daughter's reports of mean looks, whispers, and perceived slights. Normal social interaction could not take place in that class, and consequently, social dynamics were a disaster. The class ceased to be a community, and even academic progress took a hit that year. Worse, that girl came to view all uncomfortable social interaction as bullying. I am so sad for this child. Her parents mean well, but by moderating and weighing in on the subtle nuance of every social encounter, they have destroyed their daughter's confidence and convinced her that she is a helpless victim.

As adults we all have our own bullies to deal with: mean bosses, vicious enemies, and jealous peers. How your kid learns to deal with those people in their childhood, when failure means a day or two of hurt feelings or social exclusion, can mean the difference between a thin skin and a strong sense of self. As children get older, and friends play a greater role in their development of identity, it can be tempting to step in when you sense the presence of a bad influence. But before you criticize your child's friends, know this: making, keeping, and deciding when and how to part with friends is part of your child's education. Something about that most dubious of friends attracts your child, and she is simply trying to figure out what that attraction is all about. Maybe that girl who dresses all in black and paints her nails green and swears more often than you are comfortable with has talents or social skills your child is trying to learn. Maybe your child is simply feeling out the limits of what she's comfortable with in her own world. No matter how nervous these strange and different friends make you feel, it's vital that you stay out of your child's social choices, particularly in adolescence. It may seem like a simple matter of a bad friendship to you, but your child is practicing empathy and learning how to get along with people who may not share the same background and goals; these are incredibly important social skills. As adolescents move into college, they will adjust more easily to wider, more diverse, and often challenging social situations. In the business world, the ability to read all kinds of people is a sought-after character trait, particularly in women. These people, called chameleons or "high self-monitors," are better at adapting themselves to new people and to new work environments, and better at bringing other people around to their way of thinking. In sales, chameleons are able to connect to people through subtle cues of mimicry, and outperform other salespeople. In business, those who are skilled at mimicry and can adapt their behavior to diverse groups of people make the best negotiators.

So when your son comes home from school with a new group of kids who make you uncomfortable because they are simply different from anyone you have seen your child socialize with before, think of those earrings, tattoos, varying skin colors, dyed hair, and accents you can hardly understand as an education worthy of a seminar at the Harvard Business School. If your child plays with carbon copies of the same four kids every day for the rest of his life, he will never develop empathy for difference, or an understanding of how to negotiate and reason with people who come from differing perspectives, worldviews, and ethnicities. Consider your polite smile and lack of judgment as an investment in your child's education, and back off. Let him figure out for himself what he likes and does not like in people.

LEARNING FROM ADOLESCENT SOCIAL ANGST

By the time these children become teenagers, you will be glad you stayed out of their social lives, because your child will have superior skills of negotiation and self-awareness. As tweens become teens, and perceived dangers can become real dangers, parents begin to wonder when it's time to intervene. Depending on whom you ask, this question will get many different answers, from "five minutes ago" to "never." I'm always going to err on the side of trusting my child in order to preserve autonomy, but out of curiosity, I asked a group of fifteen-year-olds to answer this question. Most of the kids felt it was perfectly reasonable for a parent to snoop if that parent had a *reason* to snoop. "If someone told you that your kid was doing something dangerous," clarified one boy. In talking to these kids, I was struck by the fact that none of them said that it was never okay to snoop. One explained:

> It depends on the kid, and unless parents are being paranoid or overly protective, I think they know if they can trust their kid or not. If the kid is basically a good kid, let them figure out who they can be friends with, and even if they start acting like the bad kids, sometimes they need to do a couple of stupid things before they realize that they don't want to go down that road. Give them some space.

There was dissent among these teenagers about how far to let kids travel down the road into dangerous behaviors, but they all agreed that when parents attempt to control teenagers' social lives their children are much more likely to become deceptive.

"My friends with strict parents lie so much more than the kids whose parents let them have some freedom."

"Yeah, this one friend of mine, her parents think she's perfect and doing everything they tell her to do, but she's lying to them about *everything*, even stuff she doesn't have to lie about."

There were nods all around.

ADOLESCENT PSYCHOLOGIST JENNIFER HARTSTEIN STRESSED the importance of finding a way to support, but not control, teens through their adolescent relationships in an email.

> Adolescence is a time when friendships are the toughest, in many ways. Teens are learning who they are, what they want and how to balance that with friends experiencing the same things. It is so valuable to encourage adolescents to be interpersonally effective on their own, as they will soon be leaving home and need to do so in many aspects of their lives. For parents, this is a huge challenge, as seeing their teen in pain or struggling is terrifying. Be a guide and a safe place for problem solving, rather than the problem solver. Your teen will gain strength from knowing that he/she faced a problem with a peer directly and handled it, learning what works and what doesn't along the way, and thus being more prepared for all the challenges adulthood presents.

Yes, kids will make bad choices in friends, and some friendships will fail, but these missteps are what we look back on in order to recognize the traits of a healthy relationship versus a toxic one. As hard as it is to live up to Hartstein's challenge, the rewards—independent, courageous, and brave young adults who understand what they want and need from the friends they will make and rely on over a lifetime—are worth the restraint and patience.

I recognize, however, that the stakes are higher once kids hit adolescence. A failed relationship or social interaction as a third grader is a much less traumatic and emotional gauntlet than a hormone-fueled adolescent feud or the frightening weight for parents of dangers such as drugs, alcohol, drunk driving, and eating disorders. That said, here are some tools for meeting Hartstein's challenge while protecting your child's safety and emotional health.

If your child changes in ways that make you uncomfortable as a result of his friendships, talk to him about what he likes or is drawn to in these new friends. "What do you like about Mike? What do you two do together? You seem to be spending a lot of time around Mike; what is it that you find interesting in him?" Even if Mike grates on your very last nerve, offer to host Mike more often, not less, so you will have a front-row seat to your child's relationship. Make sure your son understands that your expectations for his behavior have not changed, and that your house rules will extend to Mike, but that he is welcome in your home. If you feel the need to make your expectations or house rules exceedingly clear to both your family and their guests, post them on the refrigerator. If your child crosses the line in your own home, make sure you follow through with consequences as well. If Mike does not like the rules in your home, he may choose to leave, but remember, your child is still your child, and the rules in your home apply to everyone you invite in.

Having a problematic kid over to your house also gives you the opportunity to get to know the proverbial enemy and understand what you are dealing with. At best, you will find that your son's new friend is a really great person who wants what's best for your son and their relationship. At worst, your suspicions will be confirmed, and you will have evidence you can point to in your discussions with your child about why he is no longer allowed to have that kid over to your house anymore. Offer to drive your son and his friend around. There's something about car trips that elicits unguarded conversation. It's as if the kids forget you are there and open up their inhibitions and conversational topics. Listen and look in the rearview mirror. Use these visits and car trips as a way to get to know the parents of these friends. You may find that these parents simply don't hold high expectations for their kids, or you may find allies who want the same things for their child that you want for yours. In the end, remember that you do not have the power to change other people's children. You can only make your expectations clear and follow through with consequences when those expectations are breached.

Don't lecture. Children, and particularly adolescents, will tune out the moment you start. Take it from a teacher. If your communication style tends toward the lecture, you are going to have to change your style, because you won't be able to force your child to start listening.

Ask an open-ended question and then listen. "Kevin seems different from your other friends. How did you guys become friends?" would be a great nonjudgmental, nonthreatening opener that gently cracks open the door for further conversation.

If unsafe behavior is the topic, talk about the safety issue rather than passing judgment on the friends. Kids get defensive and protective of their relationships the moment it seems as if their friends are being attacked. Best to stick with facts and actions as opposed to character assassination.

Adolescents have a heightened sense of loyalty, and will defend their friends' behavior even when they feel uncomfortable about it. Stick with what you know about your own child's behavior, and if she has acted wisely in the face of a dangerous or problematic situation, make sure to praise her for her judgment and fortitude. A statement such as "It must have been hard for you to say no to that party last week when you knew there would be a keg. I'm really proud of you for making such an adult decision," offers praise for character and maturity.

Once, when I shared my own worries about sending my teenager out into the world, an older mother who had been listening in on my conversation shared her personal lightbulb moment, one I've tried to keep with me every time I watch my son head out the door. She said,

> One time my teenage son was going somewhere, I don't know where, and I said on the way out the door "be careful," as I always had. I then heard my husband say, "Have fun," and for the first time, I heard the differences in our parenting approaches summed up in that one exchange. My kid had always been a careful kid, and my words, whether I said them or not, were not going to serve as some magic charm over his experience. All he heard was that I did not trust him to be careful, whereas his father did. That was the last time I ever said, "Be careful," as he left the house with friends.

As we send our kids out into the world, we need to trust them more, and when they live up to our trust, catch them doing things right and praise them. This may require changing your mindset but keep an eye out for their good judgment, character, and resilience, and let them know that's what you value above all else. Make sure they know that if events spiral out of control, and they find themselves in a dangerous or threatening situation, you will help, no questions asked . . . until the next day. Hold your comments about how on earth they ended up smoking a cigarette at the middle school dance or in the passenger seat of a car with a drunk driver. Once they are safe, and have had a good night's sleep, discuss the specifics of what happened and why. Using poor judgment is part of growing up. If they had the presence of mind to call you for help, focus on the fact that they respected and trusted you enough to say no to a situation they sensed was unsafe; now live up to that trust and help them figure out how not to get into that situation again.

Model positive and mutually beneficial friendships for your children. Talk about what makes a good friend and why you consider your friends good influences in your life. Ask them how they think their friends describe them. Eradicate toxic and harmful people from your own life before fixing your sights on the toxic and harmful elements in your children's lives, because your example is going to teach them much more about the anatomy of healthy relationships than your words ever will.

If, however, all of this careful communication and planning goes nowhere and you continue to have worries about your child's relationships, the time may come when it's appropriate to intervene. First, check your motives. Are you truly interested in the safety of your child, or are you looking for ammunition on kids you fear are bad influences in your child's life? If so, step back, take a breath, and stay out of it.

IF YOU ARE STILL WORRIED, try these alternatives before snooping and breaking your child's trust:

- Talk to other adults, the teacher, administrators, and coaches, and find out if the child in question is really a bad influence or a wolf in scary sheep's clothing.
- Go meet the friend's parents in person and share your concerns. Make sure they are clear on your house rules as well, and feel out their commitment to keep their own kid healthy and safe.

- Talk to your child about behavior you have witnessed or heard about that makes you nervous. Ask questions, and in the process, make your expectations around drugs and alcohol clear once more.
- If it becomes clear that this kid is a bad influence, based on actual evidence rather than fear, limit time with this friend. Keep in mind that this can backfire, and your child may well react poorly to your attempts to control his social life.
- Find safer, healthier things for your child to do. If you arrange other activities you know he would enjoy, the friendship with this problematic kid may just wither from inattention.

If you are still concerned, and have done that gut check to make sure your motives are pure and centered on the health and safety of your child, here are some examples of circumstances that warrant snooping:

- Sudden changes in behavior, personality, weight, sleep patterns, or general health.
- Changes in your child's communication patterns. If your child is usually willing to share with you, has she stopped doing so? Conversely, if your child never was a big talker, is he suddenly trying to tell you something? If so, make sure you are listening.
- Evidence of drugs or alcohol use (drug paraphernalia, suspicions that your child is drunk or high).
- Changes in grades or study habits.
- Hard evidence to back up your suspicions that your child's friends are a "bad influence."

If any of the above circumstances arise at your home, it might be time to take a look into your child's room, social networks, or simply Google your child's name and see what comes up. Mother, writer, and prosecutor Loni Coombs advocates for parental snooping that adheres to what criminal law calls the "Plain View Doctrine":

> The other possible source of information that isn't an unconscionable violation of trust is stuff left out by your child in plain sight. In criminal law, this is called the "Plain View Doctrine." Police officers are allowed to look at anything they find in plain sight in a location where they have a legal right to be. If you, as the parent and owner of the home, go into your child's bedroom to clean or put away clothes, or what have you, and you see things that aren't hidden away, if you have a legitimate concern, it might be okay to look.

Finally, if you decide to look, think about what you plan to do with what you might find. If you stumble upon information that needs to be dealt with immediately, such as information that your child or your child's friends might be in danger, certainly act on that information. However, if the information is not life threatening, sit on it for a while. Give your child time and perhaps he will confide in you. Also allow for the possibility that sometimes, even with proof, you can misconstrue what is happening in your child's life. Use the information to guide your parenting rather than as ammunition in a full-on assault on your child.

If your child is in trouble, or at risk for dangerous behaviors such as substance abuse, depression, eating disorders, or any number of the pitfalls that come up in a teenager's life, remember that you have the power to align yourself with your child and help him cope. Keep autonomy, love, and support at the forefront of your priorities so as not to risk alienating yourself from your child and losing the opportunity to save him from peril. At the first sign of drug or alcohol abuse, eating disorders, or self-injury, seek professional help rather than attempt to handle the situation yourself.

Above all else, do not promise your child that you can "fix" his problems, social or otherwise. You may not be able to, and it's important that your child understands that not everything can be magically remedied with a wave of the parental wand. Some problems are too big for that, and some require complex and imperfect solutions.

Fortunately, if parents have done their jobs right, kids will have the competence and courage to face these complex and imperfect solutions. As much as I wanted to grow up as Anne of Green Gables with a nut-brown-haired Diana Barry as my best friend, I didn't. I had complicated and often fraught friendships with the kids in my neighborhood. We were the fortunate prisoners of each other's constant company, and we had to cobble out our own treaties and lines of demarcation across the boundaries of our comfort zones. This is childhood. Those shifting, hotly contested, and embattled lines littered with successes and failures don't just define childhood boundaries; they define the people our children will become, and we owe them the time and space they require to explore those territories.

7
SPORTS: LOSING AS AN ESSENTIAL CHILDHOOD EXPERIENCE

WHEREVER GROUPS OF PARENTS CONGREGATE, discussion quickly turns to our children, and a recent breakfast with friends was no exception. The school year was just beginning, and the subject of fall sports came up. I had heard the horror stories before. Sports are too competitive, parents scream at children from the sidelines, and coaches dole out trophies for simply showing up. When the tone shifted from indignant to upset, and the stories took a turn I didn't expect, I finally understood who the real losers are in this era of hypercompetitive sports specialization: kids who just want to play. Here's one mom's tale of woe, told over that breakfast:

> I always loved sports, and when I was little, sports were where I established my identity, so I was thrilled when I finally convinced my daughter to get out there and give sports a shot. But instead of finding fun and exercise and identity, she's found that she's too late. Even the recreational league is so intense that the coaches

> won't work with her or let her play. We tried gymnastics, but those kids have been training since they were toddlers, so that didn't work out either. She wants to try some different sports and see what she likes, but everything is so *serious* now that she can't just try stuff out. She's nine. Isn't nine when you are supposed to be playing a lot of different sports and figuring out what you like to do?

This mom was in tears by the time she finished speaking, and the room fell silent. No one had any good suggestions for her, and everyone knew that what she was saying was true. Another mom concurred: "It's frustrating because I just want my kids to try out lots of things, learn some sports or dance basics, and have fun, but the machine of youth sports is wound so tight it is difficult to even break in."

We don't even live in a particularly intense or competitive community, yet by the time the kids hit nine or ten, many have been specializing in a sport for a couple of years. The local indoor soccer league actually starts at age three with their "Tykes" league.

How about a league called "I just wanna play"?

The next morning, I recounted this mother's story to the headmaster of a prestigious Massachusetts independent school.

"Oh, that's nothing," he said, shaking his head. "You have *no* idea how intense youth sports have become."

He spent the next two hours filling me in on the state of sports in his world. He told tales of ninth graders who have committed to colleges for lacrosse and soccer in clear violation of NCAA recruitment rules. He described high school showcase tournaments in which players attend not out of team allegiance, but in order to showcase *themselves* for college coaches. He spun tales of parents he has had to face when those verbally committed students come home with a C-plus, and the parents plead with him to have the grade changed because "Brown [or Duke or Harvard, take your pick] won't look at him unless he keeps his grade at a B-minus or higher." One parent begged him to "get their son the right set of teachers" who would not give him C's.

"It used to be that I only had to worry about my high school kids when it came to early sports commitments," said this headmaster. Increasingly, middle school students are being targeted for early recruitment. The Independent School League, composed of sixteen New England prep schools, has begun to organize the same sorts of showcase tournaments for middle school students so that secondary school coaches can scout talent among eleven- to thirteen-year-old children. When I talked to administrators and teachers in other schools to get feedback on the details of his story, all I found was further confirmation that childhood sports are no longer about play. A high school basketball coach lamented, "If only my players wanted to do it as badly as their parents do." For many kids and their parents, sports have become as much, if not more, about planning for their college applications than about fun and exercise. Competition for the top spots in high school and college sports is becoming so intense, it's no wonder children are stressed-out and under great pressure to perform at younger and younger ages.

Dr. Louis Profeta, author and emergency medicine physician in Indiana who treats these young athletes' repetitive motion stress injuries, wonders why we impose this pressure on our kids and sacrifice so much of what used to define family time:

> Somewhere along the line we got distracted, and the practice field became the dinner table of the new millennium. Instead of huddling around a platter of baked chicken, mashed potatoes and

> fruit salad, we spend our evenings handing off our children like 4 x 200 batons. From baseball practice to cheerleading, from swimming lessons to personal training, we have become the "hour-long" generation of five to six, six to seven, and seven to eight, selling the souls of our family for lacrosse try-outs.

The value of play for the sake of play, the disruption of family time, the unnecessary pressure placed on kids of all ages, are all hugely problematic issues when it comes to childhood sports, but we are forgetting that one of the most significant aspects of sports is as an arena to learn about and accept failure.

Sports psychologist Terry Orlick refers to youth sports programs as "failure factories," and if this is the case, why do we pretend that every one of the 40 million American children who play youth sports should emerge from each game a winner? If kids are inevitably going to face failure and losses in sports programs, why not embrace it? Imagine if sports could be a safe place to fail, where athletes and teams could lose and the aftermath would be all about sportsmanship rather than conflict over that last contested call or doomsday panic about the child's future. Sports should be the place and time to experience disappointment and failure in a lower-stakes environment, a brief window of time to lay down the foundation our children will need in order to grow into adults of character.

Melissa Atkins Wardy, author of the book *Redefining Girly: How Parents Can Fight the Stereotyping and Sexualizing of Girlhood, from Birth to Tween*, told me the story of her daughter's first, failure-ridden day of baseball practice.

> Amelia showed up for her first day of baseball last night and discovered she is one of two girls on a team of boys she doesn't know.

> She was very intimidated, but she got on her helmet, chose a bat, and went into the batting cage. We didn't realize "coach pitch" meant "pitching machine." We thought it meant a parent lobbing balls across the plate for the kids. Still, Amelia summoned enough courage to get in the cage and take a pitch. She only took one pitch before the tears started, but sometimes that is what courage looks like. Somedays, courage looks a lot like failure, except it is the exact opposite.

Melissa has learned how to reveal the upside of failure for her daughter, those moments that feel horrible and humiliating, when we lose the game or celebrate a goal kicked into the other team's net. Those are moments of courage and growth, and we need to teach our kids to be proud of them. Whether Amelia chooses to return to baseball practice, she's found something valuable in that scary, no-hitter experience.

THE BENEFITS OF SPORTS OFF THE FIELD

Competitive sports can be a great place to discover and learn from these moments of courage that look like failure. In *The Parents We Mean to Be: How Well-Intentioned Adults Undermine Children's Moral and Emotional Development*, psychologist Richard Weissbourd describes the empathy and appreciation that can be developed in children through sports:

> Competition challenges children to appreciate the skills of opposing players even when they seem like mortal enemies, to find weaker teammates' strengths even when those players are jeopardizing the team's chances of making the playoffs, to take the

> referee's perspective, at least after the game, even when he or she makes a bad call at a critical moment. That's the kind of demanding morality that helps to develop over time children's capacity to see beyond their own intense feelings, to tolerate others' flaws, to place others' perspectives and needs on a par with their own.

Sports also offer parents the gift of time with their children. Most sports participation requires a fair amount of car travel to practices and tournaments, and in my experience, this is where some of the most honest and unguarded conversations with my teenage son take place. So much of parenting is about being there when our kids decide they want to talk to us. I have also found that the more positive and relaxed the atmosphere in the car, the more often kids will seize the opportunity to talk about difficult subjects, topics that are not likely to come up in the usual course of a stressful, task-oriented, and tightly scheduled day. Here is a place to talk about the ups and downs of what happened at the game or at practice, a place to confide in disappointments, exhaustion, passion, or disinterest.

Unfortunately this is not the case for the majority of families, as Bruce Brown and Rob Miller, two former coaches who now run Proactive Coaching, LLC, discovered. Over the course of twelve years, Brown and Miller conducted an informal survey of athletes about what makes supportive and effective sports parents. When Brown asked college athletes, "'What is your worst memory from playing youth and high school sports?' their overwhelming response was, 'The ride home from games with my parents.'" Teens across the country are apparently sharing tense car rides home from games with parents who use the hours of travel time to criticize players, second-guess coaches, and deride referees. That's a lot of valuable parenting opportunity wasted, hours that could be used for conversation and the enjoyment of each other's company.

In an illustrative corollary to this finding, this study revealed who kids *really* want at their games and, presumably, in the car on the way home: grandparents. Grandparents don't criticize or micromanage in the moments after the game. Grandparents don't critique the coach's strategy or a referee's call. Even in the face of embarrassing failures on the field, grandparents support their grandchildren with no ulterior motive or agenda. So if you want to become the kind of person your child wants to be around after the big game, act more like a grandparent. When your kids have kids, do you imagine your response to a missed goal will be to criticize and berate your grandchildren, or are you simply going to enjoy being around them? My mother is fond of telling me that the most wonderful thing about having grandchildren is that grandparents get to enjoy the fun parts (like watching sports practice) without the anxiety and stress over the grandchild's performance. Try, fail, succeed, she doesn't care, she just wants to be there, cheering her grandchildren on through all of it. Wouldn't it be a relief to enjoy the fun parts *now*, instead of a generation down the line, and let the coach be the one in charge of how your child and his team perform at the big game? It's not an impossible dream. Let the coach be the coach, let the referee be the referee, and when it comes time for your child to play, sit on the sidelines and be the parent.

PRESSURED PARENTS ON THE SIDELINES

When parents intensify competition through hovering, yelling, berating, and second-guessing players, coaches, and referees, everyone loses. Kids are miserable, coaches are nearly apoplectic, and all that stress can't be making parents very happy, either. If you are one of these unhappy parents, you should know that the monster that emerges on the sidelines lives in all of us and is part of our basic biology. Psychologist Wendy Grolnick refers to this response as "Pressured Parents Phenomenon."

> The PPP is a visceral anxiety, triggered when the ever-increasing competition—academic, athletic, social or artistic—that our kids face today switches on our physiological hardwiring. It's an internal pressure so strong that we can't rest until we feel our child is safe—has gained admission to that certain magnet school or won a spot in the school orchestra [or made the varsity team].

The problem with feeling these completely natural feelings, Grolnick explains, is that "it alienates our children from us—a result exactly opposite of what we intended. Because, ironically, it's the absence of pressure that allows our kids to both remain close to us and to succeed." However, when we see our kids under stress, even if it's just the pressure to hit a pop fly ball, our fight-or-flight reflex kicks in. Your brain may know your kid is not in danger, but your body goes into high alert mode and cortisol levels go sky-high. Once PPP kicks in, and our stress hormones start flowing, it can be really difficult to calm down and find the lessons in failure. PPP heightens emotions and our sense of crisis, so in those moments on the sidelines when our parental anxiety and competition begin to spiral, it's especially important to recognize your surroundings for what they are: a game. Put your head between your knees if you have to, but relax. The reason children start playing sports in the first place is to have fun, exercise, and learn the invaluable lessons of sportsmanship and teamwork. This should still be the goal, even when the stakes get higher and aspirations of glory are on the line.

Parenting and competition can be a terrible mix, particularly when parents pit siblings against each other. In his book *Drive*, Daniel Pink recommends that work teams be a "no competition" zone. "Pitting coworkers against one another in the hope that competition will spark them to perform better rarely works—and almost always undermines intrinsic motivation." Families, like offices and classrooms, are best conducted in the absence of the stress of competition.

Competition, in turn, encourages overparenting, even when the competition is for approval rather than trophies or scholarships. In one study, mother-child pairs were told to complete an "About Me" questionnaire. Half of the pairs were told to complete the form "for fun," while the mothers in the other half were told that their children would be meeting a group of kids who would use the form to "rate" their children. The first group of moms, the ones who had no expectation that their child would be assessed, sat back and watched their child fill out the form on their own. However, the mothers who believed their children would be rated and scrutinized pressured their child to fill in answers that might help the child look good and be liked by the other kids. The very idea that their child would be rated or measured against other children caused those mothers to overparent. Now imagine these same mother-child pairs five or six years down the road, at the big showcase soccer tournament watching coaches take down recruiting notes on their children's prowess on the field. College admissions, scholarships, maybe even a career in sports are on the line, and players are in competition with each other. Consequently, competitive hell breaks loose, and these parents take their anxiety out on the coaches, other parents, players, and their own children.

After seeing her five children through active careers in amateur sports, one mother admitted to me that she had actively dissuaded her sixth child from going the same route. "I just could not take it anymore," she admitted. "I had spent years cheering and supporting, and I know that sports are a great way to stay fit and teach teamwork, but I could not take one more afternoon of competitive sniping on the sidelines. The lessons and the trophies are great, and I was happy my other kids got to experience that, but I was done with it all."

This mom would be happy to know that even the upsides she recounts, such as trophies and awards, may not be as positive as we are led to believe. Those trophies, medals, and scholarships that we dangle as reward for our children's athletic efforts don't just heighten a sense of competition and anxiety, they undermine drive. Just as rewards for positive behaviors are intrinsic motivation killers in academic and social contexts, they also dampen participation and enthusiasm in sports and other recreational activities. In one study, researchers asked kids ages nine to eleven to play on a stabilometer, a device that measures balance and had proven to be a lot of fun for kids of that age. Half of the children received a reward for playing on the stabilometer, and the other half did not. A few days later, these kids were asked to come back and play some more, and they were given a variety of options for play, including access to the stabilometer. The kids who had been rewarded the first time around spent less time on the device than the children who played on it for their own personal enjoyment in the first play session. This is a good example of how rewards diminish enjoyment and motivation even in fun, noncompetitive recreational activities without an obvious goal or endpoint.

I'm not proposing that we should eliminate competition and rewards altogether, but the practice of giving all children trophies simply because they show up on the playing field is equally harmful to a child's sense of self-worth. Parents need to find their own happy medium between the empty praise of participation trophies and the amped-up, competitive drive that sacrifices their child's sportsmanship, performance, and motivation. I asked Hannah Kearney, two-time Olympic medalist in freestyle skiing, to describe the ideal sports parent.

> The perfect sports parents would be ones you never hear from the sidelines. They should be there after the game, to be supportive, when the heartbreaking things happen. Kids get cut from the team, they get injured, that's just what happens in sports, but the perfect sports parent is there after that heartbreak to listen and help the kid find the positive in the heartbreak. I have to admit, my parents bribed me when I was ten with a pair of soccer shorts in order to get me to commit to my first week of practice, and I remember the adrenaline of that first goal. From that first goal on out, I was committed to sports, and they were there for me. My mom and dad sacrificed everything for my ski career and my brother's hockey. My mom drove me back and forth to Waterville Valley [a ski area in New Hampshire], held up my boom box on the mountainside so I could hear my music while I practiced routines, choreographed those routines, and copied pages from my textbooks so I could do my homework when I was traveling. They were supportive, but they never pushed me. After a kid finds a sport they love, it has to be up to the kid to go forward, or it's a disaster for everyone.

A GUIDE TO SUCCESSFUL SIDELINE PARENTING

In order to be that parent who can help a kid find the positive in the heartbreak, Kearney and the other athletes, coaches, and sports parents I interviewed offer the following guidelines on how to be the kind of parent your kids will want to ride home with, whether from their first T-ball game or a world championship final.

Be the parent, not the coach.
Unless your child's safety is at risk, don't yell from the sidelines, don't criticize coaching decisions or referee calls in the car after the game, and don't do any armchair coaching in the living room. Feel free to talk with the coach about ways to help your child improve, how your child behaves during practices or games, or ways to troubleshoot issues around injuries, but do *not* discuss other children on the team, team strategy, or your own child's playing time.

Never, ever, bad-mouth the coach in front of your child.
This destroys your child's trust, respect, and faith in his coach and creates a real emotional dilemma for your child. If he agrees with you, he's betraying his coach, and if he agrees with his coach, he's betraying you. Don't put him in that position. Talk to—and about—the coach only when your child is not around to hear it.

Don't ask your child to fulfill your own athletic dreams.
It does not matter how talented you were in softball, soccer, or chess when you were a kid; your kid is not you. Don't be the parent who attempts to relive past glory or play out unfulfilled dreams through a child. You may love baseball with all your heart

and soul, and put a Red Sox onesie on your child the moment he exits the womb, but as we are not (yet) engaging in human cloning, your child will have his own, desires, hopes, and dreams. Give him a chance to figure out what those dreams are instead of imposing yours on him.

Cultivate a growth mindset with plenty of room for failure.
Sports are hard, and only get harder as kids progress through the ranks. Caroline Gleich, professional skier and extreme athlete, explained that the transition from recreational athlete to professional athlete was hard for her at first because she was operating from a fixed mindset.

> I really had to change my mindset, because my parents had always told me I was great, and I'd never had to work at my sport. So with skiing, I thought there were things like ski jumps that I just could not do. I would see other people do these amazing tricks, but I figured, I'd never taken gymnastics, so I simply could never do those tricks. I had to shift from what I can't do to what I can do and I had to really work at it. That became part of the fun, to stay focused on the goal even when things get hard.

Gleich has excelled in her sport because she's come to understand that her initial failures are necessary steps toward eventual accomplishment, steps that make the final push to a mountain summit or the top of a glacier all the more rewarding.

Know the difference between quitting and failure.
It's easy for successful, professional athletes to look back on their failures and moments of challenge with fondness, but what if challenges prove insurmountable and it's time to accept the fact that a

career or even participation in a given sport is not to be? Michael Thompson, psychologist and author, points out that there comes a time when all of us must decide whether or not the struggle—of sports, or a relationship, or any other path we choose to take—is worth the pain. "In a broad sense, all learning and growth require struggle, but there is a difference between the experience of struggle that leads to success and the experience of struggle that leads to only more struggle." Not every child is destined to become a professional athlete, and as kids move up through the "failure factories" toward the more rarefied air of high school and college sports, nearly all of them will have to decide when to throw in the towel. When this happens, parents are tasked with the duty to help our children find the value in the experience of sports, whether that's fun, fitness, or the lessons they've learned in courage, failure, resilience, sportsmanship, and teamwork. These lessons are not lost just because they stop playing the game. I've heard many parents cite "I can't let my kid be a quitter," or "I have to teach my son that you follow through on your obligations to the team" as reasons to force children to play when they no longer love a sport. However, as K. C. Potts, basketball coach and English teacher told me, this approach can be a mistake.

> The tragedy of youth sports is that kids are often signed up with little or no sense of what playing the sport entails, and when the child has the epiphany—"I don't like this sport," the parent opts to invoke the "you can't quit during the season" clause and force the child to stick with it. There is the nobility of following through with a "commitment," yes, but often younger children have not really made a commitment, and the parents' insistence brings misery to everyone: to the coach who must find time for a player who does not want to play, to the parents who believe that

> they are somehow building the character of a child who in their eyes does not have enough, and most of all to a child who plays not for enjoyment but out of some obligation. Nobody smiles, nobody wins.

Sports are, after all, supposed to be fun. This was the number-one sentiment I heard in all the stories shared by successful athletes. Above all, they love their sport and have fun with it, even in practice. Think back to when your daughter played her first game of T-ball. Remember how she had to be reminded to pay attention to the batter while she pretended she was a water buffalo raising a cloud of red dust around the pitcher's mound? How every single player abandoned the infield in order to run down a foul ball? How you laughed about it later over ice cream because the experience and the memories were more important than the final score? That's what sports and childhood are supposed to be about, even if our children dream of Olympic glory or a full ride at Duke. As they progress from team to team, and league to league, or give up sports completely, children rely on parents to anchor their family team and provide the kind of unwavering support that can help them through their most humiliating and humbling failures. In those moments, they need us to remind them that as long as they show up on the field and do their very best, in sports or anywhere else, we will keep up our end of the bargain and show up on the sidelines to cheer them on.

8
MIDDLE SCHOOL: PRIME TIME FOR FAILURE

"YOU TEACH MIDDLE SCHOOL? REALLY?"

The question is usually punctuated by a wince, and a look of pity.

Yes, it's true. I happily spend eight hours a day in the company of "tweens," a much-misunderstood and maligned population well versed in the everyday business of academic and social failures. Even among my peers—educators who understand the joys and rewards inherent in teaching—the middle school classroom is often viewed as educational and professional purgatory. When I asked parents for their positive sentiments about middle school, one mother's submission spoke for the group: "I think I need some distance from this era before I find my anecdotes entertaining."

I wholeheartedly disagree.

Of course middle school students are challenging. They are pupa-people whose immature sixth-grade selves hardly resemble their eventual eighth-grade form. There are days when I can't imagine these mere children will ever be prepared to enter the world on the world's terms; they are demanding, curious, impulsive, and mercurial, and they can be maddening. But these same maddening traits are the very tools that will allow them to navigate the tricky waters of middle school and emerge as more fully formed people.

Here's the ugly and wonderful truth about middle school: it's a setup. Middle school teachers ask students to succeed at tasks that their half-cooked, adolescent brains are not yet able to master, and therefore, failure is not an *if* proposition, it's a matter of when. This is one of the first truths I tell my students' parents at back-to-school night, because the sooner they accept this reality, the easier everyone's life will be over the next three years. Some kids really love this challenge, and rise to it as if it's been what they have been waiting for all their lives, an opportunity to finally have some autonomy and accountability for their own actions:

> The best part of moving to middle school was the idea that you were responsible for your own actions. In lower school, teachers were always reminding you to hand your homework in, hang your coat up, pay attention, and stay organized. In a sense, fifth grade and before that were just years spent preparing ourselves for the daunting prospect that was middle school and so to finally get there was rewarding in itself.

For kids like this, who are ready, the opportunity to have control over their lives is exciting. For others, the transition is not quite so easy. Middle school demands feats of organization, planning, time management, and shifts of focus that young adolescents are not capable of mastering, at least not all at once. Some kids can handle one or two of these skills some of the time, but for most middle school students, genuine mastery of all of them doesn't come until well into high school. Think about it this way: infants can't yet speak because their brains are not yet developed enough to master the complex physical tasks of forming language. Toddlers can't plan and execute long-term projects because their brains have not yet made the neurological connections that allow for long-term planning and sequenced execution of complex tasks. We don't expect little kids to be able to do these things, but we do expect middle school students to be able to handle the complexity of middle school, even though they, too, are still lacking the neurological connections that will allow them to manage the demands we place on them.

It can be really hard to remember this fact of middle school life, particularly when, thanks to the vagaries of puberty, some students look like hulking adults by the end of eighth grade. I've taught classes where prepubertal, baby-faced children study alongside man-sized boys who need to shave every day. Despite all appearances, those physically advanced kids are still children as far as their brains are concerned, and it's important to remember this while we patiently wait for their neurons to catch up with their five o'clock shadow.

When students stumble into sixth grade on the first day of school, the faculty is ready for them. We spend the first couple of months watching them shove crumpled papers into lockers, helping them pick up the scattered remains of binder explosions, and suggesting ways to remember what class comes after English and what materials to take to science. One mother explains the chaos of middle school this way: "I fear for my hands every time I reach into his backpack. I don't know what is in there. Neither does he."

Learning to organize, plan, and conquer "what's in there" takes a concerted effort from students, parents, and teachers, and even I have my moments of doubt. I worry for their future. I worry that I have precious little time to prepare them for the more complicated and challenging world of high school and can't imagine there will be enough time to get them ready, but there almost always is. Somehow, that chronically late, perennially disorganized sixth-grade boy who can't use a planner for two days in a row is able to manage his academic life by the time I wave goodbye to him at middle school graduation.

So fear not. Failure is a fact of life in middle school, so embrace it. Everyone is doing it, even the cool kids. Even the kids who look as though they have it all figured out. The stakes are still low, the rate of failure is high, and teachers understand that small disasters happen every hour of every day, so jump in and take advantage of all those learning experiences in the guise of everyday failures, littering the middle school landscape.

THE NAME OF THE GAME IS EXECUTIVE FUNCTION

The elusive skills they will need to survive in high school and life are part and parcel of what psychologists call *executive function*, or the collection of skills and mental processes that allow us to manage our time, resources, and attention in order to achieve a goal. There are many skills that make up executive function, and I would argue that the diagnosis "executive function deficit" is merely a synonym for "early adolescence." Failure to engage or access executive function skills is what causes most middle school disasters such as late assignments, forgotten homework, and lost textbooks. An understanding of this root cause is the first step toward maintaining some perspective on this otherwise frustrating and maddening period in your child's academic life. This understanding also gives you a step up on all those other frustrated parents, as they worry and search the heavens for answers as to where they went wrong. Best of all, you will be able to respond to the inevitable failures your child will encounter as a result of executive function deficits and teach her the workarounds she will need to know in order to avoid repeating her mistakes.

While it's tempting to blame executive function deficits on a lack of intelligence, don't go there; they are not related. Executive function skills develop as the adolescent brain develops, and all we can do as teachers and parents is support kids as they learn from their mistakes. Executive function skills develop at different rates, and while some kids acquire them quickly, others continue to have issues well into high school and beyond. It's not coincidental that the students whose parents bail them out, and don't allow them to deal with the consequences of these failures, develop these skills more slowly. The key to helping kids create the systems they need to gain executive function is to let them fail, let them feel the pain and inconvenience of their mistakes, and then support them in their efforts to rework the bugs. Try, fail, suffer a little, remedy, try again. Over and over again until they learn. A few missed lunches or a zero on the homework assignment she left on the kitchen counter will reinforce these skills better than your lectures or nagging ever will. Every intervention or rescue is a lesson lost. They need every minute, every learning opportunity inherent in their failures we can grant them before they face the much greater challenges and consequences that await them right around the corner in high school.

While you are waiting for your child's brain to develop, here's a rundown on the collection of skills and habits that constitute the umbrella definition of executive function, plus tips on strengthening those skills and supporting your child while he struggles with solutions and fails in their execution.

THE STRUGGLE FOR SELF-CONTROL

One lovely spring day, while I was preparing my English class notes and the class was settling in to their desks, I felt something whiz past my head and hit the whiteboard behind me. I whirled around, trying to figure out why I was under attack, and realized that someone had thrown a mechanical pencil at me. One glance up at the class, and it was obvious who was the culprit. His eyes were wide, his mouth was hanging open, and he was doing his very best to avoid my stare. After class, I took him aside and asked him what he had been thinking.

"Well, I wasn't *aiming* at your head," he said. "I was aiming at the recycling bin."

"But a mechanical pencil isn't even recyclable. . . . No. Wait. Hold on. Let's back up. What were you *thinking* just before you threw the pencil at me?"

He looked at his feet and shuffled them around a bit. "Nothing." He looked up at me and shrugged again. "I didn't know I was going to throw the pencil until I'd thrown it, and by then, it was too late."

It was an honest answer. The key to helping kids curb their impulsive behavior is to teach them how to understand their patterns of conduct and the body language that tends to precede these behaviors. We have to catch adolescents *before* they throw the pencil or paper airplane, point out their jiggling leg or twitching fingers, in order to teach them to recognize these signs as precursors of problematic behaviors. Adolescents are a notoriously self-unaware lot, but if we point out the precursor behavior often enough, they will learn to recognize the signs themselves and redirect their focus. It's not easy; it's one of the greatest challenges teachers face when juggling the needs of twenty or more children at a time, but teaching self-awareness is an important part of helping kids gain control of their own behavior.

Even for that kid who threw that pencil at my head. It took every moment of middle school, but even he managed to head off to high school with a pretty good sense of self-control and the ability to recognize when he was beginning to lose it. There were plenty of failures along the way, but I like to think his teachers and parents helped him find a lesson in each and every one of them.

Here are some techniques that can help kids gain some self-control and awareness of their own patterns of disruptive or distracting behaviors.

- Agree on a signal: for some of my students, a light tap on the shoulder is all they need in order to regain focus and composure. Before class, when the mood is light and the student is feeling positive, I take her aside and propose that we come up with a mutually agreed-upon signal. It can be a word, a tap on the shoulder or head, or a look, whatever the student wants. When I notice the student losing focus or beginning to show signs of an impending impulsive behavior, I take a casual stroll around the room and invoke our signal. It's an amazingly effective strategy, one that can work at home as well. It saves the child from embarrassment, and can be a way to communicate without nagging or shouting.

- The Pencil Game: Child psychologist William Hudenko taught me a technique that can help kids learn how to recognize signs of impending impulsive behaviors, and then signal their brain that they need to refocus.

Give the child a set of two or three pencils and teach him to switch pencils when he feels his brain getting distracted. Now, it's not really about which pencil he uses, but switching pencils gives his brain the prompt, "Oh—I'm distracted, I need to get focused again," and switching pencils becomes the signal for his brain to refocus.

Eventually, he won't need the pencils, because his brain will learn to recognize distraction and he will begin to automatically redirect his focus, but in the beginning, the pencils offer a way to become conscious of subtle signals of distraction.

- FER: If your child is apt to lose those pencils, or is loath to carry props around with him, Hudenko suggests another technique he calls "FER," which stands for Flag, Eye contact, and Rehearse. "Flag," according to Hudenko, means to "figure out what's important to pay attention to"; for instance, if a teacher is talking in class, the student should listen for the highlights he thinks are important. "Eye contact" means, literally, that he should be making eye contact with whoever is speaking. Finally, "rehearse" means to repeat, or rehearse the important points in his mind, so they will get moved from short-term to long-term memory. This process is really for attention issues, but it also gives the student something to focus on, which helps head off impulsive behaviors.

All of these techniques will take time, practice, and patience, and there will be lots of failures along the way. The important thing to remember is that talking about the process of being in control and coming up with a plan such as the pencil game or FER will at least set the stage for an awareness of this issue.

LIMBERING UP FOR MENTAL FLEXIBILITY

If I were to walk into my son's room while he is deep into the construction of an imaginary kingdom and announce that we will be departing in five minutes for an amusement park, he'd complain about having to stop playing with his blocks. It's not that he doesn't want to go to the amusement park; he would not hear what I was saying. All he would hear was that there would be a change, and he wouldn't like it. It would take him a minute or two to make the switch from blocks to roller coaster.

At five, this cognitive inflexibility is par for the course, but once your child gets to middle school, he is going to have to learn how to switch mental gears many times a day.

One of the most difficult transitions for middle school kids is the shift from home to school. Adolescents, and particularly young adolescents, need quite a bit of time in the morning to wake up and prepare for the day. When your child barely makes it to school on time, he is being put at a major disadvantage. Kids really need a good ten or fifteen minutes to empty their backpacks, reorganize their materials, talk to their friends, adjust their outfits, and get their heads on straight before first period. Without this time of transition, that first class is a nightmare for them. Their brains, bodies, and belongings will be disorganized, and many of these kids don't really pull themselves together until lunchtime, when they get a moment to breathe, unpack, and arrange their priorities for the day.

Once he is at school, he will have to move between classes and subjects, reorient his brain from math to French, switch out his materials in his locker, and adjust to various teachers, all with their own rules, expectations, and personalities. A simple illustration of this sort of mental inflexibility arose a few years ago when my seventh-grade Latin students came to my class straight from French class. The word for "and" is spelled the same way in both languages, *et*, but it is pronounced "eh" in French and "et" in Latin. Students who never mispronounced were suddenly dropping their T's all over the place when they arrived straight from French. It became a running joke that year, and when they graduated to eighth grade, and Latin no longer followed French, the mistake disappeared as if it had never existed.

Even after they survive the many transitions in their school day, kids are then faced with shifting gears between one extracurricular and another. They must navigate the mental leaps from soccer practice to homework to dinner to television to reading to bed. If they were not already exhausted from the school-day leaps, they certainly will be by the time their heads hit the pillow. The sheer mental exhaustion of these leaps of focus, paired with the massive amounts of academic, physical, and social data adolescents are expected to assimilate and process every day, serves as yet another reason kids should be getting plenty of sleep.

HERE ARE PRACTICAL GUIDELINES FOR helping your child manage transitions:

- Create some predictability in your household. Continuity and predictability aren't just reassuring for toddlers; stability calms adolescents as well.

- Keep a family calendar and try to remind kids of appointments and schedules, particularly if a change in the routine is on the horizon.
- Kids should keep their own schedule as soon as they are able. When kids are aware of and organize their own timetables, they will gain a sense of autonomy, and that will push them toward greater independence.
- Keep your child on a regular sleep schedule, even on weekends and vacations. Studies show that it takes a long time to recover from even a small shift in sleep routines, and sufficient sleep is key to almost every aspect of developing executive function.
- When unexpected changes come up in the family's schedule, model calm. Children feed off adult cues and learn how to manage stressful situations through their parents' examples. If you handle transitions with grace, they will be much more likely to emulate that grace.

THAT POOR, POOR WORKING MEMORY

If you know anything about computers, then think of working memory as RAM. Or think about the mind of a dog. My Labrador retriever can hold one task in her mind ("retrieve the paper!") for about two seconds, or until some other task enters her brain ("chase the squirrel!"). This deficit is not her fault, and it's not because she's stupid (although she is). She has poor working memory. Similarly, when I ask my son to feed the dog while his brain is occupied with guitar practice, he will walk into the kitchen and stare blankly at me, and I can tell that in the time it took for him to walk from his room to the kitchen, he's forgotten what I asked him to do. While this behavior is irritating, it is also completely normal. A gentle reminder—best if it's handed over without irritation or judgment—will get him back on track.

A lack of working memory isn't just annoying at home; it's a real problem for kids in school. Teachers tend to give students oral information, and if the student can't keep that information in mind long enough to write it down in her notebook or planner, that information is lost forever . . . or until the student asks the teacher to repeat it and gets a dirty look for "not listening the first time around." When I give my students an assignment, I try to look them in the eyes and wait until they are paying full attention. Even then, I will inevitably have to repeat the assignment a couple of times, particularly if it contains specific details such as page numbers. In order to retain my sanity, I write it down for them on a chalkboard. Between the oral and visual command, the assignment will usually make it into their plan books.

HERE ARE SOME PRACTICAL STRATEGIES for middle school kids with poor working memory:

- Have your child's hearing tested. Hearing and working memory are unrelated, but kids with hearing deficits often look a lot like kids with memory impairment, so go ahead and check that off the list first thing.
- Be patient. Repetition is key, and even though that can get old really fast, try to remember that you are dealing with a developing brain.

- Write tasks down so your child can refer back to your instructions. Post refrigerator chore charts or checklists of tasks to be completed. I'm a huge fan of kid-generated checklists, because if kids create the list, the act of writing it down helps solidify the items in their memory banks. If you like word games and have some time on your hands, create mnemonics to help kids remember information, such as the order of tasks involved in doing a load of laundry or in loading the dishwasher. Enlist your child's help in devising these mnemonics. It's more fun that way, and again, the more involved he is in drafting these steps, the more ownership and autonomy he will have over the task.
- If your child's school allows it, look into audio-recording classes, particularly on test review days or in classes that rely on lectures to convey information.
- Keep instructions simple. If you are trying to teach your child how to do the laundry, spend one session on sorting and laundry cycles, and save the lesson on spotting stains for later. If necessary, post a checklist on the wall next to the washing machine and have him check the steps off as he completes them.
- Teach your child critical listening skills. Part of improving working memory is filtering out all of the stuff kids don't need to remember. If you listen to the news on the radio on the way to school, ask your child, "What do you think were the two most important ideas in that story?" This skill will really pay off down the road as kids get older and the amount of information they are expected to assimilate increases.

AWAKE, BUT NOT NECESSARILY AWARE

Adolescents have a lot of trouble looking at their own efforts and gauging their results against what is being required of them. Middle school teachers know that in order to receive the results we want from our students, we need to be clear about what we expect. Repeatedly. I try to be precise and painfully detailed about every aspect of my expectations, because if I am not, I risk frustration and eventual mental collapse in the face of the chaos that will ensue on due dates. When I do receive assignments that fall short of my explicit instructions, I sit down with the student and give her examples of where and how she fell short. I'm specific about expectations going in, and specific about how I will evaluate those expectations going out.

At home, deficits in self-awareness and monitoring may show up as shoddily executed bathroom cleaning or lunches packed with little more than Cheetos. In my house, the problematic task is cord wood stacking, an adventure in frustration that led to a house rule that if the woodpile falls over, the person who stacked it has to do the job all over again. Wood stacking is an exhausting and splinter-prone job, so it only took one or two stack collapses for my older son to perfect his wood-stacking technique. But let me repeat: adolescents require detailed and explicit guidance on their execution of a given task. I did not just send my kid outside with an IKEA-esque instructional packet or some loose oral directions; I stacked with him. I taught him how to properly form support towers at the end of the stack, account for the angle of the ground underneath the pile, and compensate for unevenly split wood. He gained an education in wood stacking, and I scored a day with my son, watching as he earned a sense of competence in the completion of a complex and challenging task.

Here are some tips for shoring up adolescents' self-awareness and their ability to gauge their progress on tasks:

- Make expectations crystal clear, from the get-go. Ideally, model the task with them the first time they attempt it, and talk about tricks and tips for getting the task right.
- When kids claim they are finished with a task, help them compare your (or teachers') expected outcomes with their actual outcomes.
- If they make mistakes or fail at the task, teach them step-by-step how to remedy the situation. The way to capitalize on failures is to turn them into an education in resourcefulness and remedy. Sometimes, the failure becomes a lesson in and of itself in another skill. Go with the flow, and teach the lessons as they emerge with patience and a sense of humor.
- Praise effort while supporting future improvement, and view mistakes as opportunities to learn. The more kids learn how to look at their own work and measure it against external expectations, the better they will get at measuring their own progress and working up to those expectations.

FAILURE TO LAUNCH

Kids of all ages struggle with the ability to start and get down to work on new tasks, and while this fiddling and fooling around in the face of something new looks like procrastination, psychologists call it "initiation," and it's an essential executive function skill. To initiate means to begin, to overcome entropy, launch a plan, and get down to a task. This won't come as news to any parent of an adolescent, but young teens can have trouble originating an idea, coming up with a plan for a task, and getting down to that plan, all part of executive function. Nagging seems to have the opposite of the intended effect, and this inability to initiate tasks has delayed many a school project. Sometimes it's about not being able to recognize how much time a task will take in relationship to the amount of time that's left to complete it. Sometimes it's simply a matter of inertia.

Most little kids don't initiate tasks until an adult tells them to, but as those kids get older, it will be important to transition them toward a place of independence where they initiate and complete tasks under their own power.

HERE ARE PRACTICAL TIPS FOR helping kids initiate (and follow through) on tasks:

- A clearly and carefully maintained daily, weekly, and monthly calendar is vital. Much of understanding time management flows from a clear picture of how much time there is in a day and how a specific task fits into a schedule, with real deadlines and time pressure.
- Talk about time management. If a child needs to complete three tasks before bedtime, talk about how long each task might take and how much time remains in the day.
- Timers and alarm clocks can work miracles. Set a timer for when one task needs to end and another should begin. That way, it's the timer, not the parent, who is the "nag." If the child can watch the time run down, that's

also helpful in that it makes time a real, rather than an abstract, concept.

- Again, model what you hope to teach. Show your kids how you budget your time. Let them see the wizard behind the curtain and understand how running a household and work life really happens. Help them understand that fully cooked meals don't just materialize in the half hour before dinner. Explain the process, figure out how long it will take to plan, shop, defrost, prep, and cook that meal, and then invite them into the process.

ORGANIZING FOR LEARNING AND LIFE

Okay, this is a biggie. Most students enter middle school with unformed organizational habits and resort to this mother's description: "My seventh-grade son's idea of organizing his school papers is to stuff them into his locker or backpack. Every now and then he loses something important and has to complete an archeological dig through crumpled, torn, shredded papers and tests that would better be served in papier-mâché projects."

There are some practical strategies you can try in order to help your adolescent become more organized, but even if you work as a professional organizer, mastering this executive function skill is a process, not an item on a checklist to be dealt with over the short term. Many of these skills are learned over a lifetime, so adolescents are probably only going to master the rudimentary skills at first. The goal here is not perfection, but the acquisition of basic skills and strategies that will allow them to keep their papers in order, know where their test review sheet went, and understand how much time they have to study for next Friday's Latin test on the imperfect tense. This happens through trial and error, with an emphasis on the latter.

If your child's school does not teach study skills, he is going to have to learn this essential curriculum at home. Work with your middle schooler to come up with a method for organization and planning. For example, every Wednesday, my students are required to empty out their lockers, organize their papers, and get a locker check. Some of the more disorganized students are asked to take their binders into homeroom and spend ten or fifteen minutes filing away loose papers and recycling the redundant paper that seems to accumulate in the front pocket of the binder. Often, students will find that they have three copies of one assignment—the original, and the two they were given as replacements when they were *positive* that it was lost forever because they looked for it *everywhere*. If your child's school does not encourage this practice, have him set aside fifteen minutes a week at home to clean out and file loose papers. As your child learns to organize his materials, he won't need this extra time anymore, but fifteen minutes in the beginning is about right. One middle school student mentioned this weekly check-in as an important part of her organizational routine.

> The thing that most helped me to stay organized was the weekly locker checks. It was a time in the week where you were forced to organize yourself and your whole locker and backpack. That was so helpful because it was a reserved time in the week to actually clean out your locker, throw away the loose papers in your backpack, and find the odd sheet of homework that you never handed in. Usually, we would never have had the self-discipline to actually take some of our own time and sort ourselves out.

In addition to the weekly cleanout, we also schedule some planning time once a week. Every Monday morning, we spend some time filling out plan books and transferring assignments from teachers' weekly sheets to their own calendar. My school hands out a plan book specific to our calendar at the start of every year, and middle school students are required to keep it up to date, noting all assignments and special events. Any calendar will work, though, and you should be checking over their shoulder at first in order to make sure assignments are being recorded. I make sure my students list in the appropriate boxes the names of their classes, or even better, an abbreviation that leaves lots of room for other notes, so when they need to flip to next Tuesday's French class to fill in an assignment, they can find it. The most important point here is that students should be in charge of their own schedules by the time they hit sixth grade. They will need a couple of years to get used to this process, and some time to try out a few different systems to see what works for them, so give them that time. Pushing this time management responsibility off until high school or college is doing your kid no favors. This isn't an ability that magically appears when he needs to take on the management of his own life. It's a skill that takes practice, trial and error, and patience.

Whether your child's school has a strategy or you are flying solo at home, choose a time to organize once a week. For really bad organizational cases, I have been known to check in on binders a couple of times a week, but a home check once a week should work. While this presents another opportunity for conflict, try to frame it as a way to see what your kid has been up to over the week. If all else fails, make it clear that you only have to do this irksome task together until your kid has a handle on his own organizational abilities. If getting mom's nose out of a teenager's business isn't an effective reward for positive habits, I don't know what is.

A sense of humor is essential in dealing with this task. I have one student who asks me for a locker check every week, confident that he will be given the go-ahead on the first try, free to head on out and play on the basketball court. I don't know where he gets this false sense of confidence, because every Wednesday for the past two years, his locker has been an unmitigated disaster. I point, and say "What about those papers? What are those?" Or I remove his science textbook from the locker, hold it by the binder, and shake, only to have loose folded paper flutter to the ground by his feet. This is our regular routine. He *knows* I am going to hold his binder by the spine and allow gravity to reveal which papers are secured and which are not, but every week, he's sure he has the task in hand. Believe it or not, this weekly date with his binders has become one of my favorite parts of the week. We find mangled papers, realize they were due yesterday, and together, we devise plans to ensure he won't make the same mistake next week. As he slowly learns, fails, then relearns expectations, we have laughed and rolled our eyes. While I will be thrilled when he finally masters his binders, I will miss that weekly bonding opportunity.

Expectations differ, of course, from school to school, and teacher to teacher, but that's part of the education, too. Most teachers will specify whether they want students to have a binder for each subject or a couple of huge binders segregated into core classes and "specials" such as music and art, but after much trial and error, my students have found that a smaller binder for each subject works really well. At the end of each marking period, these binders will get cleaned out and all essential papers will get filed in case they are needed for the final exam. Alison Gorman, a math teacher in New Hampshire, has an excellent method for filing necessary papers. She keeps a milk crate file box for each of her classes in the classroom itself, where students are free to file personal folders, including their important quizzes, lab sheets, or tests, until they are ready to study for the final exam. If the teacher is not willing to take up space for this system, make sure your child has a file box at home, and encourage her to clean it out from time to time in order to make space for new papers.

Within each subject binder, use a couple of those tab separators to indicate "notes," "homework," "handouts," "tests/quizzes," and loose paper. Reinforced loose-leaf paper is one of the best inventions on the planet. If you can afford to upgrade from regular loose-leaf paper and reinforcement stickers, get a couple of packages of the reinforced stuff and your kids' teachers will love you for it. One of the biggest issues I see on Wednesday morning locker cleanout are the pages of important notes that can't be filed away because the holes are all ripped out. Kids resort to punching the opposite side of the paper or making a tape edge to punch. I can't stress this strategy strongly enough: encourage middle schoolers to put reinforced binder paper at the top of their back-to-school list.

The key to learning how to organize one's materials and one's life is to try one strategy and see if it works. If it does, great; stick with what works. But if it fails, if papers are lost, deadlines are missed, and opportunities are lost as a result of flawed strategies, it's vital that the pain of that failure is felt. That pain, whether it's experienced as frustration, disappointment, sadness, or anger, is what prompts change and growth. It's what prompts the formation of a new strategy, and it's what prompts learning. I hate seeing my students or my children upset, but on the other side of that upset is the promise of improvement, one more step toward the day they will be able to successfully manage their lives. Viewed in that light, failure is progress.

FOR SOME KIDS, THEIR EDUCATION in executive function can take years (in general, girls tend to get a hold of their executive function earlier in adolescence than boys). I know adults who still struggle with these skills, and for them, calendar alarms and to-do lists are the tools that keep them from losing their jobs and their minds. That's what middle school failures provide, low-stakes testing and experimentation with the tools that will work best the next time around. Because the task of acquiring organizational skills is about as much fun as a day at the dentist, start by helping kids organize the gear and schedules for activities that mean the most to them.

Parents and teachers can help adolescents develop skills to cope with deficits in these areas, but what's needed during the middle school years is patience and a willingness to allow kids to deal with their failures and the consequences of their mistakes—whether those consequences are detention for forgetting homework, being benched at soccer for forgetting a mouth guard, or a demerit for tardiness while they learn how to organize themselves and get out of the house on time. Let them fail. Let them get upset when they make mistakes, and when they do, don't save them. Every consequence experienced will hasten your child's acquisition of these skills. Conversely, every time you rescue, you push your child's helplessness out another day. Remember how little time middle school kids have to make middle school mistakes before they are thrust into high school, and its relatively higher stakes.

Every time you feel tempted to drive that homework to school or make that lunch, just envision this beautiful scenario: Your child packs his own bag—both for soccer and class—remembers to make *and* bring his lunch to school, makes a mental note to hand in that form you signed last night, jots some detail of a long-term project down on the calendar, and loads himself and his gear in the car without being reminded or asked. Won't that be lovely? Your kids will get there, and oh, what a beautiful world it is when they do.

9
HIGH SCHOOL AND BEYOND: TOWARD REAL INDEPENDENCE

AS I ANSWERED PARENTS' QUESTIONS after a high school presentation on intrinsic motivation and autonomy, one parent lurked at the back of the group, waiting patiently for the others to ask their questions. When the last parent had left the room, she leaned in close and whispered,

"My son is seventeen and I do *everything* for him."

She paused and held my eyes, touched my arm, and said, once more for emphasis,

"Everything."

I nodded, and waited.

"I never let him fail, never, and I want to . . . I mean, he's seventeen. Even if I stop now . . . am I too late?

By the time she finished her question, she was squeezing my forearm tightly, and I was pretty sure she was about to start crying. But I could see that she was determined, so we sat down and formulated a plan that would make the most of the last year of her son's childhood.

WE USED TO CELEBRATE THE end of childhood at eighteen, the traditional age of majority, when children loosened the bonds of our apron strings and struck out into the world in search of independence and purpose. Over the past couple of generations, however, childhood has been lengthened by a protracted adolescence, and consequently, the bounds of childhood are stretched further than ever before. As a result, many young adults have no idea how to function in a world that expects them to speak and act on their own behalf, and that world is beginning to take notice. Adolescent psychologist Jennifer Hartstein reports that she's increasingly seeing the children of these parents in her practice as they struggle to find their way as emerging adults.

> When these kids are not allowed to fall and pick themselves up, they never learn how to tolerate disappointment, manage their relationships, take responsibility for themselves, or cope with the anxiety of not getting what they want. I frequently pose this question to parents who are afraid to let go: "How do you expect your child to be an adult if you never let them learn how?"

Mothers and fathers are accompanying children to college, job interviews, and salary negotiations. As the *Journal of Adolescence* noted recently, "attempts at [parental] control are linked to negative child outcomes in emerging adulthood." The authors conclude,

> It would seem that emerging adults should be personally invested in their own growth and development by solving their own problems with roommates, making their own decisions about employment, and seeking their own help from professors. By not doing so, emerging adults may be robbing themselves of the experiences

> and practice necessary to develop skills that are essential to success in marriage, careers and social interactions.

In other words, until we step back and allow teenagers to live their own lives, surviving their own failures and earning their own triumphs, they won't get a chance to experience their own sense of competence, competence they will need in order to be successful in their jobs, families, and yes, even their marriages. When I asked parents with grown children about their experiences, many acknowledged just how hard it can be to let go.

> I had a terrible time letting my children fail. So much so that my son (who is now 35) wisely told me in his early teens that I had to let him fail. And to him that meant that I had to stop cringing when he did, because then he felt like his failing (rather than being a sign that he was stretching his boundaries) was a sign that he had not lived up to my expectations. He grew up believing that he should be "perfect," and "perfect" meant that he never skinned a knee and never broke a sweat.

The process of separating from us began for our children the moment we set them down on the kitchen floor and they took their first steps away from us. Every milestone—first step, first word, first day of school, first date—marks the stages of the journey toward an independent life. Our job is not to protect them from their failures along the way, but to help them cope with setbacks as they occur, because when they move out of their childhood home and begin to forge their own path, they are going to need all the resources and tools we can give them. The road ahead is theirs, not ours, and as tempted as we may be to pave the way for them so that we can live vicariously through their successes, it's time to let them live their own lives, to unravel our own priorities and needs from theirs. One very honest mother admitted how hard this can be to do: "I am a high achiever. I come from a generation of high achievers. We are the baby boomers. When my children achieve, I have reflected glory. I am confused about where they end and I begin."

High school and college offer parents a last chance to unravel those ties that bind our kids to helplessness, but I'm not going to sugarcoat the challenges inherent in changing course so late in in the game. If you have been a directive or controlling parent for this long, both you—and your kid—are used to the dynamic, and it's going to take some work to undo the years of dependent routines and expectations. Teenagers, like toddlers, need a clear understanding of expectations and limits, and it can be hard to move the line in the sand. When parents begin to ask more of their older kids, and stop rescuing them from the consequences of their mistakes, there will be tantrums and raging and indignation. The good news is that once the initial negativity and shock subside, it's easy to hand responsibility and consequences back to older kids because they are capable of so much. It's hard to know what tasks five- or ten-year-olds can handle, but teenagers can do just about everything you can do, and sometimes better, if you give them the chance.

Adolescence may be a challenging phase of life for parents from a hormonal and emotional perspective, but in terms of learning and cognitive development, it's a time of huge mental and physical gain, the perfect time to launch a full-on push toward adult competence. Teens are deep into what's known as the "formal operational stage," when they develop their ability to think more logically, deduce outcomes based on past experience, and connect abstract concepts to their reality in a way they were not able to just a few years before. Even more important, their executive function skills are more developed, so they have a newfound ability to plan for the future and come up with systems and methods for achieving the outcomes they desire. What's really fun to watch during this stage of life is the transition from the trial-and-error methods younger kids use to get at a desired goal toward a more strategic way of thinking. Adolescents can hold multiple possibilities and ideas in their brain at once and consider how those ideas might play out before launching willy-nilly into a plan. As David Bainbridge explains in his book *Teenagers: A Natural History*, "Children may be charming little people who can talk and think a little, but we do not become fully mentally human until we are teenagers."

When I talk to parents about giving kids the room to fail in high school, they claim they want to, but can't. It's just impossible these days, they argue. The stakes have gotten too high: "It's so intense, and every grade matters!" and "I can't let [my son] fail because he only gets one shot at high school, and there's too much to lose." These parents argue that even one failure could spell the end of a scholarship opportunity, the loss of honor roll, the unerasable record of a detention, academic probation, or suspension. Yes, I nod, that's true, but the greater risk lies in sheltering and protecting kids from failures while they still are living at home, because failures that happen out there, in the real world, carry far higher stakes. One mother, whose children are now grown and settled in to their adult lives, pointed out that sometimes parents need to step back and consider what kind of "success" we really want for our children.

> The irony is that there are all kinds of ways to be successful, and they mostly boil down to being happy. If we rob our children of

> their opportunity to fail, we rob them of their opportunity to, ultimately, be happy despite the realities of the economic and political world they will live in because they won't develop the self-confidence and resilience necessary to find creative solutions to challenges in their own lives with their own realities.

At a recent conference of independent school guidance counselors, one of the counselors asked for help getting one of her advisees to understand the reasoning behind the failing grade he'd received for a plagiarized science term paper. The student was angry with the teacher and with his counselor, and viewed the failing grade as an unfair punishment that put his scholarship at risk. His parents were furious, and had threatened to sue the school over the situation.

"I just don't understand this mentality," she told the room. "Everyone is blaming me, his teacher, and the school, and no one seems to be talking about the fact that he chose to cheat. No one seems to care that this is a lesson the student needs to learn. This kid wants to be a scientist. Just imagine if he plagiarized a scientific paper in ten years in the professional world; it would mean the end of his career. Isn't it better that he learn about the consequences of plagiarism in high school rather than later?"

She was absolutely right; if we fail to teach our kids these lessons now, they will be more likely to make the same mistakes again. In adulthood, the consequences are much more dire than a failing grade or an afternoon of detention. High school is the last opportunity we have before our kids face the real world, with its real consequences.

Once kids are in high school, capable of adult cognition and reasoning, it's time to give them the trust, faith, and responsibility they deserve. According to one high school teacher and administrator,

> Responsibility is best learned when parents step back at the high school level to let the student, by trial and error, advocate, motivate, activate for him or herself. There should be a relatively moderate to high level of autonomy for a student at the high school level to begin to find his/her way to live and experience choice and to safely experience the consequences of personal actions. The important thing is that Mom and Dad are nearby to support from the sidelines, but not to be lead counsel. When parents take the supporting role, but balance it with the ability (and it is a learned skill for parents) to step aside and watch and welcome and expect the student to choose his/her way, students seem to make the better choices relatively quickly if not automatically. Students want to do well. They want to make the right choice . . . but they also want to have the ability to choose.

Given this sage advice, it's time to step back, loosen the ties, and let kids surmount the obstacles they encounter during these final four years of childhood. Each year of high school offers its own challenges and opportunities, and it's important to encourage your child to take advantage of them all.

NINTH GRADE: DEER IN THE HEADLIGHTS

The first year of high school is incredibly frightening for many students. Just a few months ago, they were the reigning kings and queens of their middle school, but come fall, they are promptly demoted to the very lowest rung of high school social life: freshmen. I always found it terribly difficult to teach ninth graders, because the fear of standing out or making a mistake is a powerful force in their decision-making process. One newly minted freshman confessed to me, "Ninth grade was not so much scary as it was intense. I was nervous all the time, worried something might happen; I just wasn't sure what."

Generalized anxiety over the perceived disasters that lurk around every corner of freshman daily life can create a heightened fear of failure early on in high school. However, as most high school teachers are aware of this anxiety, freshman year can be the perfect time to step up and grab high school by the proverbial horns. Help your child understand that her teachers, particularly the ones who have been around for a while, understand that freshmen spend the first year of high school in a state of perpetual anxiety and befuddlement, and are likely to mess up here and there. They know that freshman year requires patience, flexibility, and understanding, and they are there to help students understand what is expected of them in high school and beyond. Teacher David B. Cohen agrees.

> We build in an expectation of mistakes, or maybe another way to put it is we don't assume much about students' knowledge or skills. It's definitely a time for them to find their way. Part of my goal is to help students learn how to work with teachers, not just learn the course content.

Encourage your kids to capitalize on these sympathies and potential sources of support by talking to their teachers whenever possible. Tell them to: Ask for clarification. Admit when an assignment is confusing. Seek teachers out for extra help. Establish positive relationships. Teachers love it when students take initiative. One high school teacher cited these opportunities to help shape a students' education as his favorite part of the job: "The reason I am in education myself is because I love figuring out how

I'm going to make school work for this one kid right here in front of me." Teachers can become powerful and reassuring allies in the confusing world of high school, and these relationships can make for meaningful and emotionally powerful letters of recommendation when it's time to apply for college or scholarships.

For many ninth graders, the first high school tests, quizzes, and papers will serve as a rude awakening after the relative ease of middle school, and it's really important for parents to respond with calm reassurance and support, rather than panic. Frame ninth grade for your child as a getting-to-know-you period. Teachers and faculty are expecting first-year high school students to fail and want to help them figure out what went wrong, what went right, and how to make adjustments accordingly. If a low grade serves as a learning experience, the experience is not a failure. If, however, nothing is learned from that low grade, if it serves only as an opportunity for parents to freak out and tighten the screws, raising anxiety and a pervasive sense of failure, it becomes a lost opportunity.

Confusion and anxiety will give way to comfort and routine as the year wears on, but the sooner students learn to take advantage of the ready-made support system around them in the form of teachers, guidance counselors, and older students, the better. These mentors are well versed in the many ways freshman failures can be repurposed into shiny, bright successes, so encourage your kids to use these people and this valuable year to their advantage.

TENTH GRADE: MY FAVORITE YEAR

When I first started teaching high school, I was assigned to sophomores, and I could not have been happier. The fear and anxiety of freshman year has faded, and the much-hyped mania of junior year has not yet begun. Tenth grade is a time to settle in and enjoy high school before the pace picks up and love of learning is sacrificed at the altar of SATs and college admissions.

In most schools, sophomore year introduces the option of electives, the first opportunity students are given to exercise choice over what and when they learn. Remember that the first step toward intrinsic motivation is autonomy, and this is the first time they will have had any autonomy over academic content. Do not tread on this newfound independence: let kids choose their courses. If they don't feel ready for an honors-level course, listen to them. If they want to take on a harder course because it's a subject they love, listen to that, too.

A mother told me about a shock she received at her daughter's tenth-grade back-to-school night. The parents were assembled in an honors-level English class, and before the teacher had even introduced himself, he said,

> This is a really challenging class, and if your kids are in this class because they want to be here, it's going to be a great year. They will work really hard and learn a lot. However, if your kids are here because *you* want them to be here, this is going to be one very difficult year for your kids.

This teacher elaborated later on that students who have chosen to take a difficult class will be able to handle the constructive criticism and failures that come with that challenge, while the kids who have been forced to enroll won't feel the same investment in the class or its material. After thirty years teaching this very challenging Advanced Placement class, he'd seen the difference personal investment can make, both in grades, AP test scores, and the quality of his students' lives. Just as kids enjoy books they have selected for themselves more than a book that's been assigned to them, they are far more likely to engage in a course they have selected themselves. Let them choose their language, their musical instrument, their sport. If they want to switch things up and try something new, great. Yes, let kids quit an activity or sport if they dislike it, because quitting will free them (and you!) up to find their next big thing, something that may just shape their personalities and their passions. The fact that they have taken French since fourth grade and have invested five years in it is not a good reason to veto their desire for change. Accordingly, ten years spent playing piano will only fuel their success if they choose to switch to the guitar, or the trumpet, or even the ukulele. Knowledge in one discipline only fuels facility with another, so let them expand on their prior knowledge in French or piano by applying that learning somewhere else, if that's their choice. The key word here is *choice*. And it should be theirs, if you want them to find ownership and pride in their learning and growth.

ELEVENTH GRADE: CRUNCH TIME

Junior year is often ruined for students, thanks to the commonly held and oft-repeated perception that time is running out on transcript-padding and college prep. Juniors were always my most anxiety-ridden and panicked students, because the pressure is on from the first day of eleventh grade. Teachers and guidance counselors like to remind students that the "grades that count" are junior year grades, and if they have any chance of getting into the college of their choice, this is the *most important year of their entire lives*. Hogwash. All the years leading up to junior year are important, and yes, eleventh grade is important, but not because it's the last chance to add debate club to their résumé. I love Barnard College president Debora L. Spar's perspective on parents' efforts to cram every AP and community service group and extracurricular activity into their high school students' transcripts:

> As a college president, . . . someone who oversees the review of roughly six thousand carefully crafted applications every year, let me promise you: *We don't care.* Show me that your kid is great at math, or that she truly loves to play the cello. Tell me he edits the high school literary magazine and has an extensive stash of nineteenth-century Russian novels. But the expensive trips to far-flung poverty? Fifty-two activities scattered across the seven days of the week? Honestly. It doesn't help. Give me a kid with a passion for learning, a kid who has demonstrated some measure of autonomy and motivation. Give me a kid who knows his or her mind. But these things are harder to come by if the child has been tutored and handheld from birth.

The lesson of this college president? An emphatic no on the hand-holding, and an enthusiastic yes on every opportunity to cultivate autonomy and motivation. Fortunately, junior year offers ample opportunities for both. Yes, college-bound students will have to take the required tests this year. And yes, junior year courses are tough, particularly for students who have opted (or whose parents have opted) to push the limits of the space-time continuum and take ten courses in the nine hours of a regular school day. However, junior year is also time for more academic autonomy, and the ability to dip into electives in the arts, sciences, and literature that may ignite a passion or stir a soul. Some schools offer students opportunity for independent studies, more free periods, and the freedom to venture off campus on their own recognizance.

Junior year also marks the first time many kids can legally hold jobs, and I've met many students who have found autonomy and motivation through employment. One volunteers at her local art museum, helping out wherever she's needed among the paintings and sculptures she loves. Another interns at an aquarium as the touch-tank instructor, teaching younger kids about starfish and urchins while indulging her passion for marine biology. Another apprentices with a carpenter after school and is learning the art of constructing post-and-beam structures. These students are not learning how to pad their college applications and earn pocket money; they have found ways to turn learning into purpose and identity. One student, who works in a lab after school, describes the joy she has found there. "It is like a meditation room to me, once I get into the groove of my experiments, nothing else matters. A quiet rhythm forms and all stress and worry flows away. In the lab I feel important, I have a mission. For the first time in my life, I felt as if I could take what I was learning and use it, and be good at it."

Experiences such as these offer the perfect place to risk failure. Armed with a strengthened identity and sense of purpose, kids can handle the short-term disappointment that accompanies personal failure, and emerge stronger for it. Encourage your child to reach for things he might not usually try for: an internship, publication in a magazine or newspaper, a part in a play. Push your kid to take risks in that reach, because while he might get rejected 99 times out of 100, that one acceptance, or opportunity, or path, could be the one that leads to a lifelong passion.

Junior year goes by incredibly fast, and as college and the workforce loom ever closer, it becomes more important than ever that you encourage your child to test his own boundaries and comfort zone at every opportunity while you remain nearby and supportive of his efforts.

TWELFTH GRADE: THE FINAL FRONTIER

From the first day of senior year, everyone knows it's coming. Whether you and your teen anticipate graduation day with fear, excitement, or the usual trepidation, it is only 180 school days away. It's on students' and teachers' minds every day; I even know students who keep calendars in their locker to mark the daily countdown to the big day.

Twelfth grade offers heretofore unknown heights of independence, and every time I've taught seniors, they've reminded me of their need for it at every opportunity. They push their teachers away while simultaneously clinging to us for support, and this dance does not end until that 180th day. Some get right down to business and sever their relationships in the months leading up to graduation in order to end the dance, and others hold on tight until the moment it's time to walk away in their caps and gowns. I hear about this same dance going on at home when parents call to lament that their child alternately disengages from the family and relies on them for support and love.

One important place to start handing over some control is during the search for a college. Your child's choice of college is the first, and arguably the most, important decision she will make in her young adult life. Resist the temptation to talk up schools you wish you had attended or the school everyone in your family has attended for the past three generations. College choice is a matter of personal fit, and by personal, I'm talking about your kid, not you. Open your mind, encourage your child to open his mind, and look at schools beyond the annual top-fifty list posted on websites and in magazines. Hand your child some power over his choice of school and he will be far more likely to invest his time, energy, and intellect.

I asked a high school vice principal to tell me about the differences he sees between students who have been encouraged to grab hold of their autonomy and those who have been denied the opportunity. He said,

> The autonomous student leaves high school better prepared for the world. He or she leaves a stronger individual with strengthened social and coping skills. A more autonomous student leaves high school with a keen understanding of what works for her as a student and also as a community member in the world at large. She has a strategy to navigate the world. On the other hand, the student who leaves high school as a dependent follower is much less ready for the world at large and much less prepared.

As senior year draws to a close, students are faced with a wonderful opportunity to find joy in the process of learning. As students realize how little time they have left in school, and the heavy lifting of high school is almost over, they can relax and let go of some of their fears. Now that the results are in, let your kid have these last moments to enjoy the fruits of his labor before he moves on to the next phase of his journey.

AFTER THE POMP AND CIRCUMSTANCE

High school graduation, and the life that comes after, whether that includes college or a job, marks a hard line in the sand.

However, as childhood increasingly bleeds over into adulthood, many parents are unsure of how to stay on the appropriate side of it. The easy answer is that there are very few spheres of college life that belong to you. Your child is a legal adult, and even if you are footing the college bills, it's time to stop intervening and let her suffer the consequences of her decisions and failures. Feel free to call the financial aid office or the bursar if a bill is due, but that's it. Everything else—course selection, talking to professors about grades, negotiating roommate disagreements, and handling housing snafus—this is all stuff your kid should handle. If she has not dealt with any of this before, now is the time to let her start.

When I asked University of California, Santa Cruz professor Michael Chemers to elaborate on his experience with students who have been overprotected against failure and are consequently unprepared for the demands of life on their own, he replied,

> I know we've all heard horror stories about kids who show up to college without any clue how to do their laundry. I had a student in my office in tears because of this. But that's not really the problem—it doesn't take long to learn how to do your laundry. The real problem comes from the mindset of a student who emails a professor with a demand at midnight and is furious when it hasn't been addressed by 8:30 a.m. when class starts. It's when a student insists that having a real desire to do the work should earn the same grade as doing the work. It's when a college professor gets a phone call from an angry parent demanding to know why a student is failing. There's a terrible wake-up call coming, and it's not for the professor, because if your child can't write a 10-page research-based argumentative paper by his or her first year in college, it's too late. Elementary and secondary school teachers are professional *teachers.* Professors are professional *scholars* who share

> what they know with students as part of their agreement with the university—the rest of their commitment is to their own research and service to the university and their profession. It is not possible for a professor who is teaching a class of 300 to stay for an hour every week with each student who needs remedial help, nor is it reasonable to expect a professor to engage with a parent over every student's particular needs or problems. In fact, the law expressly forbids us to do so without express consent from the child. On the many occasions when I have been called by an angry parent, I simply say "your child is my client; you are not. You need to speak to your child."

In order to address the voluminous requests of parents who are concerned for their children, many colleges and universities have added parent resource pages to their dean of students site, and many others offer on-campus family orientation for parents. But just because these sorts of programs are offered, it does not mean you have to take advantage of them. Consider which message you want to send to your child as she heads off into the world: "I did not do the job I was supposed to do when you were in my home, so now I will follow you into your adulthood to make sure you don't mess up," or "You are now an adult, and I trust you to be able to hack it in college."

Colleges and universities are actively seeking parents out and asking them to convey this message explicitly and clearly to students before they arrive on campus. The Web page for parents at Northwestern University offers this reminder about what children really need from their parents during the college years:

- They need you to let go.
- They need to be able to make mistakes.

- They need to know that you believe in them.
- They need to know that you are interested, not intrusive.

I hope you started fostering your child's autonomy and competence well before your son or daughter left for college, but in case you are off to a late start, here are some autonomy-supportive conversations you can have in the months leading up to the fall of freshman year, discussions that can help students feel in control of their college experience.

Set goals for the first year.
Ask your child what he imagines the first year of college might look like, and then ask him what he could do to turn that perfect fantasy year into reality. Next, narrow those goals down. What specific things might he be able to do in his first month on campus in order to set the stage for a good first year? Keep in mind that these discussions should be supportive and in the spirit of guidance rather than dictatorial and controlling.

Identify allies on campus.
If she is not sure about how to reach her goals, recommend that she talk to someone who can offer guidance. Help her identify advisors, professors in areas of interest, and deans who are equipped to help. Make sure she understands the benefits of getting to know her professors. Try to come up with a few key on-campus people she can go to for advice and help so she does not have to call you in a panic in November just before final grades come out. If she is religious, find out who's who at the Newman Center, or the Hillel House, or whatever other organization might fit her spiritual needs. Look up the email of her professors, her advisor, or her department head, and find their offices on the campus map.

Draw a little red circle around student health services and mental health services. Amid the chaos of the first few months of college, your child will benefit from having some idea of the key people who are in her corner if she needs them.

Check in.
Revisit this conversation over the holidays. Is his first year measuring up to his expectations? Why or why not? What might he have done differently? You could even include younger siblings in this conversation, because it could save them many headaches when it's their turn to head off to college.

Locate your mute button.
Keep your thoughts to yourself about how you think his college career should be going. This process is about teaching him how to solve his own problems, and how to form a plan and follow it through. If that first year does look like his perfect ideal of a college freshman year, imagine how proud he will be that he made that happen. If you take over, you will turn college into your victory, not his, and once again, this will undermine his sense of autonomy and competence, putting off his eventual emergence into adulthood. He's in a race against time, and in less than four years, he's going to have to go out into the big, bad world and fend for himself. He can't afford to have any of these formative experiences taken away from him.

Roommate issues don't involve you.
As we've seen, learning how to deal with people whose ideas, background, and habits are different from your own is a great learning opportunity. Once your child has chosen (or been assigned) that roommate, do not call, text, "friend" on Facebook, or Google that roommate. You won't be living with him; your kid will.

Professors don't want parental input.
Do not get involved in disputes over grades, seating, scheduling, or incompletes. Ever. Not if your child is shy, not if your child is failing, and certainly not if your child is too busy to deal with it because she is on spring break. Not only will you be depriving your child of a valuable opportunity to learn how to stand up for herself and reason with other adults in a mature and competent manner; professors will lose all respect for you and your child if you interfere.

Kids will ask for help when they need it.
Trust that your children will call (or text) when they need you, but it might not be as often as you'd like. Keep in mind that they will call more often if you are not the type of parent to jump straight into an inquiry of grades, assignments, and whether or not your child made that appointment with the economics professor that you asked him to make last week.

These four years will provide the friendships, connections, lessons, and experiences that will shape his adult life. Support your child, but know when to step back and allow him to embark on his own life. One of Hartstein's clients, a thirty-year-old woman whose parents have managed every aspect of her life and now finds herself, in Hartstein's words, "unable to live life on life's terms," offers this warning to parents like hers: "You know, too much support isn't a good thing. It doesn't teach you anything, like how to survive in the world. It can be a really huge disservice."

Give your child the opportunity to succeed. Send him to college with a first aid kit and some emergency cash, and a confidence in all the things he will learn. Let him have the freedom to create the person he wants to be and understand the paths and influences he does not want to follow. If he fails, and he will, that will be evidence of a dead-end experience and he will learn not to go down that road again. If, however, you pave the way out of that dead end, he learns nothing new. You have lived your life and learned the lessons it has granted you. Now it's his turn.

Part III

Succeeding at School: Learning from Failure Is a Team Effort

10
PARENT-TEACHER PARTNERSHIPS: HOW OUR FEAR OF FAILURE UNDERMINES EDUCATION

IN MY TEACHING LIFE, I correspond with parents all day long, communicating news about late assignments, congratulations for hard-won victories, and updates on behavioral problems. Each time I email or call home, I struggle with the contents of those emails or phone calls, particularly when they contain bad news or criticism, and strive to keep my words gentle and measured, yet firm. I pray I've struck the right tone, and that my communication triggers the start of a great partnership, a concerted effort between parents and educator, working together to accomplish what no one person can do alone. Some go well, and some . . . well, some don't.

The example I hold up as the epitome of a great home and school partnership occurred one afternoon when a student posted something inappropriate about another student online during school hours. Teachers and administrators researched the incident, figured out who was responsible, and contacted parents within hours to let them know we would be instigating appropriate school disciplinary steps in response to their children's actions. The parents thanked us for addressing the issue fairly and quickly, for identifying the guilty parties in the situation, and assured us that they would be following up with further discussion at home. Everything went according to plan: we felt supported by the parents, the parents felt supported by the school, and the students understood that home and school were a united front. This outcome is a best-case scenario, and when it happens, it's a beautiful thing. Everyone benefits from the unified effort, and the students are held accountable and allowed to learn from their mistakes.

However, home-school communications also have the potential to go poorly, and the resulting conflict can be disastrous to home-school partnership and to the education of the student we are all working to support. Here's my own sad and humiliating account of just how far teachers and parents can fall when parent-teacher relations degrade.

It's 8:11, and I'm late for my first class. I have to teach seventh-grade Latin, but I'm trapped in my boss's office, an irate parent blocking my exit. I briefly consider climbing out the window, but the ground slopes away from the building and the fall could kill me. I'm willing to risk it, I realize, as I peek out the crack between the office door and its frame. The mom doesn't know I am in here; I could wait her out. But maybe, if I can get some momentum, and keep my eyes down, I might be able to sneak by her and escape unscathed. I check the clock: 8:12. Damn. I take a deep breath, remind myself that my students are waiting for me to teach them how to *amo*, *amas*, *amat*, and step out from behind the door. Between my self-imposed prison and freedom lies this angry mother lion, tensed and eager to eviscerate anyone who comes between her cub and a top-tier high school. Unfortunately, I'm her preferred prey today, because I'm the teacher who emailed her thirty minutes ago with news of her son's low grade in English class.

What has brought parents and teachers to this place? How could I, an otherwise confident person, a professional with more than a decade of teaching under my belt, feel compelled to hide from a woman who should be my ally in the quest to educate her child? On the other hand, I can't imagine this mother is having an enjoyable school year, either. All the worry and anxiety over every tiny detail of her son's school day, all the frustration and anger directed at his teachers for their perceived failings and shortcomings; it must be exhausting. She certainly never *looks* happy. In fact, many of my students' parents look positively overwrought and precariously close to their breaking points.

BUT ENOUGH ABOUT US. WE are merely collateral damage. The real victims in this situation are the students. Many of my students express tension and outright fear for weeks before report cards come out, and in the days before parent-teacher conferences, they look as if they are bound for the gallows. Even when they adore their parents and respect their teachers, loyalty to one gets in the way of the relationship with the other, sort of like negotiating divorcing parents. My students cannot possibly trust me completely when I am locked in battle with their parents.

Despite tensions between parents and teachers, decades of research shows that positive family-school relationships are vital to student success. Positive parent-teacher partnerships don't just benefit students; they are a boon to everyone involved. Teachers who encourage parental involvement in school are rated more favorably than teachers who do not, even in unrelated areas such as educational effectiveness. Students learn more when families are involved in their education, and parents feel more engaged and invested in their child's education when teachers invite them into the process.

If this is the case, why do so many teachers cite the challenge of dealing with their students' parents as their main reason for abandoning the classroom? Educators and education researchers advocate for home-school partnerships, and praise the value of family involvement in education, yet in discussions with other teachers, they readily admit skepticism about the potential success of that involvement. I'm not the only educator shaking in my boots, even if I am the only one who has been reduced to hiding in a dark office. However, based on hundreds of conversations with teachers and administrators on this subject, maybe I'm not.

A teacher of more than forty years explains the shift in the parent-teacher relationship this way:

> When I started teaching, the parent, schools, and law enforcement officials were all on the same side. Authority was aligned and united. It was not to be questioned. Then came the '60s and its aftermath. For the children of the '60s, especially those who spent their teens in that era, the relationship between citizen and authority became much less secure. Authority was indeed to be questioned. Differences were to be celebrated and accepted. Eventually, the children of the '60s became parents. Those who questioned authority now became the questioning authority.

Even before authority was called into question by the counterculture of the sixties, relationships between school and home had been complex. The history of education in America reveals the precarious balance of power between home and school, state and federal, public and private.

During the Colonial era, students were taught in a combination of home, church, and schools. Education was a collaborative effort, and no one organization or person took ownership over it. When everyone was in the effort together, it was much easier to cooperate and work toward common goals. Around 1840, the federal government began to make rules and regulations concerning the American educational system that created an ideological divide between home, church, and school. Early in the evolution of our educational system, open discussion between teachers and parents was the norm, and students graduated from one skill to the next rather than from one grade to the next. However, as we moved to a standardized system of differentiation by age, and report cards replaced interpersonal communication, the divide between home and school widened. Teachers were no longer simply well-read members of the community; they were formally educated, trained, and certified professionals brought in from outside and charged with the education and intellectual growth of an entire community.

Schools and parents began to clash over teachings about language, religion, ethnic traditions, and ethics. Parents perceived that schools were trying to usurp the authority of the family, and some of those families took schools to court in order to have the legal right to raise their children according to their community's traditions and values. When Jonas Yoder took the state of Wisconsin all the way to the Supreme Court in 1972 over the right of the Amish to take their children out of school after eighth grade, the United States upheld their right to do so, and with that precedent on the books, the disparate priorities of home and school came into conflict more and more often.

At the same time, respect for teachers and the teaching profession continued to fall, and in 1983, Gallup found that "fewer than half of all those it polled in 1983 wanted a child of theirs to become a teacher, down from three-quarters of those it asked fourteen years before." Teaching used to be a noble profession, one that garnered respect and fostered pride. As teachers flee the profession in record numbers, they cite frustration with legislators, administrators, lobbyists, and anyone else who seeks to push agendas on the day-in, day-out work of educating our nation's children.

The rocky transition to the Common Core State Standards has only served to highlight the deep rifts between parents, schools, and policy makers, and as the media whips everyone's dissatisfaction up to a fever pitch, it's become difficult for students to hear (or learn) much above the shouting. Teachers are angry that they were not consulted during the creation of the standards, school administrators feel handcuffed by the ham-handed manner in which the standards were rolled out, and parents are frustrated by the fact that their children's education is suffering during the transition to these new standards. It had become commonplace for parents to challenge teachers' procedures and practices before the implementation of the Common Core, but the problems exposed by its rollout have given parents cause to question just about every aspect of their children's education.

What is lost, first and foremost, in all this conflict, is the trust we must have in each other to help children through their mistakes and emerge with an education. Kids need the space to fail, and teachers need the time and benefit of the doubt to let that failure play out in the form of learning. One longtime teacher and administrator from a large public high school outlines the opportunities that are lost to teachers when they are barred from the fertile educational territory opened up when their students fail:

> When parents step in to defend a child's poor choice or mistake or failure in order to avoid the "consequence" of that action or performance, they tend to lose sight of the fact that if the student does not have the experience of making mistakes and living and

> learning with the consequence of that mistake or failure, college may be a very difficult experience thousands of miles away from the security of Mom and Dad when he eventually has to deal with an experience on his own. Mistakes are opportunities to grow. Failures or unsuccessful attempts are the same, and students need to live through those experiences to develop a toolbox of coping mechanisms to lift them and move them forward.

That toolbox, the accumulated store of skills students earn through their failures, adaptations, and growth, is more important than any mathematical formula or grammatical rule, and this is why teachers are frustrated when they are not allowed to help students stock up and hone these skills. A mother of three explained her autonomy-supportive strategy this way: "If you knew there was something that could help your child, that could give them 'tools' to help them later in life, could help them face the future with more strength, maturity to face life's challenges, wouldn't you do it?"

So, if you are ready to forge a true partnership with your child's teacher, and to give your child the tools that will help him later in life, here are some guidelines that will help you create positive partnerships with teachers and administrators from the very first day of school.

SHOW UP AT SCHOOL WITH AN ATTITUDE OF OPTIMISM AND TRUST.

Your child is listening and watching, particularly on the first day of school. If you are trusting and relaxed, he will be trusting and relaxed. If you are nervous and watching for the teacher to screw up, he will be nervous and watch for his teacher to screw up. My best student-teacher relationships have always been with the kids whose parents assume that I will take good care of their child and give him the education he deserves, and the worst were with students whose parents distrusted me from the start. You don't have to love your child's teacher, or disregard negative rumors, but if you give teachers the benefit of the doubt, they will be much more likely to give your child the same.

BE ON TIME.

I watched Judd Apatow's film *This Is 40* recently, and was tickled by a scene in which the mother character drops her kid off at school, and the homeroom teacher greets her at the door with the following exchange:

> Teacher:
> Hi—um, listen, Charlotte really needs to get here on time because she really just needs the extra time to settle in.
>
> Mom:
> [mystified] We are on time.
>
> Teacher:
> [deadpan] Being on time means being early.

Judd Apatow is absolutely right. Being on time means being early because kids require at least fifteen minutes to wrap their sleepy brains around the fact that they have arrived at school. Kindergartners need to check in with friends and stow their lunchboxes, and older kids need to unload their backpacks, hand in work, gather their materials for the day, and mentally prepare for their first class. I've watched middle school students stand in front of their lockers, hair all askew from heavy sleep, for a full five minutes, just staring at their books before they are able to muster the wakefulness required to select their materials. Adolescents are particularly challenged first thing in the morning due to the fact that teens' sleep cycles are plagued by a "phase delay," or delayed melatonin release. Simply put, adolescents get sleepy about two hours later than adults, and consequently, have a tendency to wake up later. Consider how well you would function if you woke up sleep deprived, then parked your car and ran straight into a presentation to the head of the company with no coffee, no time to take off your coat, no moment to take a deep breath and prepare for the day. Kids who rush into school at the last minute remain frazzled for much of the morning. Students who arrive on time—I mean early—and have an opportunity to take stock of the day are more prepared for class in terms of their materials and their emotional state.

If tardy becomes a habit, do not blame it on the child. You are the parent; make being on time a priority. Back your morning schedule up by a half an hour if you have to. I have been in charge of marking down tardies for the past five years at my school, and I can attest to the fact that kids who are tardy are inevitably stressed-out, particularly if the tardiness is not their fault. Children have a heightened sense of justice, and they understand that being late is unfair and disrespectful to their teachers and to the other kids who are distracted when they arrive late to class or homeroom, so don't heighten their anxiety by allowing blame for being tardy to fall on their shoulders.

READ THE SCHOOL'S ATTENDANCE POLICY AND FOLLOW IT.

Nothing is more frustrating to a teacher than a student who announces he is leaving for a week tomorrow and would like to know what he will have to do to keep up with the class. Kids suffer when parents don't plan ahead for school absences, both because they don't have time to get work done ahead of time and because teachers get frustrated and short when their best-laid classroom plans are foiled by unexpected student absences. Don't schedule vacations that will interfere with the first or last week of school. Try not to lengthen trips by taking off a day early or coming home a day late. Understand that the last days of a term or the classes just after vacation are crucial because teachers are often scheduled out to the minute when time is short and a unit needs to be completed. As teachers are expected to get through even more material just as testing steals away their class time, it has become even more important for students to be present and accounted for in class. Emergencies arise, of course, and when they do, teachers try to be as understanding as possible, so try to give them the same consideration.

BE FRIENDLY AND POLITE.

We tend to abandon good, old-fashioned friendliness and congeniality when our lives become hectic and overwhelmed. Not only does friendliness make the day flow more easily; it really does make a difference in the way teachers perceive parents and their children. I'd love to say that teachers can mentally separate even the most wonderful children from their surly parents, but it's not always possible. Alice could be my favorite student, the most incredible, charismatic, kind, and generous student I have ever taught, but if Alice's mother is abusive or unreasonable, our relationship is tainted. As much as I want to keep Alice separate from her mother, that memory of her mother coming into school and waggling her finger in my face in front of an entire class of students is always there, coloring the way I think about our relationship and my communications with the child. Even if I could banish Alice's mom from my brain and keep the two completely separate, I certainly don't want to voluntarily make contact with someone who humiliated me in front of my students.

Furthermore, when it comes time to bring up concerns—or praise—about Alice, I am going to be reluctant to pick up the phone or send an email if her mother has been rude to me. That's just basic human nature. When the mouse learns it's going to be shocked when it reaches for the tasty treat, you'd better believe that mouse will stop reaching for the tasty treat, even if it's hungry. Freud noted that it's in our basic human nature to "attain pleasure and avoid pain," and humiliation, distrust, passive-aggressive interpersonal communication, and disrespect are excruciatingly painful for teachers. Consequently, if you humiliate, distrust, or offer up passive-aggressive communications with your child's teacher, be prepared for radio silence to follow. We will continue to educate your child and hold him to the same standards, but we sure as heck will avoid talking to you about it unless we have to.

PROJECT AN ATTITUDE OF RESPECT FOR EDUCATION.

If your attitude toward teachers is one of respect for the educational process, your child will be a lot more likely to respect, enjoy, and engage in her education, and we will look forward to telling you all about it. There's nothing I love more than intercepting a parent at drop-off or pickup just to tell her about a fantastic contribution her son made in class that day, or that as I read her son's last paper, it occurred to me just how far his writing has come over the past year. Teachers cherish good relationships with parents and take great pleasure in offering up those communications. Teachers are also a lot less likely to be upset by constructive criticism or negative feedback from a parent they have come to like or admire. Some of the most effective feedback I have received about flaws in my teaching has come from parents. However, if that same feedback had come from a parent I don't respect, or a parent who cries wolf every time her son comes home with a complaint, I would be a lot less likely to take that feedback as useful or valid.

MODEL ENTHUSIASM FOR LEARNING.

Your attitudes toward education will be your child's attitude. Likewise, your enthusiasm for the process of learning for learning's sake is vital to instilling the same in your child. Let your child see you reading for fun. Pick up a book about a topic you know nothing about and become the resident expert on something, maybe Greek gods, Renaissance art, or botany. Learn to play an instrument. Go to the library and browse books in subjects you've never read or check out college courses from The Great Courses and take a class you never got to take in high school or college. Find out what your child is reading at school and get an audio version of that book for the car. Talk about the book, about the big ideas, and what the characters are up to. You will get the opportunity to understand what your child is reading and learning, which will open the door to conversations about what it would take to make Boo Radley come out, or why Holden Caulfield wears that ridiculous hunting hat.

MAKE SURE YOUR FIRST COMMUNICATION WITH A TEACHER IS POSITIVE.

One of my favorite bits of teacher advice applies to parents, and is a great way to ensure a positive relationship from your very first moments with your child's teacher. In his book *The Essential 55*, educator Ron Clark advises teachers to make sure the first interaction they have with parents is positive. This is a great guideline for parents, as well. Make contact in the first month or so of school and find something nice to say. Mention an interesting dinnertime conversation you had with your child about a book he's reading in class. "We had a great conversation last week about that Frost poem you taught Kevin," for example. As long as the feedback is genuine, it will create the beginnings of a productive bond. This sort of communication places parents firmly on the same team as teachers, and sets the stage for trust, even when students flounder or fail. Parents who sit at the back of the room at back-to-school night, fold their arms, and convey dissatisfaction, however, are not likely to get picked for the team. Willing, eager, and polite participants are the choice picks for this parent-teacher team, and teachers will fall all over themselves to make sure they end up playing with the positive, friendly parents.

INVITE TEACHER FEEDBACK.

Teacher feedback is valuable, so encourage it from day one. Let teachers know that you view both positive and negative observations as a vital part of your child's education and the parent-teacher partnership. On a practical level, let the teacher know how to reach you. If you prefer email, let her know. If you work long hours or the night shift, or would prefer that she call you at work, let her know that, too. Conversely, know how the teacher would like to receive communications and adhere to that preference. When you do reach out, understand that most teachers either cannot or will not be checking email throughout the day. They are supposed to be teaching your children, after all. Ask the teacher whether she'd prefer email or phone, and comply. Make sure the teacher knows you are not just paying lip service to the idea of feedback; let her know that you are ready and willing to listen.

WAIT A DAY BEFORE EMAILING A TEACHER OVER A PERCEIVED EMERGENCY OR CRISIS.

While you should absolutely let teachers know about emergencies at home as soon as possible, wait a day to complain about homework, assignments, disciplinary actions, and the like. These may feel like crises in the moment, but if you wait, you may just realize that they are not. Besides, as you should be moving your child toward a greater responsibility for discussing issues with her teachers, these twenty-four hours give you a perfect interval to develop a game plan with your child. Take this time to breathe and calm down. Once you and your child have distance from the emotional side of the incident, take some time to talk about what happened. Ask open-ended questions about what was happening before, during, and after the incident.

LET TEACHERS KNOW ABOUT BIG EVENTS UNFOLDING AT HOME.

Don't wait until the divorce or child custody battle or chronic nightmares or eating disorder has gotten to a crisis point before filling the teacher in on what's happening at home. If you let your child's teacher in on these things early, it will be much easier to accommodate, adapt, and help children cope at school. For many students, school provides a refuge from troubles at home, and the more teachers can create that sense of refuge and safety, the better. Make an appointment to speak with the teacher if you feel a face-to-face is important or if the situation is too sensitive to put down in writing. However you choose to do it, the goal is to communicate with the teacher so she can help your child.

EXPRESS INTEREST IN WHAT IS BEING TAUGHT.

Let the teacher know you are interested in what's going on at school, and find ways to explore that learning at home. Find opportunities to ask your child to teach you about something she learned in school. Feign ignorance about why lava forms, or how pulleys work, and allow your child to enlighten you. Ask for details about what is happening at school, and don't accept "I don't remember" as an answer. When parents complained that this was the stock answer they received from my students, I started sending home weekly bullet lists of the big ideas we discuss in class, from daily etymology or cultural literacy lessons to capsule summaries about the authors and stories we read. Once you know a little bit about what's going on at school, you can open the door to conversations about that material and how it relates to the greater world.

FIND OPPORTUNITIES TO EXPRESS GRATITUDE.

Teachers receive daily complaints, but it's rare to hear feedback about the successes. I'm not suggesting that you invent praise or compliments out of thin air, but when things are going smoothly, or if your child is talking about something she's excited about in school, thank her teacher. Better yet, write a thank-you note. I guarantee that note will either get tacked to the wall of the teacher's office or tucked in a special folder she keeps in her desk drawer. I have one of those folders in my desk drawer, and I've carried some of the notes inside it with me since my very first teaching job. The value of a thank-you cannot be overstated, and the practice of expressing gratitude is a great lesson to model for your kids. Have your child deliver that note to the teacher's mailbox or office, and make him a part of the gesture. If you are not one for expressing your emotions in writing, use someone else's. My favorite gratitude quote, one I use all the time in notes when I'm not sure of what else to say, comes from Dr. Albert Schweitzer: "At times our own light goes out and is rekindled by a spark from another person. Each of us has cause to think with deep gratitude of those who have lighted the flame within us." My students have rekindled my spark more times than I can count, and I try to remember to thank them for that as often as possible. In order to model that expression of gratitude further, I teach my students to write handwritten (not emailed) thank-you notes to someone they appreciate, and we often receive grateful thank-you notes for our thank-you notes. In an age where email, texts, and tweets dominate our lives, a proper thank-you note is a true gift. In order to feel connected, we all need to feel appreciated, and children should learn how to convey appreciation from a young age.

BEGIN WITH THE ASSUMPTION THAT YOU HAVE AN INTEREST IN COMMON—THE STUDENT.

The vast majority of teachers go into education because they care about children and are excited about the subject they teach. What struck me over and over again during interviews with teachers was the genuine concern and love most teachers feel for their students, so keep this in mind when you are tempted to assume that a teacher has it out for your child. A high school English teacher offers this advice to parents and teachers for successful parent-teacher conferences: "Begin with the common ground, the fact that both parent and teacher should truly care about the student in question; both should be seeking what is truly best for the student." There are exceptions to this assumption, of course, but if you go into the school year with this mindset, your child's teacher will be far more likely to follow your lead.

PROTECT YOUR CHILD'S RIGHT TO FAIL.

Be emotionally prepared for the challenges your child will face in the coming year, particularly as she battles her way through transitions and milestones. She will take her cues from you, so project confidence in her and in your ability to refrain from rescuing her from the challenge of these transitions and milestones. Keep your eyes on the prize of autonomy and competence, and remember that failure is going to be a vital part of her education, as vital as math or English or science.

To that end, protect her right to fail. Give her the time and space she needs to be disappointed in herself. Finally, encourage her perseverance as she picks herself up, dusts herself off, and learns from experience that she is capable of rebounding from those failures. These guidelines don't change much over the years between the first day of kindergarten and the last day of high school. Each and every first day of school offers the promise of a new beginning, a chance to be understood for who we really are, and an opportunity to learn from the mistakes we've made along the way.

GIVE YOUR CHILD A VOICE.

From the very first day of kindergarten, it is vital that children learn to advocate for themselves. According to one kindergarten teacher, "communication with teachers and peers is one of the main functions of kindergarten." She spoke with great frustration about parents who inform her on the first day that because their child is not yet capable of speaking for himself, she is going to have to "intuit" these things. When I asked her, "What would you like parents to know their child can do that they don't think their child can do?" she shook her head, laughed, and replied, "These children are able to do *so* much more than parents are willing to believe, and they can speak for themselves."

From the first day of kindergarten, she expects her students to talk to her, and politely asks parents not to speak for their children. She explains that she wants her students to feel heard and understood, and in order to do that, they must be able to communicate with her. Furthermore, she expects her students to talk to each other before seeking her intervention. "They have to spend the time trying things out and messing it up, learning how to make themselves heard, and making mistakes in those communications, or independence won't happen. Kids are not born knowing how to negotiate for themselves, it takes a long time," she said.

As social interactions get more complex with age and maturity, teachers will expect students' ability to communicate to improve along with their ability to reason and think critically. Teachers respect students who are able to stand up for themselves and self-advocate. When your child is dissatisfied with something that has happened at school, whether she is upset about a grade or feels a teacher has acted unfairly, the student should always be encouraged to speak to the teacher directly. As children move into middle school, students should be responsible for dealing with the details of their education and scheduling, including planned absence forms, permission forms, and deadlines. Certainly, once students are in high school they should be completely in charge of their schedules and the requisite school obligations and details.

If you are worried about your child's ability to conduct these more challenging middle or high school conversations, help him prepare for it. Role-play with you as the teacher, and run through the conversation. If the conflict is over an assignment, ask your child to show you why he feels he was assessed unfairly. If it is clear to you why your child missed the mark, explain the flaws you see in his work. If this is too hard for your child to hear, imagine what the teacher might have thought of the work and frame your observations in that way.

If your child still feels he is being misunderstood and has been treated unfairly, encourage him to prepare a defense. I tell my students that the skill I respect most is the ability to calm down, think logically about the situation, and then engage in a balanced and rational conversation about conflict. I am always going to be much more willing to change my mind—or a grade, for that matter—if the student approaches me with a reasoned argument for change. Have him write a script, if he is so anxious about the conversation that he does not think he can think on his feet.

REMEMBER THAT TRUTH OFTEN LIES BETWEEN TWO PERCEPTIONS.

I trust my children, and yet I am aware that truth is slippery, a subjective and elusive beast. Truth is subject to human frailty and flaws in perception, and this applies to even the most trustworthy and honest children. If you approach your child's teacher or another parent with the assertion that your child is completely free of fault, you are going to lose credibility before you've even begun to advocate for your child. Keep an open mind and hope others will do the same.

After talking with many parents about their child's behavior at school versus their behavior at home, it's become clear to me that the child you know at home may not be identical to the child his teachers and other students know at school. This is completely normal and understandable. Friends, academic pressure, chemistry between teacher and student, and a million other factors affect who we are in a given situation. When a teacher reports that something is going on with your child, at least consider that the teacher might be right. Rejecting teacher observations out of hand is a common defensive move, one I have fallen for myself, but it damages relationships and delays the opportunity for academic, psychological, or medical help for a student.

IF YOU ARE CONCERNED WITH A TEACHER'S ACTIONS, TALK TO THAT TEACHER.

Resist the temptation to go over the teacher's head to the principal, at least at first. The principal is put in an impossible position when a parent goes straight to the administration, because the principal is forced to respond in some way, and it's highly unlikely she was present for whatever altercation or conflict took place. Make an appointment to talk to the teacher sooner, rather than later, because as time passes, resentments mount, details fall away in memory, and the opportunity to make things right is lost.

THE BEST TIME TO CONDUCT A PARENT-TEACHER MEETING IS AT A SCHEDULED MEETING.

The teacher may look available first thing in the morning at school drop-off, but she's not. She's doing an essential part of her job: helping her students settle into their day and organizing her thoughts before the first lesson of the morning. The first and last moments of the day are often the most hectic for teachers, and to have an informed conversation about a student, teachers need time to mentally prepare. Even if the teacher offers to go out in the hall or in her office to talk to you right that minute, don't be tempted. And for the record, cocktail parties, the produce section of the grocery store, and the doctor's office are not appropriate places to initiate impromptu parent-teacher conferences. All three of these examples are my own, and each was awkward in its own horrifying way.

READ THE SCHOOL'S HANDBOOK AND DISCIPLINARY POLICY.

Too many parents find out about detentions, pink slips, or privilege revocation after the fact, and it's difficult to talk to your child about actions and consequences when you do not know how the school deals with these issues. If the rules are different at school than they are at home, you have to know that, too. Finally, remember that if you are incensed and upset by a teacher's actions or discipline, talk to the teacher about your concerns and refrain from trashing the teacher in front of your child. It is very confusing for children (particularly young ones) to understand when parents and teachers, their authority figures, collide.

Do not intervene in the schools' disciplinary actions unless there has been an egregious misunderstanding or something is unsafe or truly unreasonable. The school's rules may not be your rules, and you might not impose the same disciplinary action, but your child needs to understand that in the real world, people must abide by rules they don't always agree with. Your child needs to own up to the consequences of breaking school rules, rebound from that, and move on with her education.

Parenting children through school crises is an emotional, painful process. I have felt out of control, frustrated with teachers, even wanted to retaliate against some other kid in the sandbox who slighted my darling child and threw sand in his face. When I feel that way, I try to remember that I'm being a good parent every time I don't intervene in the hardships he faces in the classroom and on the playground. My child's life is only going to get harder, more emotionally complicated, more frustrating. Those mean teachers will become mean professors and mean bosses and mean neighbors, and if I allow him to sail through his childhood free of frustration and upset, I am setting him up for misery. When the stakes get higher, and the painful episodes get more painful, he's going to know how to be resilient and resourceful without me. Don't save your kids. Let them learn as early as kindergarten how to walk up to someone who has misunderstood or mistreated them, stand up for themselves, and be heard.

SUPPORT THE STUDENT-TEACHER PARTNERSHIP, EVEN WHEN IT'S CHALLENGING.

The relationships children forge with their teachers can become some of the most important of their lives. I don't know anyone who does not have fond, lasting memories of at least one teacher, and when I asked people to share their very best memories of teachers, along with why those teachers meant so much to them, the responses came pouring in.

> Honestly, the hard ones were the best ones, the ones who also seemed to take a personal interest and work with you to help you succeed.
>
> Sister John Andre, my sixth-grade English teacher, was so excited about grammar. She would turn away from the board while diagramming a sentence to literally clap her hands with excitement. That love of learning rubbed off on me, and she was the first person to call me a writer.
>
> Mrs. Peters, my high school English teacher. She gave me an F on a quiz, and I never, ever came to class unprepared again.

> My favorite teacher cared about me. It is that simple. He took the time to get to know me, and therefore I felt a strong sense of commitment to him. I knew he cared about me and I would run through a wall for him.

Over the course of a child's education, he is going to have many teachers. Some will be great, some will be adequate, and some will fall short, and your child is going to have to learn to deal with all of them. If your child is lucky, one or two of those teachers will be people your child will recall with great fondness, as role models who changed his life. But at some point during your child's education, he will be assigned teachers he doesn't like. There will be teachers he doesn't know how to talk to, teachers who are exceptionally demanding, teachers he doesn't completely understand, and teachers whose expectations are unclear. This, dear parents, is a *good* thing. These teachers will be the people who will teach your child how to deal with the many challenging, unpleasant, contrary, and demanding people he will encounter over the course of his life. He will have problematic bosses, employees, boyfriends, girlfriends, spouses, and neighbors, and your child will have to learn how to get along with all of them. As a parent, I know how painful it can be to witness our children's pain and discomfort when faced with a bad relationship. When my child is in pain, when he's frustrated or disappointed by his attempts to play the game of school according to a teacher's quirky rules, my first instinct is to cry foul, grab my kid, and flee the field. But that game will go on, with or without my kid. The sooner he learns how to adapt, the better prepared he'll be when it's his time to play, no matter what version of the rules is in force.

11
HOMEWORK: HOW TO HELP WITHOUT TAKING OVER

HOMEWORK COMES IN MANY FORMS—FROM practice to preparation, from useless to useful, from engaging to downright torturous. Whatever form it takes, and regardless of where you stand on the topic of homework's purpose and utility, homework is your *child's* job, not yours. *Your* job is to support, encourage, and redirect your children when they are young, and as they get older, to make your expectations clear and get the heck out of their way.

Yes, yes, I know; easier said than done. It's easy to stand back and give your child autonomy when homework is a simple math facts review or when long-term assignments remain safely in the distant future. However, when the whining and the complaints of "But I don't *want* to do homework!" and "It's too hard!" rise to a shriek, it is tempting to take over or simply divulge the correct answers so the torture can end and family members can get on with their lives. Don't succumb. These stressful moments, when your child's frustration levels are high, harbor the most valuable opportunities to foster diligence, perseverance, and grit in your child. Kids learn the most about sticking with a task when it's hard, when they are sure they will never figure something out, or when they are suffering the consequences of their own procrastination or botched planning. Even more important, homework that's challenging is more valuable from a learning perspective than easy homework, so stick to your guns. Be strong. When that poster for the science fair looks like a glue-smeared mess, and it's an hour past bedtime, that's precisely when you should step back and walk away.

It may seem harmless to step in, but the damage is cumulative. Every time you take over, and rescue your child from working out a challenging math problem or thesis statement on her own, you undermine your child's sense of confidence, and autonomy. Completing the task herself is its own incentive, a reward infinitely more important than grades or test scores. Think long-term goals. When tonight's stressful homework assignment has been forgotten, she may not even remember that poster, or the specific math problem that tripped her up, or the thesis statement she could not get just right. What she will retain, however, are the long-term benefits she gains when she unravels that math problem on her own or guts the science experiment out until she reaches a conclusion all on her own. She may also feel disappointed in her efforts or her abilities or embarrassed the next day when she faces her teacher and her class with an incorrect answer, but these are her lessons to learn. Your job is not to save her from disappointment or embarrassment, but to sympathize, support, and help her find the strength and skills she will need for tomorrow night's assignment. Let her find what this student found when she did battle both with math, and her better angels, in the middle of the night:

> One night when I was working on the last problem on a particularly hard math assignment, I had the thought, "What if I stopped working on this last proof? What if I gave up?" I knew I could do the work, but it would take a long time and I did not want to do that. I thought about it for a long while. I actually packed up my schoolbooks and went to bed, only to be awakened hours later by the drive to finish. I got up at about one in the morning and I finished that proof. Despite the resulting fatigue, I felt good. I knew that I had done my best. I had not felt that good about myself and my school work for a long time.

While this student clearly benefited from her evening alone with her math homework, parents, teachers, and the media have been engaged in a heated debate about whether or not homework serves a valid educational purpose. The perceived "homework crisis" in America is detailed in the documentary *Race to Nowhere* and has gained traction in the popular media. Yet the National Educational Association (NEA) observed in their "Research Spotlight on Homework," "Homework overload is the exception rather than the norm." Further, they state "the majority of U.S. students spend less than an hour a day on homework, regardless of grade level, and this has held true for most of the past 50 years." The truth of the "homework crisis" is that more homework is being assigned these days, but to only two groups: younger students (who historically were not assigned homework) and students in college preparatory schools. By contrast, homework loads in the middle and upper grades of most schools, particularly lower-achieving schools, have remained stable since the 1950s, and students in low-performing, inner-city schools do almost no homework at all. The National Parent-Teacher Association (National PTA) recommendations tend to be the yardstick by which many schools measure their homework levels, and those recommendations come out of the best available research on homework efficacy: 10–20 minutes per night in the first grade, and an additional 10 minutes per grade level thereafter. That said, if your child is being assigned unreasonable amounts of homework, particularly before middle school, it's time to talk to teachers and administrators to try to get your child's homework load in line with the PTA's recommendations.

Whenever any child is taking a long time to complete her work, or complaining that she simply can't get everything done, I suggest that parents run through this quick checklist before rushing to her teacher to complain.

- Check vision and hearing. Vision and hearing impairments can be the cause of comprehension dips and changes in school performance, a cause that's easy to miss unless schools or physicians conduct regular screenings.

- Make sure your child is getting enough sleep. According to the U.S. Centers for Disease Control and Prevention, preschoolers need 11–13 hours, children from five to ten need 10–11 hours, and teens need somewhere between 8.5 and 9.25 hours of sleep a night; less than that wreaks havoc on concentration, memory, learning, attention, executive functioning, and behavior.

- Gauge challenge. If you believe your child can't manage the work she is being given, talk to the teacher. Conversely, if the work is too easy, that is equally problematic. Research shows that children lose focus and interest when tasks are too simple and, therefore, not

> engaging. That magical "flow" of losing oneself in a task happens only when a task is challenging. Challenge and desirable difficulties trigger encoding, and if the student persists, mastery.

Once you've turned an objective eye to your child's vision, hearing, sleep, and level of challenge, look at *how* your child is doing that homework. When I hear from parents that a student is spending hours and hours on homework, I like to quietly and surreptitiously watch that student during study hall or when I have assigned an independent task in class. Some students look as if they are working, but when I pay close attention, I can see that they actually waste a lot of time, skipping around from task to task, stopping and starting, doodling—and that's without access to a computer, smartphone, or any other obvious distraction. Other students, who get down to work on an assignment, work straight through, check it off their list, and move on, get two or three times as much work done as the students who mess around. Often the parents of the students who waste time mention the huge homework load their children deal with at night, and we point out that much of their homework could be accomplished during study halls, that the students who take advantage of these periods take home much less homework than the students who do not. If homework seems excessive, try this exercise at home. Watch your child when he does his homework, and take note of when real work is getting done and when he is fiddling and fooling around with other stuff. Once you've taken an objective look at the accumulated time of "real work" your child is doing, and the amount still seems excessive, then, by all means, figure out which subjects are the biggest offenders and talk to those teachers about their homework load.

If teachers claim your child is in the minority, and homework takes a reasonable amount of time for others in the class, try the Timer Cure, in honor of one of my personal heroines of children's literature, Miss Piggle-Wiggle. Credit for the Timer Cure goes to math teacher Alison Gorman, a middle school math teacher who noticed that some students were taking a long time to do problem sets at home, but in study hall, where there are no distractions and a set time limit, those same students managed to finish the entire assignment, often with time to spare.

The Timer Cure works like this: Determine which subject is taking up most of the student's homework time, and then figure out how much time it's taking each day. Let's pretend, for the purposes of illustration, that it's algebra. If the student is spending 90 minutes on algebra alone, cut that in half. Set a timer for 45 minutes and make it clear that once those 45 minutes are up, algebra is over and your child must move on to another subject. Make sure your child can see the timer so that he knows when time is running out. Remind him that he can't spend a half hour on one problem and expect to finish the entire problem set in the time allotted, so he is going to have to budget his time. Nine times out of ten, the student will meet the clock.

Speak to the teacher ahead of time to let her know that you are going to perform this exercise, and often that teacher will give the student a little leeway for a couple of days. At the very least, the teacher will know why a problem or two remained unfinished, and that will be valuable information for her, as well. She will be able to tell which concepts are giving your child fits, and help reinforce the exercise from her end.

Now for the practical details: when you should help and what that help should look like, when is it time to back off, and how to help children find the silver lining around their homework failures. The key is to stay focused on the endgame rather than the moment-to-moment play-by-play, and keep those long-term goals of a growth mindset, autonomy, competence, mastery, and diligence in mind.

Here are some practical steps you can take to help children of all ages learn how to organize, strategize, and take responsibility for their homework. For young children, parents will need to teach these steps at first, in order to form good habits, but over time, you should expect your child to take ownership of these tasks. If your child is older and she has never had to step up and take charge of her own learning, giving her control over these first steps can be an ideal place to start.

- Fuel up. Our brains can't work well unless we are nourished and hydrated. Prepare—or encourage your child to prepare—a healthy snack and drink of water in order to top off the energy his brain needs to be alert and awake for the work ahead.

- Get rid of distractions. Even small distractions, such as switching between tasks, or a momentary lapse in concentration can lead to mistakes. A recent study showed that even a three-second distraction can double the number of mistakes people make on tasks, likely because the distraction caused the details of those tasks to slip out of short-term memory. Find a quiet, distraction-free space for homework time.

- Understand expectations. Know what teachers expect from your child. Many teachers send home or publish weekly plans online to keep parents apprised of assignments, so use those to clarify expectations and plan ahead for the rest of the week. Elementary school teachers will often provide a "family letter" explaining the concepts being taught at school. If older children are not clear on expectations, encourage them to follow up with their teachers at school.

- Organize and strategize. In study halls, I have students write a checklist on the whiteboard in the front of my classroom so they are all held accountable for what they need to do. This also allows for reminders from classmates not to forget about the math or French homework. At home, you could ask, "What about English? Isn't Monday grammar day?" and help your child prioritize.

- Suggest your child do the hardest work first. Research shows that self-control is a limited commodity in the human brain, and reserves are likely to be at their highest levels at the start of homework time.

- Evaluate the end product. Teach kids to pause at the end of an assignment, and at the end of the homework period, and evaluate if the assignment has been completed according to instructions. Some teachers ask parents to sign off on homework, but move kids in the direction of being able to evaluate on their own whether or not their work meets expectations. Once children are able to do this, inform the teacher that you will no longer be signing off on their work, that the child is responsible for signing off on her own homework.

- Complete what can be completed. If, after repeated attempts, your child cannot complete all of the work, encourage her to break the assignment down and do what she can. Here is where it's important to speak with elementary school teachers about expectations. Some teachers would like parents to talk the child through the work, and others prefer that the sections that the child could not complete be left blank so that the teacher can see what the child does or does not know. My personal preference is that the child do *something* even if he or she can't complete the entire task. In a challenging Latin translation, for example, I ask students to look up the words and list their definitions, or label the parts of speech of the words, even if they can't figure out the precise or complete English translation. The more evidence I have of where the student is going wrong, the more I am able to help get the student back on track.

- Aim for learning, not for perfection. Try to keep the focus on what's really important about homework. Homework is not only about finding the right answers; it's about giving kids an opportunity to practice and expand skills they learned today and to prepare for the skills they will learn tomorrow.

SUPPORT, ENCOURAGE, AND REDIRECT

When children are young, your job during homework time is to be nearby, busy with other activities, while the child is doing homework. You are present, but not hovering. Supportive, but not intrusive. I often prepare dinner while my younger son does his homework at the kitchen counter. That way, I'm there if he needs support, encouragement, or redirection, but I'm busy and won't be tempted to intervene every time he hesitates or makes his attention-seeking moans of frustration. Until he was nine or ten, I checked in on his progress every ten minutes or so, just to make sure he was on track, but now that he's able to identify when he's really stuck, as opposed to momentarily hung up on a concept or instruction, he asks me for help as needed.

It's really important that kids know we have other things to do in our lives than sit next to them and wait for them to get stuck and ask questions. I've spoken with many parents who admit this is how homework happens every night in their homes. One mother, whose children are six and nine, told me, "We sit down as a family at homework time so my husband and I can both be there to help them when they get stuck." Another parent, when we sat down together to problem-solve the nightly tantrums and anxiety attacks his children were having at homework time, painted a similar picture. Each night he and his wife would spend hours struggling through their eight- and ten-year-old daughters' homework assignments. In both cases, the parents would stay present for *when* a child became stuck, feeding a self-fulfilling cycle of dependency and an expectation that their children will, sooner or later, get stuck and need adult help.

Some parenting books advise that kids should do homework first, then have the freedom to play as a reward, while other books recommend that kids have the "reward" first, so they are not rushing through homework in order to get to the reward as quickly as possible. Let me propose a novel concept: ask your child where and when she would like to complete her homework. If homework time is a nightly battle, ask the question she may be yearning to answer: "How would *you* like to complete your homework?" Every child is different. Some need time after school to run around and vent some pent-up energy and heebie-jeebies, and others like to get straight down to business and get homework out of the way. Author and parenting expert Vicki Hoefle tells a story in her presentations and in her book *Duct Tape Parenting* about the nightly battles she and her husband used to fight with their then second-grade daughter. Vicki and her husband wanted their daughter to do her homework, and she flat-out refused to comply. Finally, in Vicki's words, "it clicked."

> The next morning, at breakfast, I asked her the magic question.
>
> "K, in a perfect world, on a perfect day, how would you take care of your homework?" She did not hesitate. She had been waiting for us to listen to her.
>
> "I would get up at 4:30 a.m. and do it. I can't do it at night. My brain just won't do it."
>
> "Okay," I said. "How about for the next week, you do your homework whenever you like. Your dad and I will not get in your way. Here's the thing, though. We have to leave the house at 7:15 a.m. No exceptions. Can do you that?"
>
> She thought for maybe ten seconds and then said, "YES."

Vicki and her husband were prepared for this plan to fail, but it did not. Not only did their daughter set her alarm clock and get up the next morning to do her homework; she continues to be an early riser and, according to Vicki, continued to do her homework at four thirty in the morning throughout college.

Once your child has selected a time and place of his choosing, give him time and space to struggle. Make it clear that you are nearby, taking care of your own responsibilities, while he takes care of his. If you have been helping with homework up until this point, this switch-up is going to be a real challenge, but like those toddler temper tantrums that required you to stick to your guns until the battle passed, the homework temper tantrum will end as well, and your student will be more independent and confident for your efforts.

While studies on homework effectiveness in children reveal that homework before middle school has little academic value, there are nonacademic benefits to be gained from the nightly task of homework. The ability to initiate, delay gratification, see a task through to completion, and persist through frustration and challenge are incredibly important executive function skills, and homework encourages their development.

While research shows that there is little or no evidentiary link between elementary school homework and achievement, I can support one benefit of homework: it gives teachers feedback on how students are doing in terms of their progress toward mastery. When parents step in and "help," however, teachers get an inaccurate representation of that mastery. One middle school math teacher told me the story of a seventh-grade student whose parents "helped" so regularly and extensively with his homework that while his answers were always correct in his notebook, the work often contained advanced math concepts, ideas the student was rarely able to explain to the teacher or class when he copied his work on the board. This teacher lamented that she was never really sure where his level of mastery fell, but she quipped that it must be "somewhere between his brilliant and suspiciously above grade-level homework and his spotty and below average in-class work."

As children get better at taking responsibility for homework, and sticking with it even as the going gets hard, they can begin to experience the real rewards of their persistence: pride and confidence. Kay Wills Wyma recounts the following story about her daughter Snopes in her book *Cleaning House: A Mom's 12-Month Experiment to Rid Her Home of Youth Entitlement.*

> Once, when Snopes asked for help on a fifth-grade English paper, I couldn't stop myself from progressively increasing my involvement. I tried to guide her in coming up with descriptive language, but it took too long. I didn't have time to weather stammering and searching for words. Screaming siblings were vying for my attention. So rather than stand behind her, let her type (as slow as that might be), encourage her to struggle through word choices, and make her correct the errors, I literally pushed her aside and took over the helm in front of the computer. I corrected every grammatical error, filled in missing details, and added creativity to pull the reader into her story. Her report on *Redwall* emerged from its cocoon a beautiful butterfly, a far cry from the hairy caterpillar she had shown me moments earlier.
>
> When she came home from school with the paper that not only sported a huge "97" in glaring red marker (firework marks exploding around the number) but also a note from the teacher on how proud she was of the terrific effort, Snopes looked embarrassed, not proud. It wasn't her work being praised, and she knew it.

Snopes lost out on more than genuine, earned praise. She missed out on all those desirable difficulties that would have really solidified the skills she was supposed to be learning as she completed the assignment. Consider the classic example of parental overinvolvement: the science fair project. If there's one arena where failure is most desirable and productive, it's in the process of scientific inquiry. Even if the science project is a grand failure, even if the hypothesis is flat-out wrong, that's a good thing. In science, negative results are not failures, they are useful data.

As you support your children through their nightly homework efforts, keep their need for desirable difficulties at the top of your list of parenting priorities. When frustrated, kids gripe, whine, wail that they are hopelessly stuck, and otherwise give up, hoping you will intervene and save them. In these moments, resist the temptation to do so. Psychologist, author, and school counselor Michael Thompson suggests that children's struggles become more manageable when we support their efforts to work through it. "Children need us to recognize their struggle and pay attention to it. That doesn't mean to intervene immediately, or to start yelling or panicking, or to come to a premature conclusion." As you recognize and empathize, remain autonomy-supportive and support by redirecting your child's focus and effort. If he is really stuck, give him a new way to think about the problem, but do not step in to solve the problem for him.

Of course, there's a fine line between struggles that promote learning and struggles that doom learning and intrinsic motivation. First-year Latin students can't translate *The Aeneid*, and asking them to do so would not result in learning but frustration and anger. Just as we learn the difference between cries that indicate our child is really hurt versus the cries that signal momentary frustration or a call for attention, we need to learn how to hear pleas for homework help that indicate insurmountable difficulties as opposed to transitory, desirable challenges. This is no easy task, and a constantly moving target. Young children have diverse and ever-changing skills and needs, and some children are more independent than others. As their idiosyncratic cognitive and emotional talents and deficits emerge, your role will ebb and flow with their needs. Your role in homework won't be the same in first grade as it is in fifth grade, but keep your eye on the future. You are there to help your children become independent and rely on their developing skills.

Finally, when the homework session is at an end, remember the lessons of Carol Dweck and the growth mindset. Praise your child for the effort he put into his assignments, particularly when he encountered those frustrating difficulties that pushed him to the limits of what he thought he could do. Make sure he knows that you value his persistence as much as, if not more than, you value the answers he wrote after each problem. Whenever possible, reiterate the concept that the harder we work, and the more we stretch our brains, the smarter we become.

CLEAR EXPECTATIONS AND ROOM TO LEARN

Once your child is in middle and high school and those executive function skills have started to kick in, it's time to remove yourself from your child's homework duties. Around the beginning of middle school, when research shows that homework begins to have an academic benefit, homework takes on increasing academic relevance. Homework, when carefully planned and prepared, is not busywork. Quality homework shores up knowledge that has already been encoded, and pushes students to apply that knowledge to new contexts. This final aspect of learning, in which students create answers rather than merely recalling them, is called *generative learning.* Homework that promotes generative learning offers students opportunities to play with skills, exercise some trial and error, and create their own answers. While generative learning is vital to mastery, it is also *hard.* Generative learning does not come easily, and when this valuable and precious kind of learning is going on, expect to see some blood, sweat, and tears. It won't look like elementary school homework, in which answers fit tidily in squares preprinted on math worksheets. Generative learning, when done right, should travel outside the lines, disregard boundaries of subject matter, and stretch students' abilities to the limit.

I had the opportunity to witness a particularly messy display of generative learning recently when I served as a practice judge for a middle school FIRST Lego League team. FIRST Lego League is an educational robotics program in which teams of kids invent a solution to some problem they have identified out there in the world. When it came time for the students to run through their presentations, I squirmed in my seat and held my tongue as the students tried, and failed, and tried again to communicate solutions to the problems they had identified. It was all I could do to keep from holding my head in my hands as their prototypes failed to work as planned and they argued about workarounds and last-second improvisations these mishaps caused. I was anxious about how they would fare in the real competition the next day, as these prototypes were clearly not ready to be deployed in the real world, let alone in front of a panel of judges. The next day, I received an email from the team's parent supervisor to thank me for my help and to announce that the kids had received an award for their work. Specifically, they were honored for the way they approached the challenge they were given and for the manner in which they embodied the FIRST Lego League core values. Notably, the core values state, "What we discover is more important than what we win." All of that failure, failure that nearly gave me an ulcer, resulted in a great learning experience for the students.

In order to take advantage of the more complex generative learning assignments kids face in middle and high school, some students may continue to need guidance where the executive function skills come into play, such as with long-term planning and time management. However, these maturing students should be maintaining their own plan book or calendar and beginning to take responsibility for their work and deadlines. Certainly once high school begins, homework should be completely under students' control, and unless they want to talk through an assignment or get your feedback on an idea, parents should not be involved in homework at all.

THINK BACK TO YOUR CHILDHOOD, to those days when you simply felt ready for the school day, when you had worked hard on your homework and felt *really* confident and prepared. Remember those mornings walking to school or riding the bus, when you could not wait for the day to start because you were not just willing to be called on, but eager to show off what you'd accomplished the night before? Keep that feeling in mind when you are tempted to take over your child's homework. Don't deprive her of those feelings of competence. Let her experience both her failures and her successes, and let her take ownership and pride in her work and abilities. You can cheer her on as she progresses, but you can't sit next to her at the dining room table and hold her hand forever. This is her journey, her personal quest to slay her dragons and secure her just rewards.

12
GRADES: THE REAL VALUE OF A LOW SCORE

I RECEIVED AN EMAIL LAST YEAR from Maggie, a worried and desperate mother who wrote to ask my advice about her son, John, who was about to be kicked out of his gifted magnet school due to his failing grades. As the other schools in her family's district were dreadful (so dreadful the principal and many of the teachers had just been fired), she was desperate to keep him enrolled at his current school. A meeting had been set for the following morning with John's teachers to decide his future.

I admit that I am guilty of all sorts of overparenting crimes, like catering to my kids for picky eating, or bringing my son his lunch if he forgets it. His shelves are lined with trophies and he has several medals for perfect FCAT scores and Math Meet competitions. He has never had to study or barely lift a finger in order to achieve high marks or win his school's PRIDE award (highest mark). Gifted school is making him work like he has never had to in his life and he's been failing his strongest subjects, math and language arts. I think I have done all I can without actually following him to class and listening in. I nag, and push, and keep my fingers crossed. Now that John has received these failing grades, and the consequences might just be expulsion, he claims that he really wants to stay at his current school. He has never expressed actually wanting to go to school—any school—so I think this is a good sign.

I suggested the following plan to Maggie:

First, she should sit down for a serious talk with John in order to figure out whether or not he is truly dedicated to keeping his place in his current school. I told her to be honest, to explain how dire the situation has become, and describe his other school options in the district. Finally, she should tell him she has a plan, but only if he is truly willing to do what it takes to reclaim his spot at the gifted and talented school.

If John says yes, that he is ready and willing to do what it takes to stay in his current school, then it's time to reveal Maggie's new expectations for John.

- School, and all it entails, will be John's responsibility—the homework, organization, planning, all of it.
- Maggie will not nag, remind, cajole, or otherwise interfere in his efforts to succeed.

John agreed to these new expectations, and they shook on it. The next day, Maggie met with John's teachers, described his newfound drive to earn his place at the school, and made the case for a probationary semester, three more months for John to prove himself and his commitment. John's teachers, sensing her desperation, granted her wish. Maggie promised to keep in touch, and my three-month wait for news began.

IN MY EXPERIENCE, EVEN PARENTS who are enthusiastic about promoting autonomy in their kids get nervous and start second-guessing themselves when actual failing grades are at stake. Even the most stalwart, autonomy-supportive parents can be tempted to fall back on controlling and directive behaviors when failing grades mar their child's grade report. However, these D's, and yes, even those ugly, frightening F's, can prompt a child to step up, take charge, and find his drive. These failing moments are, more often than not, metaphorical roads diverging in a yellow wood, chances for children to decide what's important to them, and whether or not they want to invest in their own learning.

I'm going to point out the gigantic elephant standing in the middle of this chapter right away. Grades. There's no way around this unfortunate reality, so I'm just going to face it head-on. Grades are extrinsic rewards for academic performance. Extrinsic rewards undermine motivation and long-term learning. Ergo, grades undermine motivation and long-term learning. There. Elephant identified. I'd love to remove the elephant from the room altogether and replace it with something less unwieldy and more attractive, but as our system of education is currently based on the exchange of grades for performance, I have no choice but to talk about how to retrain our brains and our children to look past the beast and see the other, more meaningful rewards that grades obscure.

Over the years, my students have shared their many frustrations with grades and the impact they have on learning and motivation with me in conversations, and more often, in essays and journaling exercises. Their collective frustrations are beautifully summed up in an essay this high school student wrote about her experience of elementary and middle school.

> Before third grade, when scores and percentages did not matter, I wrote freely and honestly about what made me happy. But then foreign numbers began appearing on my papers, numbers representing other people's approval or disdain. At first those numbers were inconvenient little shapes that hindered my ability to write without care. But soon I began to rely on those numbers. I became addicted to A's, craving more when I got snatches of praise. And I started to drift away from what I had been writing as a younger child. Before I realized it, I was writing for those little, crawling black shapes and red marks.

Students are not the only ones acknowledging the detrimental effect of grading. Teachers are increasingly writing and talking about the harm grading does to their students' learning and the fragile student-teacher bond. High school English teacher K. C. Potts repeats some version of the following speech to his students at the beginning of each school year:

> I will say many times that grades are the worst thing that ever happened to learning, and until you find a way to establish a healthy relationship with them, they will torment and frustrate you, have you worried and stressed-out, will make you sometimes feel not so good about yourself. Of course, you are better at some things than you are at others. One of education's tasks is to help you recognize your strengths and weaknesses. Try to avoid the compare game whereby you judge your performance by comparing it to that of others. Doing so is both inevitable and counterproductive. The issue is not what others can do but what *you* can do.
>
> Many of you aspire to high grades because you see them as a ticket to the college of your choice. And yes, grades do matter. But are they an indication of what you can do? The better motivation:

> learning how to do something well. Getting an "A" measures that the student "knows how to play the game of school." It does NOT always, as practiced, demonstrate real mastery of material.

Even parents admit that grades get in the way of their relationships with their children. "I never thought I'd be this kind of mom, but here I am. Grades are stressing me out. I think about my kids' grades all the time, every day. I know it's wrong, and it's stupid, and I know the kids get mad at me when I do it, but I can't help it, and these days, I feel like it's all I talk about with them."

Grades, or any other attempts to classify students according to achievement, have been a thorny reality of academic life since the first days of education in America. The earliest examples of report cards come from 1817 and focus mainly on how attentive, orderly, and prepared students were for their classes, and don't contain any mention of academic achievement. This was judged based on end-of-term examinations, or as the president of Harvard called them in 1857, a "test of scholarship." They were conducted as written examinations, one-on-one discussions with an instructor, or before a panel of examiners, much like a modern dissertation defense. Even in the early days of grading, teachers and administrators were dubious as to their utility in measuring learning and mastery. The president of Yale, Rev. Timothy Dwight V, expressed his concerns about the imperfections of the emerging examination and grading system in 1898.

> There are, to say the least, two or three very marked evils and imperfections in the system. One of them has already been hinted at—the impersonality, if the expression may be allowed, which is inseparably connected with them; that is to say, the necessary

absence of personal communication between the mind of the examiner and the mind of the one who is examined.

Given the long-standing discontent with our system of grading, it's odd that test scores and grades have gained such power in education. We talk about them every time our kid walks through the door at the end of the day ("How did you do on that French test?"). We get reminders of them in the mail in the form of progress reports, midterm reports, and report cards. Modern software platforms give parents the ability to check in on grades 24/7 from the comfort of their homes. We have to talk about them at parent-teacher conferences, and even when there's nothing more we, or our children, can do to improve those grades, we have to share them with colleges and hope they are good enough to invite admission.

Teachers, parents, and students rely on them and hate them at the same time, and there's plenty of evidence to show that grades are just about the worst way to promote learning through intrinsic motivation. Researchers asked a group of fifth graders to read a passage from a textbook. It was one of those classic samples given on standardized tests, something that's not very interesting and requires paying attention. One third of the kids were told to read the passage and nothing else, the second third were told they would be tested on their comprehension for a grade, and the final third were told that they would be tested but would not receive a grade. Everyone was tested in the end. The two groups who had no expectation of a grade did better on the test than the kids who knew they were going to be graded. Furthermore, they were more interested and curious about the reading. In another study conducted in Japan, a researcher gave middle school students weekly math quizzes. He told half the kids that the grades would not count, that the quizzes were just to monitor their learning and progress. The other group of kids was told that the quizzes would impact their final grade. Again, the kids who were not concerned about the impact on their final grades learned more and had higher levels of interest and curiosity. These differences endured over time, too. When the researchers returned at a later date to test these same kids again, the ones who had no expectation of being graded retained more of the material than the students who read with the fact that they would be graded in mind.

GRADES ARE AN ANNOYING AND exhausting fact of life, and despite debate over more effective alternatives, they are not going away anytime soon. But there are ways to promote intrinsic motivation and long-term learning in spite of them.

KEEP GRADES IN THEIR PROPER PERSPECTIVE.

Grades are not a measure of our children's worth, and often they are not even an accurate measure of their ability. Teachers know this, but even we fall into the trap of equating our students with their grades. While grades *can* be a measure of ability, more often they are a measure of the skills that make for successful students: solid executive function skills, compliance, willingness to please, ability to follow directions, and self-discipline. When I listen in on students as they debate the merit of grades, it's clear that kids understand this reality. If you catch an honest and forthcoming teacher at the right moment, she may even reveal that she knows it, too. Grades, for all the weight they carry in our culture, are less important than learning. Learning is the key to understanding our world, and the universe beyond; to communicating with other people, and to innovating for the future of our society. Grades are the key to certain academic institutions and a few office doors. I'd prefer my children and my students to value the former rather than the latter.

If that's not incentive enough, consider this: your child might just want to spend more time with you if you lay off the topic of grades. At a local high school orientation, a parent asked a student on a panel, "What's the piece of advice you'd give us parents about how to help our kids have a great freshman year?" Her answer:

> I'd say, give your kids some space and don't always talk about school and grades and stuff. Be there, and talk to them, like at dinner and in the car, but talk about the things they want to talk about. My family eats dinner together every night, and I really wanted to be around my parents and talk to them, but not about school or grades, just about my life and what's going on. When they just talk about grades, it makes me not want to be around them, and it makes me feel like that's all they care about.

As my sons get older, and I compete with their friends, technology, and all the other diversions in their lives for attention and conversation, I find this advice heartening. If all I have to do is lay off the topic of grades in order to warrant more time and attention, I'm in.

EMPHASIZE GOALS RATHER THAN GRADES.

One way to keep grades in their proper perspective and help kids gain control of their education is to shift your family's focus off grades and onto goals. Because goals are self-determined rather than teacher-determined, they can be a much more useful measurement of success. When kids establish their own goals for learning, they gain a sense of ownership and competence. Earning high marks can provide a temporary high, particularly when a kid has worked hard, but achieving a specific and self-determined goal always transcends the rush of a straight-A report card.

Goals can be a great way to motivate and maintain engagement in school, but in order to be effective, the goals must belong to your child. No matter how small or how nonsensical your child's goals may seem to you, they are his goals, and you should respect that. Even nonacademic, seemingly frivolous goals are important, because the process of setting goals is not about the goal itself, but the grit required to put a name to an ambition and see it through to fruition. Simply taking the time to talk about the things they want to achieve over time shows kids that we respect their needs and aspirations.

As your family sets their goals, work on your own. Any time you feel yourself taking over or offering too much advice, go into the other room for a drink of water or excuse yourself to use the bathroom. Take a few deep breaths, and remind yourself of the goal here: autonomy over self-directed goals leads to intrinsic motivation, which leads to better learning and life success. And then breathe.

But in between those breaths, don't forget to praise effort, diligence, and perseverance. "I'm so proud of you for keeping yourself organized this week and getting your papers put away. I know that's a pesky job, but you really stuck with it." A common refrain in our house has been "I'm really impressed with how hard you are working on your goal of keeping your room clean," and "It must be nice to be able to do your drawing on a clean desk."

SEEK FEEDBACK RATHER THAN SCORES.

While scores and grades prioritize grades over learning, there is one aspect of modern report cards that is actually quite helpful, particularly when done well. Narrative comments and feedback on students' performance, according to research, are "better than grades at both promoting kids' self-motivation to learn and boosting their achievement." Elementary school teachers do a good job of providing feedback on report cards, but as soon as grades take over from narrative comments as the main method of evaluation, students and parents begin to lose out. When teachers offer information such as "You did a great job of planning your ideas for this paper, and formulating your thesis, but your body paragraphs don't address the question raised by the thesis," in response to a rough draft of a paper, the student has information that praises the positive elements of her work, addresses failures, and gives useful information she can use to improve performance. In this way, informational feedback works much like praise for effort, and similarly boosts intrinsic motivation, enthusiasm for the task, and performance on subsequent post-tests.

Because grades don't give parents or students any information about the specific skills (or in education lingo, "competencies") a given student has achieved mastery of, many schools are moving to an assessment method called "standards-based grading" and abandoning point-based grading altogether. Standards-based grading assesses students on the skills or competencies a school has decided that student should learn in a given year. For example, if a school is using the comprehensive list of skills outlined in the Common Core State Standards, and the second-grade math standard requires that a student know how to represent one hundred in groups of tens, the teacher will be able to report to parents on whether or not their child has mastered that particular skill. Whereas a B grade says nothing about a child's mastery of particular skills, the standards-based system is a boon to parents and administrators for just that reason. It conveys specific, useful information we need to know in order to determine how students are progressing toward mastery of their grade-appropriate skills.

If your child's school uses solely grades as a summative measure of learning, ask for more information at parent-teacher conferences and report that information back to your child. Make sure you share the criticism as well as the praise, because it's the criticism that offers the most useful information for your child's evolution. Communicate to the teacher that your family favors constructive feedback over grades, as the former is more helpful, and plant the seeds for information- or standards-based grading for future mention at faculty meetings. If the current move toward these grading systems gains momentum, more schools will be making the switch in this direction in the coming years. I know I'm a fan of more information when it comes to children's progress, deficits, and strengths.

LET KIDS STEER THEIR OWN COURSE.

Another opportunity to give kids autonomy and control over their learning is in course selection. As soon as your child has a choice about what classes to take, usually in middle school or early on in high school, course selection should be his job, not yours. When he sits down with the high school course catalog and prioritizes language and music and math selections, he begins to form expectations and goals for himself in his own mind. Choice is one of the most important aspects of establishing autonomy, and if kids have a say in which classes they take, at what time, and with which teachers, they will have so much more ownership over their education.

Yes, I know you want your child to get into a great college and your son's guidance counselor stressed that he *must* take a specific balance of classes designed to thrill those college admissions officers. However, which would you prefer: a child who is excited because she has ownership over her education and therefore works hard to reach her own goals, or a disengaged child who feels as if his educational path is not his own? That first kid is going to do better in school, report more happiness in her educational experience, and be much more likely to meet the goals she's created for herself. You can have total control over your child's every move, or you can have an autonomous, intrinsically motivated kid, but you can't have both.

As you watch your child work toward her goals, make sure she hears that your definition of success includes perseverance in the face of failure. I'd much rather teach a kid who takes risks in his education, even when those risks fail to bear fruit in the end. Students who are too afraid to fail tend to produce boring, uncreative, and mediocre work. I try to push those students to take risks, be unconventional in their thinking, and approach the assignment as if they were not being graded.

FIND ALTERNATE DECORATIONS FOR THE REFRIGERATOR.

As you shift your family's thinking away from grades and toward goals and learning, try not to deify report cards as the end-all, be-all arbiter of accomplishment. It might be tempting to post that straight-A report card on the refrigerator, but doing so conveys the message that you love your children for their grades, not for themselves. What do you plan to do with "bad" report cards, papers, and tests, if you don't post those on the refrigerator as well? The message is clear to your child when you gush over high grades with "Oh! I'm so proud of you! You are so smart!" and frown over C's. A better way to approach grades and report cards is to talk to kids about what went well with a particular assignment or class when they receive a high grade. Ask what approaches worked for your child as he prepared for that French test, and what approaches did not work as well. If he gets a low grade on a test, ask what he might do differently next time, strategies that were successful or problematic. Grades should be a measure of progress, not a destination, so give them the weight and attention they deserve, no more.

BEWARE GRADING SOFTWARE PORTALS.

As schools adopt PowerSchool, iParent, and the other grading software systems for the use of teachers and staff, they must also decide whether to grant students and parents 24/7 access to grading and attendance records. If your child's school offers this option, consider carefully the role such access will play in your family before logging on. While I have used these programs in a couple of different schools and am a big fan of their utility for teachers, I am not a fan of parent portals. Many teachers I spoke with feel that logging in has taken the place of conversation and feeds both student dependency and parent overinvolvement. As one teacher told me,

> Teachers today are asked more and more to keep students and their parents informed. From giving out long-term assignment

packets, to keeping updated phone or email lists of assignments, and posting grades every few days, these tasks lower the need for students to be autonomous. Instead, they encourage dependence on an outside agency telling you what to do.

When the letter arrived containing the user ID and password for my older son's PowerSchool records, we already knew what we would do with it. The envelope was handed over to our son, unopened, in exchange for his solemn promise that he would talk to us about school, and that we would not be the last to know if he was in academic trouble. While we decided to maintain actual conversation with our son as our default method of access to his academic information, many of my friends were shocked and appalled, as if we were defaulting on our parental duty.

I disagree. Checking in on children's grades is a type of surveillance, which is one of the forms of control that is often mentioned in the research as an enemy of autonomy and intrinsic motivation. I would have rejected my access to the grading portal for that reason alone. However, checking in on your child's grades, particularly without making an agreement in advance, communicates a lack of trust that makes me, for one, very uncomfortable.

If you are not ready to give up access to your child's PowerSchool records, there are other ways to handle the access that includes your child. Some parents decide to log on to the program only under strict parameters and engage their children in a discussion of how those parameters might work. For example, you could say to your child, "I plan to log on to PowerSchool today. Is there anything you want to talk to me about?" or "I'd rather hear about grades from you, but will check in next week at the midterm, so why don't you take a look at PowerSchool yourself and let me know what you find?" This way, your child can be in control of the information and learn how to rise to the challenge of initiating hard (or great) conversations.

If you do decide to forgo the parent portal, you might want to send a note to your children's teachers explaining your decision to make your child responsible for communicating information. If I know a student is responsible for talking to his parents about grades, I make sure to check in with the parents from time to time if something has gone wrong or if his grade is in decline. If the teacher does not know that the parents are not checking in online, she won't take responsibility for encouraging the student to rise to the occasion from her end.

REINFORCE FAILURE AS OPPORTUNITY.

When students admit to me that they are scared to death to fail, I can sympathize.

Of course they are afraid of failure. Most students are. They have been told that to fail is to shatter dreams of college, employment, and ultimately, happiness. I am absolutely aware of the stakes faced in college admissions today, but I still maintain that learning for learning's sake, and the opportunity to establish intrinsic motivation early in a child's education, far, far outweigh the impact of a few low grades, and in fact those low grades are necessary and beneficial lessons. However, how a child reacts and adapts to failures can mean the difference between soul-crushing despair and the impetus to step up his game. All of the research, interviews, and anecdotes I've read about successful people and their failures reveals that people who don't identify themselves as failures just because they have failed, who face their failures head-on and look for lessons in the mistakes, are the ones who emerge triumphant. Those who equate failures with being a failure, who go into denial, or seek to blame others for their failures are doomed to repeat their mistakes over and over again, gaining nothing from the experience. Ken Bain, author of the book *What the Best College Students Do*, describes people who see themselves as failures when they fail as people with "contingent self-worth."

> If you have a sense of contingent self-worth, if your attitude toward yourself depends on whether you "succeed" or "fail," in a certain domain in comparison with other people, you may stop trying. Subconsciously you decide that the best way to avoid losing is to stay out of the game.

Teach your children to face failure and accept it as valuable feedback. Let them see you taking risks and failing, and talk about those failures as opportunities to better yourself. Tim Harford, author of the book *Adapt: Why Success Always Starts with Failure*, puts this approach simply: "Biologists have a word for the way in which solutions emerge from failure: evolution." When viewed in that light, the proper reaction to failure is not to deny that it exists, or to kill the messenger, but to evolve in response.

THREE MONTHS LATER, MAGGIE EMAILED back to thank me for my advice and fill me in on John's progress. As per their agreement, Maggie stopped nagging and interfering and gave John the reins to his education. She successfully lobbied John's school for a probationary period of one semester. The result? Maggie stepped back, and as she did, John stepped up. Maggie wrote,

I think John really needed that bad year to learn how to study and do things for himself, rather than to be accustomed to everything being done for him. I don't even have to prompt him to work, which I was fully prepared to do. He does it all on his own. Until now, it's been a total struggle for him to prove his answers and show his work. This year he's finally getting it right.

I'm glad he had his "fail" time at an earlier point rather than later. We all have to face it at some point in our lives, and I think he now understands what he's capable of.

So far so good!

At the end of the school year, John was nominated for the school's "Turnaround Student" award, and he continues to impress his teachers with his drive and determination. John's struggle was not, at its essence, about grades. Sure, those failing grades precipitated his transformation, but failing grades were merely a byproduct of John's inability to be responsible for his learning. Now that Maggie has agreed to step back, she's no longer his to-do list, alarm clock, chef, chauffeur, and tutor. She's simply his mom.

Like most kids, John takes his cues from his parents. Your attitude about autonomy and grades will inform your child's attitude. It's that simple. She spends her days immersed in academic competition with her peers, fully aware of the relevance of grades to honor rolls and colleges, so why not be the one person in her life who doesn't fuel the raging fire of academic pressure and insecurity? I'd much rather be the person my kid wants to talk to over dinner about that funny thing that happened to his friend after math class, the movie he wants to see next weekend, his hopes and dreams. We have such a limited amount of time with our children as it is, so we might as well enjoy it while it lasts. My favorite view on the value of failing in high school comes from longtime high school teacher Jonathan Shea, who has seen the pattern of try, fail, and try again play itself out over and over:

> Students recover. People do it all the time. And the failure helps them learn about themselves. First, they learn that people want them to be okay. Second, they learn that they can overcome a problem, but that work and attention are more important than genius or perfection. Students need to fail, because this is when they learn to succeed.

CONCLUSION: WHAT I'VE LEARNED FROM LETTING GO

I LOVE A GOOD PARABLE; I am an English teacher, after all. My life is spent in pursuit of the stories that can help my students connect their individual journeys to the larger experience of being human. When we read the story of Pip's departure from home and return to redemption in *Great Expectations*, for example, Dickens reveals one potential path through childhood, a route for rectifying our own missteps and a glimpse of a possible ending. Pip, like us, is imperfect, so it's reassuring to know that he finds his way through the mist and the danger and heartbreak of growing up.

All this imperfection is rendered more tolerable when couched in fiction, or fixed safely in the distant past. Our history textbooks are full of these stories, some accurate, some apocryphal, all of them meant to shore up our identity as a culture based on a tradition of bootstrapping, invention from necessity, and the great comeback. The oft-cited story of Edison's education in ten thousand failed lightbulbs, for example, has become one of the most famous stories of failure-turned-success in American history.

Edison is quoted, misquoted, and paraphrased all over the Internet regarding the lessons of those ten thousand failed lightbulbs and the triumph of that one successful attempt. Google "famous failures," and you'll find an entire day's reading, from the well-worn (Steve Jobs, J. K. Rowling, and Albert Einstein) to the obscure (Alan Hinkes, S. A. Andrée, Akio Morita).

We reprint and repeat these tales of failure because we know they end well. They may contain plot twists and surprise endings, but before we even begin reading, we can bet hard money on the outcome. Against all odds, the invention will work, the championship game will be won, and the astronauts will make it back to Earth. We don't share these stories for their surprise endings, but to remind us that our own mistakes might just be worthwhile in the end. We need to know that our suffering, humiliation, and pain will prove valuable in the final accounting.

If the unpredictability of our own journey is frustrating, the suspense that parents experience as we watch our children's stories unfold is downright unbearable. Because we can't possibly know how their stories will end, their failures are all the more acute, immediate, and treacherous; more Shakespearean tragedy than quaint anecdote.

When my children make mistakes that endanger their own happy endings, the bottom drops out of my world, and in those moments there's nothing I'd like more than to be able to flip to the end of their story and reassure myself that everything turns out okay. Sadly, that's not how parenting works. We don't have access to spoilers, and we can't skim through the uncomfortable chapters in our children's story arcs in order to skip to the happy ending. Worse, we can't even know if there will *be* a happy ending.

What we can do, however, is be patient, and trust in our kids. As I watch my own children make their way toward their dénouements and strategize goals that I may not even be around to witness, I have no choice but to focus on the details of their journey. They are writing their own stories, in their own voices, with plot points of their own invention. Their narrative is not mine, and I can't edit them into perfection. The author Richard Russo wrote, "Great books are not flawless books," and he's right. In order for my children to become masterpieces, their flaws must be allowed to remain, and serve as an essential part of their tale.

ACKNOWLEDGMENTS

WRITING MAY BE A SOLITARY endeavor, but the publication of a book is a mass effort. There's no possible way to thank every person who helped transform a late-night idea for a blog post into a book.

The next morning, in between teaching English and Latin classes, that blog post morphed into an article, and K. J. Dell'Antonia suggested I submit it for publication somewhere. Around lunchtime, *Pound Foolish* author Helaine Olen supplied me with Jennie Gritz's email address at the *Atlantic.* By the end of the day, Jennie had accepted, edited, and posted the article "Why Parents Need to Let Their Children Fail." These three women changed the trajectory of my life, and no matter how many times I thank them, it will never be enough.

A good editor is hard to find, and yet I have been fortunate to work with many: K. J. Dell'Antonia at the *New York Times*, Jennie Gritz, Eleanor Barkhorn Britton, Heather Horn, James Hamblin, Ashley Fetters, Julia Ryan, and Emma Green at the *Atlantic*, Betty Smith at Vermont Public Radio, and Cassie Jones Morgan at William Morrow.

The editor who labored over this particular book deserves more than a full paragraph of thanks, but she would inevitably make me omit what she would interpret as repetitive and unnecessary sentiments. So thank you, Gail Winston. Thank you. You are a wise and wonderful woman.

When I became a professional writer, I dreaded meeting those territorial, underhanded, catty women writers I'd heard so much about. It seems it's past time to kick that tired stereotype to the curb. These brilliant women have been nothing but kind and generous with their time, quotes, advice, and support: Carol Blymire, Marilyn-Price Mitchell, Michele Borba, Katie Hurley, Andrea Nair, Betsy Lerner and her FTF Writers, Jacoba Urist, Jennifer Hartstein, Christine Gross-Loh, Jennifer Senior, Ashley Merryman, Isabel Kallman, Lisa Belkin, Lisa Heffernan, Launa Schweizer, Naomi Shulman, Kimberly Williams, Jeanne Eschenberg Sager, Catherine Newman, Galit Breen, Aviva Rubin, Laura Vanderkam, Asha Dornfest, Blair Koenig, Amy Gutman, Alicia Ybarbo Zimmerman, Julie Cole, Nancy Rappaport, Jennifer Senior, Gretchen Rubin, Catherine Newman, Priscilla Gilman, Annie Murphy Paul, Kendall Hoyt, Holly Korbey, Avital Norman Nathman, Sarah Buttenwieser, Megan Rubiner Zinn, Melissa Atkins Wardy, Naomi Shulman, Sue Scheff, Elizabeth Green, Kay Wills Wyma, Ruth McKinney, Kristen Laine, Lisa Damour, Susan Cain, Joanne Wyckoff, Joanne Jacobs, and so many others. I promise to be horrified and embarrassed when I realize my omissions.

And no, I have not forgotten about the boys. Huge thanks to Robert Pondiscio, my first editor on matters educational. I could not have had a more able and wise mentor. Thanks also to A. J. Jacobs, Jim Collins, Tom Ryan, John Tierney, Mike Winerip, Paul Tough, Jay Mathews, Greg Toppo, Smoker Shulman, Jeff Valence, Michael Petrilli, K. C. Potts, Don Cannon, Zach Galvin,

Dan Willingham, John Boger, Alexander Russo, Larry Ferlazzo, Jordan Shapiro, Matthew Levey, Nikhil Goyal, Ron Lieber, and Scott Barry Kaufman.

Thanks to all the parents, teachers, and students who shared their stories with me. I could not have written this book without you.

To the Writerdinner ladies: K. J. Dell'Antonia, Sarah Stewart Taylor, Sarah Pinneo, Jenny Bent, and Sarina Bowen, thank you for listening to my fears and shoring up my hopes.

Thanks to the Laheys and the O'Haras, family by marriage and temperament. I could not have in-lawed myself to a more loving and supportive cast of characters.

Thanks to my students at the Duke Talent Identification Program, Rowland-Hall/St. Mark's School, Highland High School, Hanover High School, Crossroads Academy, and Valley Vista. You have made me a better educator, writer, parent, and human being.

Thanks to the staff of Crossroads Academy, who supported me when I suddenly and unexpectedly morphed from teacher to teacher/writer.

Thanks to Victoria Pipas for giving over her summer to do some painfully boring administrative grunt work when the demands of writing this book eclipsed just about everything.

Thanks to my agent, Laurie Abkemeier, for continuing to answer my emails, read my queries, and share my hope that someday, somehow, we would have the chance to work together.

Thanks to my mom and dad, who let me have my autonomy, encouraged me to become a competent human being, and reminded me that they loved me, no matter what my grade, point total, high score, or salary turned out to be.

Finally, thanks to my husband, Tim Lahey, because I'm the lucky one in this equation.

NOTES

xv **trend that's been rising for decades** "A Rising Share of Young Adults Live in Their Parents' Home," August 14, 2013, http://www.pewsocialtrends.org/2013/08/01/a-rising-share-of-young-adults-live-in-their-parents-home/.

xvii **both parents working outside the home** Judith Warner, *Perfect Madness: Motherhood in the Age of Anxiety* (New York: Penguin Books, 2006), 138.

xx **"the same biological trigger"** Wendy Grolnick and Kathy Seal, *Pressured Parents and Stressed-Out Kids* (Amherst, NY: Prometheus Books, 2008), 74.

5 **most of them children** Steven Mintz, *Huck's Raft: A History of American Childhood* (Cambridge, MA: Harvard University Press, 2004), 15.

5 **"no more surprising than a broken pitcher"** Ibid., 14.

5 **"do not instruct children"** Paula S. Fass and Mary Ann Mason, ed., *Childhood in America* (New York: New York University Press, 2000), 45.

5 **"title and right to it"** Ibid., 47.

6 **"harden them for the future"** Ibid., 48

6 **"keeping up the distinction too long."** Mintz, *Huck's Raft,* 52.

7 **added display of individuality** Ibid., 59.

8 **"useful to useless"** Viviana Zelizer, *Pricing the Priceless Child,* (New York: Basic Books, 1985), 56.

9 **"everything about babies"** Ann Hulbert, *Raising America: Experts, Parents, and a Century of Advice About Children* (New York: Vintage Books, 2003), 70.

10 **"psychologizing of childrearing"** Mintz, *Huck's Raft,* 219.

13 **"during adolescence"** Ibid., 316.

13 **increased sixfold** Ibid., 313.

16 **"How will I know if I am a good parent?"** "The Top 10 Concerns of New Parents," accessed January 1, 2014, http://www.parenting.com/article/the-top-10-concerns-of-new-parents?page=0,0.

26 **"sad state of apathy"** Edward Deci, *Why We Do What We Do: Understanding Self-Motivation* (New York: Penguin), 31.

27 **Detrimental** Ibid., 31.

28 **not given any choice** Ibid., 33.

31 **"but only for boring material"** K. Murayama and C. Kuhbandner, "Money Enhances Memory Consolidation—But Only for Boring Material" *Cognition* 119, no. 1 (April 2011): 120–24.

33 **"falls short of their vision"** Anne Sobel, "How Failure in the Classroom Is More Instructive than Success," *Chronicle of Higher Education*, accessed May 5, 2014, http://chronicle.com/article/How-Failure-in-the-Classroom/146377/.

38 **more is always possible through effort and personal development** Carol Dweck, *Mindset: The New Psychology of Success* (New York: Ballantine, 1978), 6–7.

38 **"persist in the face of obstacles"** Carol Dweck, *Self-Theories: Their Role in Motivation, Personality, and Development* (New York: Psychology Press, 2000), 1.

40 **"desirable difficulties."** Peter C. Brown, Henry L. Roediger III, and Mark A. McDaniel, *Make It Stick: The Science of Successful Learning* (Cambridge, MA: Harvard University Press, 2014), 69.

41 **As the authors** Ibid.

48 **"striking"** Wendy S. Grolnick, *The Psychology of Parental Control: How Well-Meant Parenting Backfires* (New York: Psychology Press, 2003), 16.

63 **"It just takes effort"** Christine Gross-Loh, *Parenting Without Borders* (New York: Avery, 2013), 106.

64 **"inaccurate statements about themselves"** William Damon, *Greater Expectations* (New York: Free Press, 1995), 72.

66 **"telling them they were smart"** Carol Dweck, *Mindset: The New Psychology of Success* (New York: Ballantine Books, 2006), 73.

80 **"lack of purpose"** L. L. Harlow, M. D. Newcomb, and P. M. Bentler, "Depression, Self-derogation, Substance Abuse, and Suicide Ideation: Lack of Purpose in Life as a Meditational Factor," *Journal of Clinical Psychology* 42, no. 1 (January 1986): 5–21.

99 **"time unproductively spent"** Hara Estroff Marano, *A Nation of Wimps: The High Cost of Invasive Parenting* (New York: Broadway Books, 2008), 257.

104 **when they witness the emotional healing** Patrick T. Davies, Robin L. Myers, and E. Mark Cummings "Responses of Children and Adolescents to Marital Conflict Scenarios as a Function of the Emotionality of Conflict Endings," *Merrill-Palmer Quarterly* 42, no. 1 (1996).

116 **"if you have a legitimate concern, it might be okay to look"** Loni Coombs, *"You're Perfect . . ." and Other Lies Parents Tell* (Los Angeles: Bird Street Books, 2012), 157–58.

121 **"Somewhere along the line"** Louis M. Profeta, "Your Kid and My Kid Are Not Playing in the Pros," April 7, 2014, http://www.dgiwire.com/your-kid-and-my-kid-are-not-playing-in-the-pros/.

124 **"place others' perspectives and needs on a par with their own"** Richard Weissbourd, *The Parents We Mean to Be* (Boston: Mariner Books, 2009), 146.

124 **"The ride home from games with my parents."** Steve Henson, "What Makes a Nightmare Sports Parent," February 15, 2012, *http://www.thepostgame.com/blog/more-family-fun/201202/what-makes-nightmare-sports-parent.*

126 **"won a spot in the school orchestra"** Wendy Grolnick and Kathy Seal, *Pressured Parents, Stressed-Out Kids* (Amherst, NY: Prometheus Books, 2008), 26.

126 **"remain close to us and to succeed"** Ibid., 27.

127 **"undermines intrinsic motivation"** Daniel Pink, *Drive: The Surprising Truth About What Motivates Us* (New York: Riverhead Books, 2009), 174.

127 **caused those mothers to overparent** Grolnick, *Pressured Parents*, 99.

132 **"only more struggle"** Michael Thompson, *The Pressured Child: Freeing Our Kids from Performance Overdrive and Helping Them Find Success in School and Life* (New York: Ballantine Books, 2004), 106.

159 **"careers and social interactions"** L. M. Padilla-Walker and L. J. Nelson, "Black Hawk Down?: Establishing Helicopter Parenting as a Distinct Construct from Other Forms of Parental Control during Emerging Adulthood," *Journal of Adolescence* 35 (2012): 1177–90.

161 **"until we are teenagers."** David Bainbridge, *Teenagers: A Natural History* (Vancouver: Greystone Books, 2009), 132.

168 **"handheld from birth"** Debora L. Spar, *Wonder Women: Sex, Power, and the Quest for Perfection* (New York: Farrar, Straus & Giroux, 2013), 164.

183 **invite them into the process** Joyce L. Epstein, *School, Family, and Community Partnerships: Preparing Educators and Improving Schools* (Philadelphia: Westview Press, 2011), 39–40.

185 **"fourteen years before"** Ibid., 174.

207 **"this has held true for most of the past 50 years"** "Research Spotlight on Homework: NEA Reviews of the Research on Best Practices in Education," National Education Association, accessed April 12, 2013, http://www.nea.org/tools/16938.htm.

208 **less than that wreaks havoc on concentration, memory, learning, attention, executive functioning, and behavior** "How Much Sleep Do I Need?," Centers for Disease Control and Prevention, accessed July 1, 2013, http://www.cdc.gov/sleep/about_sleep/how_much_sleep.htm.

227 **"test of scholarship"** Mary Lovett Smallwood, *An Historical Study of Examinations and Grading Systems in Early American Universities* (Cambridge, MA: Harvard University Press, 1935), 39.

228 **"the one who is examined"** Ibid.

232 **"boosting their achievement,"** Deborah J. Stipek and Kathy Seal, *Motivated Minds: Raising Children to Love Learning* (New York: Holt, 2001), 179.

238 **"stay out of the game"** Ken Bain, *What the Best College Students Do* (Cambridge, MA: Harvard University Press, 2012), 119–20.

243 **"Great books are not flawless books,"** Mary McDonagh Murphy, ed., *Scout, Atticus & Boo: A Celebration of Fifty Years of To Kill a Mockingbird* (New York: Harper, 2010), 170.

BIBLIOGRAPHY

Adkins, Elaine K. *How to Deal with Parents Who Are Angry, Troubled, Afraid, or Just Plain Crazy*. Thousand Oaks: Corwin Press, 1998.

Alsop, Ronald. *The Trophy Kids Grow Up: How the Millennial Generation Is Shaking Up the Workplace*. San Francisco: Jossey-Bass, 2008.

Anderegg, David. *Worried All the Time: Overparenting in an Age of Anxiety and How to Stop It*. New York: Free Press, 2003.

Apple, Rima D. *Perfect Motherhood Science and Childrearing in America*. New Brunswick: Rutgers University Press, 2006.

Ariely, Dan. *The (Honest) Truth About Dishonesty: How We Lie to Everyone—Especially Ourselves*. New York: Harper Perennial, 2012.

Arnott, Alastair. *Positive Failure*. Cambridge: Cambridge Academic, 2013.

Bain, Ken. *What the Best College Teachers Do*. Cambridge: Harvard University Press, 2004.

Bainbridge, David. *Teenagers: A Natural History*. Vancouver: Greystone Books, 2009.

Barnes, Christie. *The Paranoid Parents Guide: Worry Less, Parent Better, and Raise a Resilient Child*. Deerfield Beach: Health Communications, 2010.

Bender, Yvonne. *The Tactful Teacher Effective Communication with Parents, Colleagues, and Administrators*. White River Junction: Nomad Press, 2005.

Berman, Robin E. *Permission to Parent: How to Raise Your Child with Love and Limits*. New York: Harper Wave, 2014.

Bohlin, Karen E., Deborah Lynn Farmer, and Kevin Ryan. *Building Character in Schools Resource Guide*. San Francisco: Jossey-Bass, 2001.

Borba, Michele. *The Big Book of Parenting Solutions: 101 Answers to Your Everyday Challenges and Wildest Worries*. San Francisco, CA: Jossey-Bass, 2009.

Borba, Michele. *12 Simple Secrets Real Moms Know: Getting Back to Basics and Raising Happy Kids*. San Francisco: Jossey-Bass, 2006.

Brafman, Rom. *Succeeding When You're Supposed to Fail: The 6 Enduring Principles of High Achievement*. New York: Three Rivers Press, 2011.

Brewer, Elizabeth. *Talking to Tweens: Getting It Right before It Gets Rocky with Your 8- to 12-year-old*. North American ed. Cambridge: Da Capo, 2005.

Brighton, Kenneth L. *Coming of Age: The Education and Development of Young Adolescents: A Resource for Educators and Parents*. Westerville: National Middle School Association, 2007.

Bronson, Po, and Ashley Merryman. *NurtureShock: New Thinking about Children*. New York: Twelve, 2009.

Bronson, Po, and Ashley Merryman. *Top Dog: The Science of Winning and Losing.* New York: Twelve, 2013.

Brooks, Robert B., and Sam Goldstein. *Nurturing Resilience in Our Children: Answers to the Most Important Parenting Questions.* Chicago: Contemporary Books, 2003.

Brown, Dave F., and Trudy Knowles. *What Every Middle School Teacher Should Know.* 2nd ed. Portsmouth: Heinemann, 2007.

Brown, Peter C., Henry L. Roediger III, and Mark A. McDaniel. *Make It Stick: The Science of Successful Learning.* Cambridge: Harvard University Press, 2014.

Cairns, Warwick. *How to Live Dangerously: The Hazards of Helmets, the Benefits of Bacteria, and the Risks of Living Too Safe.* New York: St. Martin's Griffin, 2009.

Campbell, Joseph. *The Hero with a Thousand Faces.* 2d ed. Princeton: Princeton University Press, 1972.

Clark, Ron. *The Essential 55: An Award-winning Educator's Rules for Discovering the Successful Student in Every Child.* New York: Hyperion, 2003.

Clark, Ron. *The Excellent 11: Qualities Teachers and Parents Use to Motivate, Inspire and Educate Children.* New York: Hyperion, 2004.

Coburn, Karen Levin, and Madge Lawrence Treeger. *Letting Go: A Parents' Guide to Understanding the College Years.* 4th ed. New York: Quill, 2003.

Cohen, Harlan. *The Naked Roommate: For Parents Only.* Naperville: Source Books, 2012.

Coles, Robert. *The Moral Intelligence of Children.* New York: Random House, 1997.

Coombs, Loni. *"You're Perfect—" and Other Lies Parents Tell: The Ugly Truth about Spoiling Your Kids.* Los Angeles: Bird Street Books, 2012.

Cooper-Kahn, Joyce, and Laurie Dietzel. *Late, Lost, and Unprepared: A Parents' Guide to Helping Children with Executive Functioning.* Bethesda: Woodbine, 2008.

Csikszentmihalyi, Mihaly. *Flow: The Psychology of Optimal Experience.* New York: Harper & Row, 1990.

Cushman, Kathleen, and Laura Rogers. *Fires in the Middle School Bathroom: Advice for Teachers from Middle Schoolers.* New York: New Press, 2008.

Cutler, William W. *Parents and Schools: The 150-year Struggle for Control in American Education.* Chicago: University of Chicago Press, 2000.

Damon, William. *Greater Expectations: Overcoming the Culture of Indulgence in America's Homes and Schools.* New York: Free Press, 1995.

Deci, Edward L. *Why We Do What We Do: Understanding Self-Motivation.* New York: Penguin Books, 1995.

Dewey, John. *Experience & Education.* New York: Touchstone, 1938.

Duckworth, Eleanor Ruth. *"The Having of Wonderful Ideas" & Other Essays on Teaching & Learning.* New York: Teachers College Press, 1987.

Duhigg, Charles. *The Power of Habit: Why We Do What We Do in Life and Business.* New York: Random House, 2012.

Dunnewold, Ann, and Sandi Kahn Shelton. *Even June Cleaver Would Forget the Juice Box: Cut Yourself Some Slack (and Still Raise Great Kids) in the Age of Extreme Parenting.* Deerfield Beach: Health Communications, 2007.

Dweck, Carol S. *Mindset: The New Psychology of Success.* New York: Random House, 2006.

Dweck, Carol S. *Self-theories: Their Role in Motivation, Personality, and Development.* Philadelphia: Psychology Press, 1999.

Eagleman, David. *Incognito: The Secret Lives of the Brain.* New York: Pantheon Books, 2011.

Elkind, David. *The Hurried Child: Growing Up Too Fast Too Soon.* Reading, MA: Addison-Wesley Pub., 1981.

Epstein, Joyce Levy. *School, Family, and Community Partnerships Preparing Educators and Improving Schools*. 2nd ed. Boulder: Westview Press, 2011.

Epstein, Robert. *The Case against Adolescence: Rediscovering the Adult in Every Teen*. Sanger: Quill Driver Books, 2007.

Esquith, Rafe. *Real Talk for Real Teachers: Advice for Teachers from Rookies to Veterans: "No Retreat, No Surrender"* New York: Penguin Group, 2013.

Faber, Adele, and Elaine Mazlish. *How to Talk So Kids Will Listen & Listen So Kids Will Talk*. New York: Scribner, 1980.

Fass, Paula S. *Childhood in America*. New York: New York University Press, 2000.

Fay, Jim, and David Funk. *Teaching with Love & Logic: Taking Control of the Classroom*. Golden: Love and Logic Press, 1995.

Feldman, David B., and Lee Daniel Kravetz. *Supersurvivors: The Surprising Link between Suffering and Success*. New York: HarperCollins, 2014.

Fried, Robert L. *The Passionate Learner: How Teachers and Parents Can Help Children Reclaim the Joy of Discovery*. Boston: Beacon Press, 2001.

Fried, Robert L. *The Passionate Teacher: A Practical Guide*. Boston: Beacon Press, 1995.

Friedman, Hilary Levey. *Playing to Win: Raising Kids in a Competitive Culture*. Berkeley: University of California Press, 2013.

Galinsky, Ellen. *Mind in the Making: The Seven Essential Life Skills Every Child Needs*. New York: HarperStudio, 2010.

Gardner, Howard, Mihaly Csikszentmihalyi, and William Damon. *Good Work: When Excellence and Ethics Meet*. New York: Basic Books, 2001.

Gawande, Atul. *The Checklist Manifesto: How to Get Things Right. New York*: Metropolitan Books, 2010.

Gill, Tim. *No Fear: Growing Up in a Risk Averse Society*. London: Calouste Gulbenkian Foundation, 2007.

Ginsburg, Kenneth R., with Martha Moraghan Jablow. *Building Resilience in Children and Teens: Giving Kids Roots and Wings*. 2nd ed. Elk Grove Village: American Academy of Pediatrics, 2011.

Ginsburg, Kenneth R., and Susan FitzGerald. *Letting Go with Love and Confidence: Raising Responsible, Resilient, Self-sufficient Teens in the 21st Century*. New York: Avery, 2011.

Glenn, H. Stephen, and Jane Nelsen. *Raising Self-reliant Children in a Self-indulgent World: Seven Building Blocks for Developing Capable Young People*. Rocklin: Prima Publishing & Communications, 1988.

Goldberg, Donna. *The Organized Student: Teaching Children the Skills for Success in School and Beyond*. New York: Fireside, 2005.

Goleman, Daniel. *Focus: The Hidden Driver of Excellence*. New York: HarperCollins, 2013.

Gray, Peter. *Free to Learn: Why Unleashing the Instinct to Play Will Make Our Children Happier, More Self-reliant, and Better Students for Life*. New York: Basic Books, 2013.

Grolnick, Wendy S. *The Psychology of Parental Control: How Well-meant Parenting Backfires*. Mahwah, N.J.: L. Erlbaum Associates, 2003.

Grolnick, Wendy S., and Kathy Seal. *Pressured Parents, Stressed-out Kids: Dealing with Competition While Raising a Successful Child*. Amherst: Prometheus Books, 2008.

Gross-Loh, Christine. *Parenting without Borders: Surprising Lessons Parents around the World Can Teach Us*. New York: Avery, 2013.

Harford, Tim. *Adapt: Why Success Always Starts with Failure*. New York: Picador, 2011.

Hartley-Brewer, Elizabeth. *Talking to Tweens: Getting It Right before It Gets Rocky with Your 8- to 12-Year-Old*. Cambridge: Da Capo Press, 2005.

Hays, Sharon. *The Cultural Contradictions of Motherhood.* New Haven: Yale University Press, 1996.

Hazard, Kris. *The Hazard of the Game: The Dangers of Over-Parenting in Sport and Life.* North Word Communication, 2012.

Heath, Ralph. *Celebrating Failure: The Power of Taking Risks, Making Mistakes, and Thinking Big.* Pompton Plains: Career Press, 2009.

Hodgkinson, Tom. *The Idle Parent: Why Laid-back Parents Raise Happier and Healthier Kids.* New York: Tarcher Penguin, 2009.

Hoefle, Vicki. *Duct Tape Parenting: A Less Is More Approach to Raising Respectful, Responsible, and Resilient Kids.* Brookline: Bibliomotion, 2012.

Holt, John. *How Children Fail.* New York: Da Capo Press, 1982.

Homayoun, Ana. *That Crumpled Paper Was Due Last Week: Helping Disorganized and Distracted Boys Succeed in School and Life.* New York: Penguin Group, 2010.

Honoré, Carl. *Under Pressure: Rescuing Our Children from the Culture of Hyper-parenting.* New York: HarperOne, 2008.

Hulbert, Ann. *Raising America: Experts, Parents, and a Century of Advice about Children.* New York: Vintage, 2003.

Icard, Michelle. *Middle School Makeover: Improving the Way You and Your Child Experience the Middle School Years.* Brookline: Bibliomotion, 2014.

Kahn, Joyce, and Laurie C. Dietzel. *Late, Lost and Unprepared: A Parents' Guide to Helping Children with Executive Functioning.* Bethesda: Woodbine House, 2008.

Kaufman, Scott Barry. *Ungifted: Intelligence Redefined: The Truth about Talent, Practice, Creativity, and the Many Paths to Greatness.* New York: Basic Books, 2013.

Kilpatrick, Haley, and Whitney Joiner. *The Drama Years: Real Girls Talk about Surviving Middle School: Bullies, Brands, Body Image, and More.* New York: Free Press, 2012.

Klee, Mary Beth. *Core Virtues: A Literature-based Program in Character Education, K–6.* Redwood City: Link Institute, 2000.

Koenig, Blair. *STFU Parents: The Jaw-dropping, Self-indulgent, and Occasionally Rage-inducing World of Parent Overshare.* New York: Perigree, 2013.

Kohn, Alfie. *Punished by Rewards: The Trouble with Gold Stars, Incentive Plans, A's, Praise, and Other Bribes.* Boston: Houghton Mifflin, 1993.

Kohn, Alfie. *What Does It Mean to Be Well Educated?* Boston: Beacon Press, 2004.

Lareau, Annette. Unequal Childhoods: Class, Race, and Family Life. 2nd ed. Berkeley: University of California Press, 2011.

Lawrence-Lightfoot, Sarah. *The Essential Conversation: What Parents and Teachers Can Learn from Each Other.* New York: Ballantine, 2003.

Lee, Ellie, Jennie Bristow, Charlotte Faircloth, and Jan MacVarish. *Parenting Culture Studies.* Hampshire: Palgrave Macmillan, 2014.

Levine, Alanna. *Raising a Self-reliant Child: A Back-to-basics Parenting Plan from Birth to Age 6.* Berkeley: Ten Speed Press, 2013.

Levine, Madeline. *Teach Your Children Well: Parenting for Authentic Success.* New York: Harper, 2012.

Levine, Madeline. *The Price of Privilege: How Parental Pressure and Material Advantage Are Creating a Generation of Disconnected and Unhappy Kids.* New York: HarperCollins, 2006.

Levine, Mel. *A Mind at a Time: America's Top Learning Expert Shows How Every Child Can Succeed.* New York: Simon and Schuster Paperbacks, 2002.

MacDonald, Betty Bard. *Mrs. Piggle-Wiggle.* Philadelphia: J. B. Lippincott Company, 1947.

Magary, Drew. *Someone Could Get Hurt: A Memoir of Twenty-first Century Parenthood.* New York: Gotham Books, 2013.

Marano, Hara Estroff. *A Nation of Wimps: The High Cost of Invasive Parenting.* New York: Broadway Books, 2008.

Mathews, Jay. *Work Hard. Be Nice: How Two Inspired Teachers Created the Most Promising Schools in America.* Chapel Hill, NC: Algonquin Books of Chapel Hill, 2009.

McArdle, Megan. *The Up Side of Down: Why Failing Well Is the Key to Success.* New York: Viking, 2014.

McEwan, Elaine K. *How to Deal with Parents Who Are Angry, Troubled, Afraid, or Just Plain Crazy.* Thousand Oaks: Corwin Press, 2005.

Medina, John. *Brain Rules: 12 Principles for Surviving and Thriving at Work, Home, and School.* Seattle, WA: Pear Press, 2008.

Mintz, Steven. *Huck's Raft: A History of American Childhood.* Cambridge: Harvard University Press, 2004.

Mogel, Wendy. *The Blessing of a B Minus: Using Jewish Teachings to Raise Resilient Teenagers.* New York: Scribner, 2010.

Mogel, Wendy. *The Blessing of a Skinned Knee: Using Jewish Teachings to Raise Self-reliant Children.* New York: Scribner, 2001.

Nelson, Margaret K. *Parenting out of Control: Anxious Parents in Uncertain Times.* New York: New York University Press, 2010.

Nichols, ML. *The Parent Backpack for Kindergarten through Grade 5.* Berkeley: 10 Speed Press, 2013.

Payne, Kim John, and Lisa M. Ross. *Simplicity Parenting: Using the Extraordinary Power of Less to Raise Calmer, Happier, and More Secure Kids.* New York: Ballantine Books, 2009.

Payne, Ruby K. *Working with Parents: Building Relationships for Student Success.* Highlands: Aha! Process, 2006.

Peskowitz, Miriam. *The Truth behind the Mommy Wars: Who Decides What Makes a Good Mother?* Emeryville: Seal Press, 2005.

Phelan, Thomas W. *Surviving Your Adolescents: How to Manage and Let Go of Your 13–18 Year Olds.* 3rd ed. Glen Ellyn: ParentMagic / EBL, 2012.

Pincus, Donna. *Growing up Brave: Expert Strategies for Helping Your Child Overcome Fear, Stress, and Anxiety.* New York: Little, Brown and, 2012.

Pink, Daniel H. *Drive: The Surprising Truth about What Motivates Us.* New York: Riverhead Books, 2009.

Quart, Alissa. *Hothouse Kids: The Dilemma of the Gifted Child.* New York: Penguin Press, 2006.

Reichert, Michael, and Richard A. Hawley. *Reaching Boys, Teaching Boys: Strategies That Work and Why.* San Francisco: Jossey-Bass, 2010.

Rosenfeld, Alvin A., and Nicole Wise. *The Over-scheduled Child: Avoiding the Hyper-parenting Trap.* New York: St. Martin's Griffin, 2001.

Sarkett, John A. *Extraordinary Comebacks: 201 Inspiring Stories of Courage, Triumph, and Success.* Naperville: Source Books, 2007.

Savage, Marjorie. *You're on Your Own (but I'm Here If You Need Me): Mentoring Your Child during the College Years.* New York: Fireside Book, 2003.

Schipani, Denise. *Mean Moms Rule: Why Doing the Hard Stuff Now Creates Good Kids Later.* Naperville: Source Books, 2012.

Schwartz, Natalie. *The Teacher Chronicles: Confronting the Demands of Students, Parents, Administrators and Society.* Millwood: Laurelton Media, 2008.

Senior, Jennifer. *All Joy and No Fun: The Paradox of Modern Parenthood.* New York: Ecco, 2014.

Shumaker, Heather. *It's OK NOT to Share.* London: Penguin Books, 2012.

Siegel, Daniel J. *Brainstorm: The Power and Purpose of the Teenage Brain*. New York: Penguin, 2013.

Silverman, Scott, ed. *How to Survive Your Freshman Year*. 5th ed. Atlanta: Hundreds of Heads Books, 2013.

Skenazy, Lenore. *Free Range Kids: How to Raise Safe, Self-reliant Children (without Going Nuts with Worry)*. San Francisco: Jossey-Bass, 2010.

Smallwood, Mary Lovett. *An Historical Study of Examinations and Grading Systems in Early American Universities*. Cambridge: Harvard University Press, 1935.

Spar, Debora L. *Wonder Women: Sex, Power, and the Quest for Perfection*. New York: Sarah Crichton Books, 2013.

Stearns, Peter N. *Anxious Parents: A History of Modern Childrearing in America*. New York: New York University Press, 2003.

Steinberg, Laurence. *Age of Opportunity: Lessons from the New Science of Adolescence*. New York: Houghton Mifflin Harcourt, 2014.

Steinberg, Laurence D., and Ann Levine. *You and Your Adolescent: A Parent's Guide for Ages 10 to 25*. New York: Harper & Row, 1990.

Stipek, Deborah J., and Kathy Seal. *Motivated Minds: Raising Children to Love Learning*. New York: H. Holt and, 2001.

Taylor, Jim. *Positive Pushing: How to Raise a Successful and Happy Child*. New York: Hyperion, 2002.

Thompson, Michael. *Homesick and Happy: How Time Away from Parents Can Help a Child Grow*. New York: Ballantine Books Trade Paperbacks, 2012.

Thompson, Michael, and Teresa Barker. *The Pressured Child: Helping Your Child Find Success in School and Life*. New York: Ballantine Books, 2004.

Thompson, Michael, Lawrence J. Cohen, and Catherine O Grace. *Mom, They're Teasing Me: Helping Your Child Solve Social Problems*. New York: Ballantine Books, 2002.

Thompson, Michael G., and Alison Fox Mazzola. *Understanding Independent School Parents: The Teacher's Guide to Successful Family-School Relationships*. Wise Teacher Press, 2012.

Tingley, Suzanne Capek. *How to Handle Difficult Parents: A Teacher's Survival Guide*. Fort Collins, CO: Cottonwood Press, 2006.

Tobias, Cynthia Ulrich. *I Hate School: How to Help Your Child Love Learning*. Grand Rapids: Zondervan, 2004.

Tough, Paul. *How Children Succeed: Grit, Curiosity, and the Hidden Power of Character*. Boston: Mariner Books, 2012.

Tulgan, Bruce. *Not Everyone Gets a Trophy: How to Manage Generation Y*. San Francisco, CA: Jossey-Bass, 2009.

Twenge, Jean M. *Generation Me: Why Today's Young Americans Are More Confident, Assertive, Entitled—and More Miserable than Ever Before*. New York: Free Press, 2006.

Twenge, Jean M., and W. Keith Campbell. *The Narcissism Epidemic: Living in the Age of Entitlement*. New York: Free Press, 2009.

Ungar, Michael. *Too Safe for Their Own Good: How Risk and Responsibility Help Teens Thrive*. Crows Nest: Allen & Unwin, 2008.

Ungar, Michael. *The We Generation: Raising Socially Responsible Kids*. Cambridge, MA: Da Capo, 2009.

Vuko, Evelyn Porreca. *Teacher Says: 30 Foolproof Ways to Help Kids Thrive in School*. New York: Perigee Books, 2004.

Wagner, Tony, and Robert A. Compton. *Creating Innovators: The Making of Young People Who Will Change the World*. New York: Scribner, 2012.

Walsh, David Allen, and Nat Bennett. *Why Do They Act That Way? A Survival Guide to the Adolescent Brain for You and Your Teen*. New York: Free Press, 2004.

Walsh, David Allen. *No: Why Kids—of All Ages—Need to Hear It and Ways Parents Can Say It*. New York: Free Press, 2007.

Warner, Judith. *Perfect Madness: Motherhood in the Age of Anxiety*. New York: Riverhead Books, 2006.

Weissbourd, Rick. *The Parents We Mean to Be: How Well-intentioned Adults Undermine Children's Moral and Emotional Development*. Boston: Houghton Mifflin Harcourt, 2009.

Wilde, Jerry. *An Educator's Guide to Difficult Parents*. New York: Kroshka Books, 2000.

Willingham, Daniel T. *Why Don't Students like School?: A Cognitive Scientist Answers Questions about How the Mind Works and What It Means for the Classroom*. San Francisco: Jossey-Bass, 2009.

Wiseman, Rosalind, and Elizabeth Rapoport. *Queen Bee Moms & Kingpin Dads: Dealing with the Parents, Teachers, Coaches, and Counselors Who Can Make—or Break—Your Child's Future*. New York: Crown Publishers, 2006.

Wood, Chip. *Yardsticks: Children in the Classroom, Ages 4–14: A Resource for Parents and Teachers*. Expanded ed. Greenfield: Northeast Foundation for Children, 1997.

Wyma, Kay Wills. *Cleaning House: A Mom's 12-month Experiment to Rid Her Home of Youth Entitlement*. Colorado Springs: WaterBrook Press, 2012.

Zelizer, Viviana A. Rotman. *Pricing the Priceless Child: The Changing Social Value of Children*. New York: Basic Books, 1985.

INDEX

abstract concepts, 160–61
accountability, 50–51, 82–83
achievement
  love of learning sacrificed for, 20
  peer play as predictive of, 99
  and sports, 121
  and struggle, 21
adolescents. *See also* high school; middle school
  and brain development, 139, 140
  communication with, 112
  and competence, 160
  and executive function, 138
  and expectations, 160
  and formal operational stage, 160–61
and friends, 98, 100, 106, 107, 108–17
  and household duties, 91–92
  and judgment, 112, 113
  and lack of purpose, 80–81
  and mental flexibility, 143–45
  and organization, 151–55
  and overparenting, 109
  and peer pressure, 103
  rebellion of, 12, 13
  and self-control, 140–43
  and sleep schedule, 189, 208
  and strategic thinking, 161
adulthood, 158–59, 172
Advanced Placement classes, 166–67, 168
alcohol use, 110, 115, 116, 117
Amish children, 185
Andrée, S. A., 242
anxiety, and high school, 163, 164, 165, 167
Apatow, Judd, 188
attachment parenting, xvi, xvii, 13, 14
Auckland University of Technology, 100
audio recordings of classes, 147
autonomy. *See also* parenting for autonomy
  and college, 174–76
  and friends, 105, 109, 117
  and goals, 33–35, 231, 236
  and grades, 225, 233–34, 239
  and high school, 163, 166, 167, 168–69, 171, 233
  and homework, 28, 205–7, 211, 214–15, 218
  independence compared to, 29–30
  and intrinsic motivation, 26, 27, 28, 29–35, 47, 51
  and middle school, 136, 145, 233
  and play activities, 102
  and unsolicited advice and direction, 53

Bain, Ken, 238
Bainbridge, David, 161
Bjork, Elizabeth, 40
Bjork, Robert, 40
Bowlby, John, 10–11, 13
brain development, 139, 140
Branden, Nathaniel, 14
Brazelton, T. Berry, 13
Brown, Bruce, 124–25
Buchan, William, *Domestic Medicine,* 10
bullying, 100, 103, 104, 106–7

Campbell, W. Keith, 14–15
cause and effect, 90
challenges
  and desirable difficulties, 40
  and growth mindset, 38–39
  of high school, 163
  in homework, 208–9, 218
  and learning, 41
  of middle school, 136–37
  and praise, 65
  and self-awareness, 148
  and sports, 131–32
chameleons, 108
checklists, 44, 52, 81, 147, 151, 208–9, 212
Chemers, Michael, 172–73
child care, 10
child development
  and emotional needs, 9, 10–11
  failure's role in, xix–xxi, xxiii
  and play activities, 97
child labor, history of, 7–8, 9
childrearing manuals, 10
choices
  and autonomy, 26, 28, 233–34
  of college, 170–71
  and high school, 163, 167, 168–69, 170
chores. *See* household duties
Clark, Ron, xxiv, 193
cliques, 105
Cohen, David B., 164
Cole, Julie, 101–2
college
  choice of, 170–71
  and failure, 172–73, 177
  and parenting for autonomy, 174–77
  and role of parents, 172–74
college admissions
  and autonomy, 234
  and grades, 228, 237
  and high school, 167–68, 169
  pressures of, xvi, 237
  and service projects, 79–80, 168
  and sports, 120–21, 127
  and teachers' letters of recommendation, 165
Common Core State Standards, 186, 232–33
communication
  with adolescents, 112
  and car travel involved in sports, 124–25
  changes in patterns of, 115
  and independence, 199
  in parent-teacher partnership, 181–83, 185, 190–91, 192, 193, 194–95
  and play activities, 98, 99
competence
  and adolescents, 160
  and adulthood, 159
  and college, 174
  and homework, 211, 221
  and household duties, 75–78, 79, 84, 89, 91–92, 148
  and intrinsic motivation, 35–37
  and parenting for autonomy, 37, 43
  and relationships, 37
  and unsolicited advice and direction, 53
competition
  competitiveness of youth sports, 119–22, 127, 128, 129, 132–33

intrinsic motivation undermined by, 127, 128, 129
competitive parenting
and protection of children from failure, 78
and sports, 119, 125–29
symptoms of, xv–xvi, xviii–xix
confidence
and competence, 35–37
and high school, 162
and homework, 206, 221
and praise, 65
consequences of actions
and executive function, 139, 156
and failure, 59, 60
and high school, 160, 162, 163
and household duties, 88
consolidation, and learning, 40
contingent self-worth, 238
control
and autonomy, 30, 31, 51
and goals, 33
and grades, 225, 236
and high school, 170
and household duties, 31–32, 76, 77, 84, 86
and independence, 160
and relationships, 37
and rewards, 26, 27, 30–31, 59
self-control, 140–43
Coombs, Loni, 116
counterculture of the sixties, 184
creative problem-solving, xix, xxii, 21, 32
creativity, rewards inhibiting, 31, 32
critical listening skills, 147
cues, for creating new habits, 51–52, 89

Damon, William, 64
Deci, Edward, 22, 26–27, 28, 29, 31, 32, 35
decision-making, 55–56, 163
Dell'Antonia, K. J., 78–79
depression, 80, 116
desirable difficulties
in homework, 209, 217, 218
and mastery, 39–41, 209
Dickens, Charles, 241
Disney American Teacher Award, xxiv
distractions, and homework, 211
divorce rates, 13, 15
drug use, 110, 115, 116, 117
Duckworth, Angela, xxi
duct-tape parenting, 84
Duhigg, Charles, 51
Dweck, Carol, 38, 63–64, 66, 68, 219
Dwight, Timothy, V, 227–28

eating disorders, 116, 117
Edison, Thomas, xxiii, 241–42
Einstein, Albert, 242
empathy
and friends, 107–8
with frustration, 57–58
and peer feedback, 104
and play activities, 98
and sports, 123–24
employment, 169, 171
encoding, 40, 209
enmeshment, xv
executive function
gender differences in, 155–56
and grades, 229
and high school, 137, 138, 139, 156, 161
and homework, 216, 219, 221
and initiation, 149–51
and mental flexibility, 143–45
and middle school, 138–40
and organization, 151–55
and self-awareness, 141, 148–49
and self-control, 140–43
and working memory, 145–47
expectations
and accountability, 50–51, 82–83
and adolescents, 160
and friends, 105, 111, 112
and homework, 28, 211–12, 213, 219–21

expectations *(continued)*
and household duties, 82–83, 86
as nonnegotiable, 28
and organization, 154
and parenting for autonomy, 47, 49–50
and perfectionism, 159
and praise, 65
and self-awareness, 148, 149
and student-teacher relationship, 204
and teachers' classroom management, 30
experience, and competence, 35–37
extracurricular activities, 105, 144, 168

failure
anecdotes of, 241–42
and autonomy, 39
and college, 172–73, 177
consequences of, 59, 60
and creative problem-solving, xxii, 21
fear of, xxiii, 20, 21, 41, 164
feelings of disappointment from, 70
and grades, 33, 223–24, 225, 237–40
and growth mindset, 38, 66
healthy reactions to, 69
and high school, xxv, 157, 159, 161, 165, 169, 240
and household duties, 77, 81–82, 92–93
and learning process, 32–33, 41, 69, 70, 138, 154, 155, 187, 220, 221, 240
love and emotional connection buffering, 69
and middle school, xxv, 138, 139, 141, 154, 155, 156
as opportunity, 237–38
and parenting in Colonial New England, 6
parents' role in allowing failure, 44–46, 59–60, 70, 156, 157, 159, 161, 197–98
and parent-teacher partnership, 186–87
as part of child development, xix–xxi, xxiii
protection of children from, 78
and self-awareness, 149
and sports, 122–23, 125, 131–33
value in, xxi–xxiii, xxv, xxvii
failure to launch, xv
family calendar, 145
feedback
and failure, 238
and grades, 232–33
of habits, 51
homework as feedback, 216
and parenting for autonomy, 58
and parent-teacher partnership, 192, 194, 196–97
peer feedback, 104
feminism, 13–14
FER (Flag, Eye contact, and Rehearse), 142, 143
fighting fair, 102
fight-or-flight reflex, 126
FIRST Lego League, 220
fixed mindset, 38, 63–64, 66, 67–68, 131
formal operational stage, 160–61
Freud, Sigmund, 10, 191
friends
and adolescents, 98, 100, 106, 107, 108–17
and autonomy, 105, 109, 117
concerns about, 114–17
and conflict, 104–5
and middle school, 98, 104, 105–8
and overparenting, 95–96, 98–99, 106–8, 109
and preschool children, 100–101
and school-age children, 102–5
and social interaction, 96–97, 98, 99, 103, 104, 107–8, 110

frustration
and grades, 225–26
and homework, 205–6, 218, 219
and middle school, 139
and parenting for autonomy, 48, 57–58

gender differences, in executive function, 155–56
generative learning, 219–21
germ theory, 10
Gleich, Caroline, 131
goals
and advisory system, 33–34
and autonomy, 33–35, 231, 236
for college, 174, 175
and grades, 230–31, 234
and household duties, 82
and social interaction, 100
Gorman, Alison, 154–55, 210
grades
and autonomy, 225, 233–34, 236
changes in, 115
effect of praise on, 67
extrinsic rewards for, 24, 25–26, 31
and failure, 33, 223–24, 225, 237–40
and feedback, 232–33
and frustration, 225–26
and goals, 230–31, 234
and high school, 161, 162
history of, 227–28
and learning, 228–30
and overparenting, 223–24, 225, 235–37
and parenting for autonomy, xxii, 223–24, 225, 230, 231, 234–35
and parent-teacher partnership, 182, 183, 185, 223–24, 228, 233, 237
perspective on, 229–30, 235
risk-taking as factor in, 33, 234
software platforms for, 228, 235–37
standards-based grading, 232–33
grandparents, 125
Grolnick, Wendy, 48, 126
Gross-Loh, Christine, 63
growth mindset
adults modeling, 68–69
and challenges, 38–39
and failure, 38, 66, 131
and homework, 211, 219
and praise, 63, 67–68, 71

habits
creating new habits, 51–53
and homework, 211
and household duties, 88, 89
Harford, Tim, 238
Harlow, Harry, 13, 22–23, 26
Harris, Judith, 97
Hartstein, Jennifer, 91, 110–11, 158, 176
hearing tests, 146, 208
Heffernan, Lisa Endlich, 64–65
Henry, Jules, 13
high school
eleventh grade, 167–70
and executive function, 137, 138, 139, 156, 161
and failure, xxv, 157, 159, 161, 165, 169, 240
and friends, 103, 106
and grades, 161, 162
graduation from, xvi, 171–77
and homework, 207, 219, 220–21
ninth grade, 163–65
and responsibility, 44, 160, 163, 199
and self-control, 141
and teachers, 162–67, 170
tenth grade, 165–67
and time management, 153
twelfth grade, 170–71
high self-monitors, 108
high-stakes standardized testing, xxii
Hinkes, Alan, 242

Hoefle, Vicki, 84, 215
homework
autonomy for completing, 28, 205–7, 211, 214–15, 218
checklist for evaluating problems with, 208–9
completion of, 213
and executive function, 216, 219, 221
expectations concerning, 28, 211–12, 213, 219–21
and generative learning, 219–21
and learning, 213
and organization, 211, 212
parents' support for, 213–19
recommendations on, 207–8
students' evaluation of, 212
Timer Cure for, 210
household duties
and accountability, 82–83
and checklists, 147
and competence, 75–78, 79, 82, 89, 91–92, 148
and control, 31–32, 76, 77, 84, 86
and expectations, 82–83, 86
failures in, 77, 81–82, 92–93
importance of household participation, 77, 81, 83, 85, 91–92, 93
and parenting for autonomy, 49
for preschool children, 85–88
and purpose-driven life, 80–81
rescuing children from household disasters, 79
rewards for, 54–55, 82–85, 89–90
for school-age children, 88–92
and self-awareness, 148
and skills of children, 79–80
house rules, 111, 114
Hudenko, William, 142
Hurley, Katie, 86

identity
and friends, 107
and high school, 169
and praise, 65, 66
impulsive behavior, 140–43
independence
and adulthood, 158–59
autonomy compared to, 29–30
and communication, 199
and decision-making, 55–56
and high school, 166, 170
and homework, 219
and initiation, 150
and play activities, 102
as reward, 52
and testing limits, 50, 160
Independent School League, 121
initiation, and executive function, 149–51
intelligence, views on, 63
intermittent rewards, effect on motivation, 32, 89
intrinsic motivation
and autonomy, 26, 27, 28, 29–35, 47, 51
and competence, 35–37
competition undermining, 127, 128, 129
control undermining, 26, 27
and creative problem-solving, xix, 32
extrinsic rewards contrasted with, 22–29, 32, 41, 85
overparenting inhibiting, 38
and parenting for autonomy, 48
promoting, 229
and relationships, 37–39
rewards diminishing, 128
role of grades in, 228–29, 236
iParent, 235

Japan, 63
Jobs, Steve, 242
Journal of Adolescence, 158–59

Kearney, Hannah, 129, 130
Kennedy, John F., 12
Korea, 63

Lang, James M., 66–67
latchkey kids, xvii
learning
and challenge, 40
and control, 27, 31
generative learning, 219–21
and grades, 228–30
and homework, 213
love of learning, xxii, 19–20, 22, 166, 192–93
modeling enthusiasm for, 192–93
project-based learning, 29
role of failure in, 32–33, 41, 69, 70, 138, 154, 155, 187, 220, 221, 240
role of mistakes in, 41, 53, 57, 139, 149, 156, 182, 186–87, 237, 242
Locke, John, 5–6, 9
long-term memory, 40, 142
love of learning, xxii, 19–20, 22, 166, 192–93

Mabel's Labels, 101–2
McCready, Amy, 81
mandatory school attendance, 8
Marano, Hara Estroff, 99
mastery
and competence, 36–37
desirable difficulties leading to, 39–41, 209
and grades, 227, 233
and homework, 211, 216
and intrinsic motivation, 36, 39–41
praise for, 52
memory
long-term memory, 40, 142
working memory, 145–47
mental flexibility, and executive function, 143–45
metacognition, 67
middle school
and being on time for school, 189
challenges of, 136–37
and cycle of testing limits, 50
and executive function, 138–40
and failure, xxv, 138, 139, 141, 154, 155, 156
and friends, 98, 103, 104, 105–8
high school compared to, 165
and homework, 207, 219, 220–21
and mental flexibility, 143–45
and organization, 138, 143, 151–55, 156
and peer pressure, 103
and planning, 138, 152, 153
and puberty, xxv, 137
and self-control, 140–43
and sports, 120, 121, 124, 132
and teachers, 135–38, 144, 146, 148, 154–55
and time management, 138, 153
and working memory, 145–47
Miller, Rob, 124–25
mimicry, 108
mindsets, 38–39, 63–64, 66
Mintz, Steven, 7
mistakes
adults modeling attitude toward, 32, 33
and autonomy, 39
and distractions, 211
and high school, 164
and learning, 41, 53, 57, 139, 149, 156, 182, 186–87, 237, 242
and parenting for autonomy, 56, 57, 242
and parenting in Colonial New England, 6
mnemonics, 147
modeling
attitude toward failure, 32, 33
as educational strategy, 33
enthusiasm for learning, 192–93
and growth mindset, 68–69
and initiation, 151
and mental flexibility, 145
mutually beneficial friendships, 114
risk-taking, 238

Morita, Akio, 242
motivation. *See also* intrinsic motivation
Deci's studies on, 22, 26–27, 28, 29, 31, 32
effect of intermittent rewards, 32, 89
Grolnick's studies on, 48
Harlow's studies on, 22–23, 26

nagging
and executive function, 139
and grades, 224, 238
and household duties, 83–84, 86, 89
and initiation, 150
and parenting for dependence, 20, 47, 53
and signals for impulsive behavior, 141
and timers, 150–51
Nair, Andrea, 98–99
narcissism, 14–15, 17, 79
National Educational Association (NEA), 207
National Education Association, xxiv
National Parent-Teacher Association (National PTA), 207–8
NCAA recruitment rules, 120
New Zealand, 100
nursery schools, 10

open-ended questions, 112
organization
and homework, 211, 212
and middle school, 138, 143, 151–55, 156
Orlick, Terry, 122
overparenting. *See also* parenting for dependence
and attachment parenting, xvi, xvii
and autonomy, 30
and bullying, 106–7
characteristics of, 53–56
and competition, 127
and decision-making, 55–56
and extrinsic rewards, 54–55
and friends, 95–96, 98–99, 106–8, 109
and grades, 223–24, 225, 235–37
and household duties, 78
intrinsic motivation inhibited by, 38–39
making amends for, xxv–xxvii
and parental fears, xiv
parenting for autonomy contrasted with, 48–49, 53–59
and play activities, 95–96, 97, 98, 104
providing solutions, 55
and sports, 125–29
and taking over, 54
and trust, xxi
and unsolicited advice and direction, 53
validation of, xv, xviii–xix
withdrawal symptoms from, 52

Paine, Thomas, 6
Parenting, 16
parenting for autonomy
acknowledging feelings of frustration, 48, 57–58
characteristics of, 56–59
and children's success, xxii, 17
and college, 174–77
and competence, 37, 43
and expectations, 47, 49–50
and goals, 35
and grades, xxii, 223–24, 225, 230, 231, 234–35
and guiding principles, 30
guiding toward solutions, 56
and homework, 218
and limits, 30, 37, 50, 160
and mistakes, 56, 57, 242
offering support, not control, 84
overparenting contrasted with, 48–49, 53–59
and parental oversight, 47
and relationships, 37, 38

role of parents in allowing failure, 44–46, 59–60, 156, 157, 159, 161, 197–98
and trust, 242–43
parenting for dependence. *See also* overparenting
and fear of failure, 20–21
and nagging, 20, 47, 53
overprotective, failure-avoidant style, xi–xv, xxi–xxii
and parenting experts, 9
parenting for autonomy compared to, 44
and self-esteem movement, xii, xxv
parenting styles
history of, 3–8
parenting experts, 8–13, 16
pendulum swings in, xvi–xvii
Spock's common sense approach, 11–12, 13
and work/family balance, xvi, xvii–xviii, 13, 14–16
parents and parenting. *See also* overparenting; parenting for autonomy; parenting for dependence; parent-teacher partnership
and children's goals, 34–35
and college, 172–74
and competence, 35–36
and control, 31–32
fears of parents, xiv, xx–xxi, xxiv
and mistakes, 58
modeling attitude toward failure, 32, 33
modeling growth mindset, 68–69
parents' arguments, 104
reluctance to teach household duties, 81
role in allowing failure, 44–46, 59–60, 70, 156, 157, 159, 161, 197–98
and science fair projects, 217–18
supportive role in homework, 213–19
supportive sports parents, 124–25, 129, 130–33
Parents magazine, 8
parent-teacher partnership
and allowing children to speak for themselves, 198–200, 203
and attendance policy, 190
and authority, 184, 202
and being on time for school, 188–89
and common interest in student, 197
communication in, 181–83, 185, 190–91, 192, 193, 194–95
and conferences, 183, 201–2, 228, 233
cooperation in, xxvii, 184–85, 187–88
and expressing gratitude, 196–97
and feedback, 192, 194, 196–97
and grades, 182, 183, 185, 223–24, 228, 233, 237
history of, 184–85
and information about events at home, 195
and interest in classroom activities, 195–96
and modeling enthusiasm for learning, 192–93
opposing forces in, xxv, 24–25, 184, 185–86
and parental involvement, 47–48, 183, 184
and perceived emergency or crisis, 194–95
and perception of truth, 200–201
and politeness, 190–91
and protecting children's right to fail, 197–98
and respect for education, 191–92
and school's handbook and disciplinary policy, 202–3
and support for student-teacher partnership, 203–4
trust in, 19, 186–88, 191, 193, 200–201
pediatric medicine, 9–10

peer pressure, 102–3
Pencil Game, 142, 143
perfectionism
and control, 86
and expectations, 159
and household duties, 93
and overparenting, 78
performance
affection contingent on, 58–59
effect of praise on, 62, 67
and grades, 225
permissive parenting, 12–13, 47, 49
Pink, Daniel, 22, 127
"Plain View Doctrine," 116
planning
and homework, 206, 221
and middle school, 138, 152, 153
play activities
and human development, 97
and overparenting, 95–96, 97, 98, 104
and playdates, 100–101
play for the sake of play, 122
and school-age children, 102–5
and social interaction, 96–97, 98, 99, 103
uninterrupted, unrestricted free play, 97, 99, 100, 104
political activism, 12
Positive Parenting Solutions, 81
Potts, K. C., 132–33, 226–27
PowerSchool, 235, 236–37
praise
and competence, 35
Dweck's studies on, 38, 63–64, 66, 68
for effort, not inherent qualities, 68, 70–71, 231
as extrinsic reward, 30, 41
for good judgment, 112
and grades, 226
and growth mindset, 63, 67–68, 71
and homework, 217, 219
honesty in, 36, 64–65
for mastery, 52
negative consequences of, 65, 66–67
and participation trophies, 129
role of, 61–63
and self-awareness, 149
and self-esteem, 62, 64, 65, 67
predictability, 145
preschool children
and friends, 100–101
household duties for, 85–88
Pressured Parents Phenomenon, xvi, 126
Proactive Coaching, LLC, 124–25
procrastination, 149, 206
Profeta, Louis, 121–22
project-based learning, 29
psychosexual development theory, 10
puberty, xxv, 137
purpose-driven life, 80–81, 169

Race to Nowhere (documentary), 207
relationships. *See also* friends
effect of empathizing on, 58
effect of unsolicited advice and direction on, 53
and intrinsic motivation, 37–39
love and emotional connection buffering failure, 69
and sibling rivalry, 101–2
repetitive tasks, rewards for, 31, 51–52
resilience
and experience of failure, xxii
and high school, 162
and parenting for autonomy, 48
praise for, 36
rediscovery of, 22
responsibility
and grades, 224, 239
and high school, 44, 160, 163, 199
and homework, 211, 216–17, 221
and household duties, 76, 82, 83, 85–86, 87, 88, 91, 92
and middle school, 136

and parenting for autonomy, 44, 47, 49, 239
retrieval, and learning, 40, 41
rewards
and control, 26, 27, 30–31, 59
for creating new habits, 51, 89
as default strategy, 85
delaying of, 85
extrinsic rewards, 22, 23, 54–55, 225
for grades, 24, 25–26, 31
grades as extrinsic rewards, 225
of homework, 216–17
for household duties, 54–55, 82–85, 89–90
intrinsic motivation contrasted with, 22–29, 32, 41, 85
intrinsic motivation diminished by, 128
for repetitive tasks, 31, 51–52
and sports, 128, 129
teachers' use of, 22–23, 26
risk-taking
adults modeling of, 238
and competence, 35, 36
and connectedness in relationships, 39
as factor in grades, 33, 234
and goals, 34
and high school, 169
and praise, 65
rewards inhibiting, 32
routines
for creating new habits, 51, 52, 89
and high school, 165
and household duties, 77, 89
Rowling, J. K., 242
Russo, Richard, 243

Schofield, Grant, 100
school-age children
and friends, 102–5
and household duties, 88–92
Schweitzer, Albert, 196
science fair projects, 217–18
security, children's sense of, 59, 69
self-abuse, 117
self-awareness, and executive function, 141, 148–49
self-control, 140–43
self-determination, 26, 231
self-efficacy, 67, 68
self-esteem
and household duties, 92
and praise, 62, 64, 65, 67
self-esteem movement, xii, xxv, 14–15, 17
self-regulation, 102
Shea, Jonathan, 240
sibling rivalry, 101–2
signals, for impulsive behavior, 141
Skinner, B. F., 31
sleep schedule, 144, 145, 189, 208
Sobel, Anne, 33
social groups, 105
social interaction
and adulthood, 159
and communication, 199
and friends, 96–97, 98, 99, 103, 104, 107–8, 110
and goals, 100
and teachers, 106
Soma (game), 26–27, 28
Spar, Debra L., 168
Spock, Benjamin, 11–12, 13
sports
benefits of sports off field, 123–25
and communication during car travel, 124–25
competitiveness of youth sports, 119–22, 127, 128, 129, 132–33
and competitive parenting, 119, 125–29
and failure, 122–23, 125, 131–33
and high school, 167
and injuries, 121–22
and quitting, 131–33
and rewards, 128, 129
supportive sports parents, 124–25, 129, 130–33

sportsmanship, 122, 126
standards-based grading, 232–33
structure, and parenting for autonomy, 49–50
study skills, 152
success, xiii–xiv, xv, xxi–xxii, 17, 161–62
suicidal ideation, 80

Taylor, Sydney, 89
teachable moments, 56, 83
teachers and teaching. *See also* parent-teacher partnership
  and bullying, 106–7
  classroom management skills, 30
  effect of parenting on, xxiii–xxv
  and extrinsic rewards, 22–23, 26
  and high school, 162–67, 170
  and intrinsic motivation, 29
  and limits, 30
  and middle school, 135–38, 144, 146, 148, 154–55
  modeling attitude toward failure, 33
  and praise, 64, 67
  respect for, 185–86
  and skills of children, 79
  and social interactions, 106
  student-teacher partnership, 203–4, 226–27
teamwork, 126, 128
technology, creating new habits with, 52
Thompson, Michael, 132, 218
time management
  and high school, 153
  and homework, 221
  and initiation, 150
  and middle school, 138, 153
Timer Cure, 210
timers, 150–51
transitions, managing, 144–45
trust
  and autonomy, 34, 43, 109
  and friends, 113–14, 115, 116
  and overparenting, xxi
  and parental experts, 9, 11, 13, 16
  and parenting for autonomy, 242–43
  in parent-teacher partnership, 19, 186–88, 191, 193, 200–201
  and praise, 64–65
Twenge, Jean, 14–15

U.S. Centers for Disease Control and Prevention, 208

victim mentality, 106
vision tests, 208

Wardy, Melissa Atkins, 122–23
Weissbourd, Richard, 123–24
Wilder, Laura Ingalls, 3–4, 37, 52
work/family balance, xvi, xvii–xviii, 14–16
working memory, 145–47
working women, 13–14
Wyma, Kay Wills, 217

Yoder, Jonas, 185

ABOUT THE AUTHOR

JESSICA LAHEY is an educator, speaker, and writer. She writes the biweekly "Parent-Teacher Conference" advice column for the *New York Times*, is a contributing writer at the *Atlantic*, and appears as a commentator on Vermont Public Radio. She currently teaches English and writing, but retains a special place in her heart for Latin. Jessica earned a J.D. from the University of North Carolina at Chapel Hill with a concentration in juvenile and education law. She lives in New Hampshire with her husband and two sons.